Best Laid Plans

Best Laid Plans

Cultural Entropy and the Unraveling of AIDS Media Campaigns

TERENCE E. McDONNELL

The University of Chicago Press
Chicago and London

Terence E. McDonnell is the Kellogg Assistant Professor of Sociology at the
University of Notre Dame.

Unless noted otherwise, photographs reproduced in this book are by the author.

The University of Chicago Press, Chicago 60637
The University of Chicago Press, Ltd., London
© 2016 by The University of Chicago
All rights reserved. Published 2016.
Printed in the United States of America

25 24 23 22 21 20 19 18 17 16   1 2 3 4 5

ISBN-13: 978-0-226-38201-2 (cloth)
ISBN-13: 978-0-226-38215-9 (paper)
ISBN-13: 978-0-226-38229-6 (e-book)
DOI: 10.7208/chicago/9780226382296.001.0001

Library of Congress Cataloging-in-Publication Data

Names: McDonnell, Terence E. (Terence Emmett), author.
Title: Best laid plans : cultural entropy and the unraveling of AIDS media campaigns /
    Terence E. McDonnell.
Description: Chicago : The University of Chicago Press, 2016. | Includes
    bibliographical references and index.
Identifiers: LCCN 2015048929 | ISBN 9780226382012 (cloth : alk. paper) |
    ISBN 9780226382159 (pbk. : alk. paper) | ISBN 9780226382296 (e-book)
Subjects: LCSH: AIDS (Disease) in mass media. | Mass media in health education—
    Ghana—Accra. | Communication in public health—Ghana—Accra. | AIDS
    (Disease)—Ghana—Prevention.
Classification: LCC P96.A392 G46 2016 | DDC 362.19697/92009667—dc23 LC record
    available at http://lccn.loc.gov/2015048929

♾ This paper meets the requirements of ANSI/NISO Z39.48-1992 (Permanence of
Paper).

For Erin

Contents

Abbreviations

A I D S : acquired immunodeficiency syndrome

A R T : antiretroviral therapy (treatment for people living with HIV)

B C C : behavior change communication

C D 4 : Cluster of Differentiation 4 (a glycoprotein measured to assess progression of HIV)

D F I D : Department for International Development (of the United Kingdom)

F D B : Food and Drugs Board of Ghana

F H I : Family Health International

G A C : Ghana AIDS Commission

G S C P : Ghana Sustainable Change Project

G S M F : Ghana Social Marketing Foundation

H I V : human immunodeficiency virus

H P U : Health Promotion Unit (of the Ghana Ministry of Health)

J H U : Johns Hopkins University Bloomberg School of Public Health Center for Communications Programs

K A P : Knowledge, Attitude, and Practice survey

N A P + : Ghana Network of People Living with HIV/AIDS

N G O : nongovernmental organization

P E P F A R : United States President's Emergency Plan for AIDS Relief

P P A G : Planned Parenthood Association of Ghana

S H A R P : Strengthening HIV/AIDS Response Partnerships

S T I : sexually transmitted infection

U N A I D S : Joint United Nations Programme on HIV/AIDS

U N F P A : United Nations Population Fund

U S A I D : United States Agency for International Development

V C T : voluntary counseling and testing

W H O : World Health Organization

Introduction

Organizations endeavor to influence us by harnessing and manipulating meaning. The state mobilizes patriotic sentiment to persuade you to act in the national interest. Corporations entice you to buy their products by telling you how to look more beautiful. Activists cajole you into protesting the status quo by promoting a sense of collective grievance. Political parties depict their candidates as people with whom you'd want to have a drink so that you'll vote for them. Charities coax you to donate money by making you feel guilty. AIDS organizations convince you to use condoms by telling you that real men wear protection. Organizations attempt to engender these behaviors by using culture instrumentally; they align their messages with the culture of the target audience, systematically shaping meaning as a means to their institutional ends. They communicate these messages by embedding them in objects that circulate through the public sphere: billboards, TV ads, political speeches, protest signs, bumper stickers, and the like.

As Max Weber foresaw, organizations take an increasingly rational approach to their goals, and the people engaged in these persuasion projects share a conviction that culture is a tool to be honed (Weber 1978). Organizations devise methods to assess how best to brand a product, redevelop a neighborhood, or frame a politician's stance on an issue. Across these diverse goals, organizations identify success cases, establish best practices, and then diffuse these insights throughout the field. Organizations systematically gather and use data on a community's knowledge and practices to design better-informed, evidence-based campaigns. They vet campaign ideas with community members to find a campaign message that works. Then, after following these steps, they expect these efforts to produce the intended results.

Culture, communication, and meaning making have become more science than art for these organizations, more instrumental than expressive. This is a recognizably modern project, rooted in the Enlightenment belief that people can shape the world through human reason, invention, and intervention. Under the mantra of "evidence-based" design, organizations adopt the logic of scientific measurement, craft campaign objects they believe will produce consistent and predictable results, and compete for clients and funding by selling a unique approach to design that purportedly produces the intended effects.

This book challenges this instrumental vision of culture and offers an alternative perspective: *Objects are disruptive and culture is difficult to tame.* Rather than being an efficient, predictable way to shape people's behavior, campaigns often do not work as intended. Messages that by all measures *should* change belief and behavior ultimately break down, make wrong turns, or collide with other cultural objects along the organization's carefully mapped-out route. People misinterpret, ignore, or change their opinion of a campaign. Unexpected and ironic uses of campaign objects overtake the intended uses. Campaign objects fall apart or move from their intended sites of reception. Paradoxically, the routinized design practices that organizations adopt to improve campaign effectiveness often inhibit it. Even when efforts appear successful, appearances can be deceiving: the potential effectiveness of a campaign is either short-lived or a fiction of which designers have convinced themselves. Through a deep dive into the production, circulation, and reception of AIDS media campaigns in Ghana, this book demonstrates how these attempts to steer culture are disrupted at each stage of the life course of a campaign. These disruptions are indicative of what I call *cultural entropy*: the process through which the intended meanings and uses of a cultural object fracture into alternative meanings, new practices, failed interactions, and blatant disregard.

Theorizing cultural entropy offers new ways to explain the unintended consequences communication projects face (Merton 1936). AIDS campaigns purposively manipulate culture to achieve particular ends. They seek to narrow meaning, constraining the ways audiences will interpret and use their campaigns. The instrumental view of culture that these organizations take—that they can manipulate culture as a means to the end of persuading people to adopt alternative practices or ways of seeing the world—has serious flaws. Following the life course of these campaign objects—from design to circulation to reception—reveals just how unrealistic these expectations are and how often unintended consequences emerge.

Modern Interventions and Unintended Consequences

Merton suggests that unintended consequences are often a problem of knowledge: either not knowing enough or having a system so complex that it precludes knowing.[1] This is true for AIDS organizations, in part. Organizations do not know enough about people's culture to communicate and persuade effectively; nor could they, given the complexity of people's culture and the process of communication. The methods used to imagine audiences are low resolution, providing oversimplified visions of people's motivations and practices. Even if people were as one-dimensional as organizations' formative research often suggests (and they're not), the objects in which organizations put their faith regularly fail them or behave in unexpected ways. No matter how persuasive a message, objects disrupt, sabotage, and undermine the intended meanings and uses they carry. The careful planning, design, and resources that organizations invest in campaigns appear to stabilize meaning and align a community's understandings and practices around AIDS. The *appearance* of stability obscures important sources of instability that become visible only when following campaigns over time and across settings.

The field of health communication—a discipline based on social scientific models of human behavior developed by psychologists, public-health scholars, and other experts—ushered in an era of best practices.[2] Informed by scholarship and lessons learned from successful interventions around the world, best practice reports diffuse to practitioners proven ways to make campaigns effective. Following these best practices has become standard practice for organizations on the ground. When campaigns fail to meet expectations, organizations endeavor to learn from their mistakes and make best practices *better*, believing that improving the design process will improve the effectiveness of future campaigns.

By learning as much as they can about their population, designers decide what audience to target, what information that audience needs to know, and how to best present that information. Then, they test their message with the audience to see if it resonates. This approach reflects the design strategies disseminated in "evidence-based" logic of best practices. When designers confront unintended outcomes, they believe they missed something. They believe they didn't *know enough*. They respond by learning from their mistakes, acknowledging their gaps in knowledge, refining their practices to collect more or better information that fills those gaps. Because organizations see campaign failures as a problem of knowledge, their solution is to collect increasing amounts of data over time. Data collection offers an additional benefit to organizations by proving to funding agencies that designers are doing their due diligence. This evidence assures both AIDS campaign designers and their funders that they've created a clear, culturally sensitive, and resonant campaign. This instrumental-rational logic gives designers (false) confidence in their ability to direct the audience's interpretation of their message and behavioral response. Knowing more—by collecting more evidence, learning from past mistakes, and refining design practices—gives designers a sense of control. Knowing more about one's target audience and crafting campaigns that align with their beliefs and practices improves campaigns, but campaign effectiveness is more than a knowledge problem.

I argue that these efforts are asymptotic. Organizations have reached the limit of their capacity to improve communication by collecting more data and tweaking design practices. Organizations control the message to the degree they can, but they can never fully capture the complexity of people's beliefs and practices or account for the complex heterogeneity of people's culture. Despite considerable alignment between the message and local culture, organizations can never eliminate the potential for campaign objects' misinterpretation and misuse. While cultural objects appear to stabilize meaning, organizations miss how objects are always open to disruption.

These efforts to control meaning grow expensive as best practice reports mandate the addition of more constraints to the design process. Every additional best practice requires more time, money, and labor. All this effort makes AIDS organizations less nimble, less able to adapt to changing situations. Campaigns often take more than a year to design, and a community's needs may have changed by the time a campaign is launched. This overinvestment in design leads AIDS organizations to miss the ways campaigns succumb to cultural entropy and reduces their ability to adapt on the fly. As designers routinize their actions around best practices, they lose their capacity to develop new creative insights into how to reach their goal of effective communication. The costs of following best practices often outweigh the benefits for organizations.

Rationality becomes irrational as the means of design become the ends.[3] Despite expressing faith in best practices and the process of design, designers' comments to me about their limited creativity suggest that they are well and truly stuck in an "iron cage" (Weber 1992; DiMaggio and Powell 1983). The organizational focus on design draws attention away from evaluation, which in turn prevents organizations from seeing how people misinterpret and misuse campaigns. Practitioners of campaign design then convince themselves they are making progress when, really, they've been running on treadmills.

Though best practices attempt to limit what I'm calling cultural entropy, organizations haven't accounted for the full range of sources of disruption. Cultural entropy, then, offers a new explanation for why so many campaigns fail to make the intended impact, despite the recent improvements in campaign design. People will always misinterpret and misuse campaign objects, *no matter how carefully designed or persuasive*. In many cases, these disruptions and divergences undermine the capacity of campaigns to achieve the desired changes in sexual behavior. The lens of cultural entropy, then, challenges the logic of modern interventions that view culture as something easily molded and put to instrumental ends. Rather than laboring to stave off entropy through better design, this book suggests that organizations need to treat unintended consequences as more than just a knowledge problem: they should view misinterpretations as typical and probable. The reality of cultural entropy will force organizations to question the belief that increasingly rational systems will lead to increasingly predictable results. When attempting to use culture instrumentally, "all hits" really are "flukes."[4]

The failed promise of AIDS communication efforts in the developing world resembles other failed modernist projects. James Scott explains how rationalized attempts to create social order often fail because states neglect local informal practices and cultural knowledge, or they overlook hidden resistance by local communities.[5] Scott argues that the technologies states use to make populations "legible" can lead to unintended consequences because they cannot capture the complexity of human action and "mētis"—the "forms of knowledge embedded in local experience" (Scott 1998, 311). For example, AIDS campaigns based on such technologies as Knowledge, Attitude, and Practice (KAP) surveys produce abstract knowledge that cannot adequately capture local culture, which, in turn, creates unintended consequences in the Mertonian sense. Elites need to simplify a complex world, making it legible so they can intervene with confidence, but this simplification insufficiently incorporates important cultural knowledge (mētis). Their inability to work within practical cultural knowledge, Scott argues, dooms interventions to fail.

As important as these ideas are for understanding why interventions fail, Scott's argument cannot fully explain the disruptions I observed in Ghana. Rather than dismiss the local cultural knowledge that comes from lived experience, the organizations I studied sought to understand local beliefs and practices. Organizations had a deep commitment to adapting campaigns to local cultures and more often than not incorporated community members into the design process. Additionally, Ghanaians do not actively resist interventions. The Ghanaians I spoke with wanted more campaigns and expressed a desire to do something about AIDS. Community groups I visited clamored for AIDS campaign materials. Even when organizations and public interest align, communication disruptions are commonplace. These disruptions are more than just a problem of imposing legibility. This presents a puzzle: Why do I find so many communication disruptions even when AIDS organizations go above and beyond to align interventions with local culture, and when Ghanaians desire to do something about AIDS?

I find that everyday life disrupts communication. For Michel de Certeau, as people go about their lives, they "enunciate" the world around them. Rather than passively read their surroundings as intended by those with power, people elaborate upon it and take alternative paths. People

> make use of spaces that cannot be seen; their knowledge of them is as blind as that of lovers in each other's arms. The paths that correspond in this intertwining, unrecognized poems [*sic*]in which each body is an element signed by many others, elude legibility . . . the networks of these moving intersecting writings compose a manifold story that has neither author nor spectator, shaped out of fragments of trajectories and alterations of spaces. . . . Escaping the imaginary totalizations produced by the eye, the everyday has a certain strangeness that does not surface, or whose surface is only its upper limit, outlining itself against the visible. (de Certeau 1984, 93)

In this passage, de Certeau vividly captures the elusive, creative poetry of everyday life. Everyday life resists interventions that impose totalizing visions. Such resistance is not necessarily about *active and oppositional* individual resistance but more about systemic resistance. Everyday life is fragmentary, constantly changing, made and remade by a multitude of authors who imaginatively write and enunciate the world around them. Everyday life evades containment, reorganization, and imposed order. Everyday life makes its own way, providing a more complex, contingent, and powerful engine of action than any ordered, tested, and well-resourced mass media campaign could muster.

This unpredictability of the everyday is more than just a knowledge problem. Even if an organization understands and adapts to local cultural knowledge and practice, that culture is always unstable and subject to change. Stability, when it emerges, is often temporary. More than just complex and hard to know, culture is *dynamic* and a constantly moving target. Even when culture appears patterned, it is always at risk of instability and open to disruption, innovation, and fragmentation. This tendency toward disorder of cultural entropy frustrates attempts to impose order.

The concept of cultural entropy, then, orients us to the myriad ways that communicating seemingly clear and culturally sensitive messages through objects is open to disruption. Modern interventions such as AIDS campaigns fail because cultural objects are always open to entropy. Organizations assume that culture is stable and static, failing to recognize how meanings change over time and across context. Understanding the ins and outs of cultural entropy improves our understanding of other failed modernist projects by suggesting how culture mediates the effectiveness of these rational interventions (Ferguson 1994; Pressman and Wildavsky 1984; Vaughan 1996).

HIV/AIDS Campaigns as Persuasive Communication

The rationalized techniques designers use to amplify the effects of AIDS media campaigns originate out of propaganda, what Harold Lasswell defined as "the technique of influencing human action by the manipulation of representations" (Lasswell 1995, 13). Throughout World War I and II, nations saw great potential in propaganda to control populations by telling people what to believe and how to act. Following the systematic uses of wartime propaganda, such media scholars as Paul Lazarsfeld began to study media effects between the 1940s and 1960s. Despite beliefs by elites and earlier scholars that propagandistic media could powerfully influence the public, these scholars concluded that the media had "limited effects," rather than the direct effects previously assumed (Klapper 1960). Although effects were limited, scholars posited that organizations could make messages more persuasive if they employed existing ways of seeing the world, received support from opinion leaders and peers, and had a monopoly over the message (Lazarsfeld and Merton 1948; Katz 2001; Katz and Lazarsfeld 2005). These insights pointed toward ways to refine messages in order to maximize effects. Once established, the fields of political communication, advertising, and health communication brought a scientific logic to improving media campaigns through design. Spurred by the incorporation of insights from social science, professional communicators have expanded their efforts from the 1960s into the twenty-first century (Packard 2007).

Public-health interventions have long used media to persuade, from pamphlets promoting smallpox vaccinations in 1721 Boston to antismoking TV ads today. Since the late twentieth century, health communication has grown exponentially. The establishment of health communication in public-health schools and communications programs, the appearance of scholarly journals in the late 1980s and 1990s, and a corps of practitioners working for global health organizations have all stimulated the growth and significance of the field.[6] With the rising AIDS epidemic, health communication techniques and standard procedures spread rapidly through the developing world via the diffusion of professionals and best-practice documents. Broadly, the current persuasion-enhancing strategies promoted by the field of health communication resemble those initially advocated by Lazarsfeld. AIDS organizations tie messages to local beliefs and practices, they recruit opinion leaders to shepherd and support the messages, and they coordinate efforts so all organizations communicate the same message. Incorporating evidence-based practices and empirically validated social scientific theories of behavior change into campaign design, practitioners feel confident that they can have more than just limited effects (Backer, Rogers, and Sopory 1992). As one how-to book suggests, "Modern-day campaigns can still fail, but the likelihood of success overall is greater. Such optimism is one reason for the large number of mass media health campaigns that are currently being carried out" (Backer, Rogers, and Sopory 1992, xv).

Despite this confidence, I find that cultural entropy often undermines campaigns. The study of cultural entropy, then, extends scholarship regarding how and why attempts to induce direct effects through media campaigns are so often fruitless (Klapper 1960; Katz and Lazarsfeld 2005; Schudson 1986). As Michael Schudson once argued, "Advertising is much less powerful than advertisers and critics of advertisers claim, and advertising agencies are stabbing in the dark much more than they are performing precision microsurgery on the public consciousness" (Schudson 1986, xii). Despite decades of research on persuasion, misinterpretation and misuse are common, and such unintended consequences can overwhelm the intended effects (Pratkanis and Aronson 2001; Cialdini 2006).

The concept of cultural entropy builds on media scholarship that these persuasion industries have ignored. Rather than having homogenizing effects by aligning people with the message, circulating campaign objects tend to encourage creative and diverse interpretations.[7] Media campaigns do less to shape behavior in accordance with organizational goals than they do to create opportunities for innovation and hybridization. In this way, I follow Arjun Appadurai, who suggests that the "media provide large and complex repertoires of images" which people use to "construct imagined worlds that are chimerical" (Appadurai 1996, 35). As cultural "flows" become increasingly complex, available local narratives multiply and diverge (Appadurai 1996; Hannerz 1992; Larkin 1997). The concept of cultural entropy, then, draws on "images of flow and uncertainty, rather than on older images of order, stability, and systematicness" (Appadurai 1996, 47). Building on these ideas, cultural entropy identifies and explains the emergence of alternative meanings and uses. Unlike this earlier work, I identify new mechanisms unaccounted for by media studies and cultural sociology, moving beyond such mechanisms as diffusion, globalization, and audiences-based approaches that explain instability through the movement of objects across cultural boundaries.

HIV/AIDS Prevention in Ghana

HIV prevention interventions take many forms, from subsidizing preventative technologies (e.g., condoms or vaginal microbicides) to setting up HIV-testing centers to media campaigns. Funding for these activities has ballooned since the 1990s, especially for prevention efforts in the developing world. The rise of such organizations as the Global Fund and Gates Foundation, country-based international aid programs such as the United States President's Emergency Plan for AIDS Relief (PEPFAR), and support from multinational organizations including the United Nations and the World Health Organization (WHO) have all directed massive resources toward HIV prevention, supplementing local efforts by the state and nongovernmental organizations (NGOs) in Ghana and many other countries. For instance, PEPFAR committed $414 million toward HIV prevention activities in its focus countries in 2007 alone (PEPFAR 2007). For Ghana, PEPFAR invested an average of $11.1 million per year between 2007 and 2013 (PEPFAR 2015). In Ghana, between the years of 2001 and 2004, the World Bank dispensed almost $22 million to the Ghana AIDS Commission for prevention activities, helping to establish the commission as the coordinating body for AIDS interventions in Ghana (World Bank 2007). During that same period, other aid agencies such as the United States Agency for International Development (USAID) and the United Kingdom's Department for International Development (DFID) were investing comparable amounts into prevention efforts in Ghana. These monies filtered down to state actors (e.g., the Health Promotion Unit of the Ghana Ministry of Health), local NGOs (e.g., Ghana Social Marketing Foundation and Planned Parenthood Association of Ghana), and subsidiaries of international health and development organizations (e.g., Family Health International and the Academy for Educational Development).

While these funds supported a range of prevention activities, communication efforts were the central component in Ghana's strategy to limit HIV transmission. Organizations can subsidize condoms or build HIV testing facilities, but such interventions are bound to fail unless organizations can persuade the public to buy condoms or get tested. Ghana's National HIV/AIDS Strategic Frameworks (2001–2005 and 2006–2010) recognized this, naming behavior change communication (BCC) interventions as the primary strategy to limit the spread of HIV (Ghana AIDS Commission 2000; 2005a). In 2005 Ghana increased its commitment to communication, crafting the National Integrated IEC/BCC Strategic Framework, which standardized best practices of design for interventions across the country (Ghana AIDS Commission 2005b). Communication campaigns attempt to reach audiences through a variety of means, including peer education, community networks, traditional media, and mass media campaigns (FHI 2002). Although I focus primarily on the production and effects of media campaigns, the organizations I studied often used multiple paths to reach audiences. To put the media campaigns in context, I also report on the peer education and community-level efforts I observed.

Ghanaian public-health campaigns have ramped up beginning in the 1990s, with campaigns promoting mosquito nets (to prevent malaria), family planning services, and HIV prevention becoming increasingly visible. This rise of Ghanaian public-health campaigns accompanied the growth of Ghana's media infrastructure. As in the rest of sub-Saharan Africa, Ghana's media infrastructure is rapidly improving. Ghana's shift to democracy in 1992 led to the privatization of the media and subsequent growth, and by the late 1990s, diverse television and radio offerings were available (Buckley et al. 2005). The practice of broadcasting TV or radio spots as part of national health campaigns was novel in the late 1990s but is now standard practice. Similarly, billboard communication increased in the first decade of the twenty-first century. Organizations used to pay to build (not rent) billboards, and these owned billboards were few but long-standing. In the years I was in Ghana, between 2003 and 2008, I saw the dramatic rise of leased billboard space and the saturation of Accra with advertising, especially in high-traffic areas. The rapid expansion of media platforms made media campaigns a viable communication path for AIDS organizations.[8] Ghanaians seem to have accepted these channels as appropriate means to communicate about AIDS: survey responses from my focus group participants suggested that media campaigns were their most common and most trusted source of information about HIV/AIDS.[9]

HIV prevention campaigns in Ghana respond to the epidemiological reality on the ground. Ghana has a "generalized" epidemic and, like most developing countries, HIV is most often transmitted through heterosexual sexual intercourse in Ghana.[10] Transactional sex and migratory patterns drive Ghana's epidemiological patterns.[11] Epidemiologists link the majority of cases of HIV infection to "high-risk" groups, such as commercial sex workers, and mobile populations: "uniformed service personnel, teachers, and miners, prisoners, long-distance truck drivers, national service volunteers, cross-border traders, and female long-distance traders" (World Bank 2005, 4) Globally, communication through the media is increasingly "narrowcast" and targeted at specific audiences. This trend reached Ghana in the first decade of the twenty-first century, and since then campaigns have become tailored for high-risk populations. Nonetheless, high-level Ghanaian officials and influential cultural leaders often desired campaigns aimed at a broad public because the epidemic is generalized. This call for general campaigns conflicted with designers' desire to increase impact by targeting specific audiences. Given this context, organizations often adopted both broadcast and narrowcast strategies: national campaigns preaching abstinence, faithfulness, and condom use to everyday Ghanaians, along with narrower campaigns aimed at youth, commercial sex workers, the military, and men who have sex with men.

HIV prevalence in Ghana is low compared to other sub-Saharan African countries—for example, Uganda, Botswana, and South Africa—but higher than such West African neighbors as Benin, Burkina Faso, and Senegal (UNAIDS 2012). During the years of this study, prevalence ranged between 3.6 percent in 2003 and 2.9 percent in 2009, according to HIV Sentinel Survey Data (Ghana AIDS Commission 2014). More recent data suggest that HIV prevalence has continued its decline to 1.7 percent as of 2012 (Ghana AIDS Commission 2014). Some observers may interpret these broad trends as evidence that HIV prevention campaigns have worked and that Ghanaians have made changes to their sexual behavior in response to these interventions. I advise against this conclusion. A number of other causes might explain this drop in prevalence: from the increasing availability of treatment to lowering transmission, to improving economic conditions and life expectancy, and people's subsequent adoption of protective strategies at higher rates.[12]

Additionally, if communication campaigns drove the decline in prevalence, we'd expect to see improvements in the outcomes more proximate to campaigns themselves—for example, increases in HIV knowledge, decreased stigma, and increased use of condoms during high-risk sex. Looking at Ghana's Demographic Health Survey results over time suggests that HIV prevention campaigns' effects on knowledge and stigma have been slow to emerge. Between 2003 and 2008 the number of men in Accra who had comprehensive knowledge declined, from 53.1 percent to 47.4 percent, with many men believing that HIV was transmitted via mosquito bites or witchcraft.[13] HIV-related stigma—a major focus of campaigns—was also high in Accra. In fact, acceptance of people living with HIV *declined* over that same time among both men and women in Accra. Among women, acceptance dropped from 16.0 percent to 14.3 percent, and among men, the decline in acceptance was even more dramatic, plunging from 24.7 percent to 17.4 percent.[14] Though campaigns promoting condoms to prevent HIV accelerated around 2000 with the "Stop AIDS Love Life" campaign, there was no increase between 2003 and 2008 in the percent of Accra residents who knew condoms prevent HIV.[15] Other statistics that suggest campaigns in Ghana have had success—such as increasing condom sales—are also poor indicators because they do not reflect actual condom use and may measure only the aid money invested to increase the availability of condoms (Meekers and Van Rossem 2004).

When I began this research, most Ghanaians did not know someone who was HIV positive (Ghana Statistical Service et. al. 2004). With such a low prevalence, firsthand experience with HIV was uncommon and the disease remained hidden and marginalized. Stigma abounded, and the informal spread of quality medical knowledge was limited. In such a context, media campaigns should play an important role in promoting official, medically informed HIV prevention knowledge and behavior. This is why Ghana makes such a great case for this study of HIV prevention campaigns. I could have studied a country with high HIV prevalence, but people in those countries have firsthand experiences with the disease that shape their attitudes and behavior more than media campaigns do. In a country—such as Ghana—with a generalized epidemic but limited firsthand exposure, people have real concerns about HIV spreading but rely on media sources for answers. As media campaigns are the primary source of AIDS medical knowledge for most Ghanaians, campaigns in Ghana are more likely to shape belief and behavior in this context than in others. Though Ghanaians rely on media campaigns for HIV/AIDS information, they do not always interpret and use campaigns as intended. Cultural entropy diminishes the capacity of AIDS campaigns to accomplish organizations' goals.

Data and Methods

Explaining whether and how AIDS campaigns do the work organizations design them to do required me to analyze the entire life course of campaigns. To identify instances of cultural entropy, I first had to know the designers' intentions: how did they expect audiences to interpret or use their campaign? When I knew producers' intended meaning and use, I could compare those intentions to how audiences actually interpreted and used campaigns, whether campaign objects circulated as expected, how settings mediate communication, and more. When audiences missed, misinterpreted, or misused campaigns (from the designers' perspective), I knew I had an instance of cultural entropy. I then compared instances of cultural entropy to discern patterns and common mechanisms.

Scholars of media and cultural objects have adopted a life course approach to great effect.[16] In particular, I follow Wendy Griswold's cultural diamond model, articulating the links between the social world, practices of production, the qualities of cultural objects and their circulation, and the ultimate reception by audiences (Griswold 1986).[17] Elaborating each point of the diamond required me to employ a variety of methods of data collection and analysis. I introduce my data and methods briefly here, but the book includes a more complete discussion in the methodological appendix.

To capture the social world, I extensively explored the city, traveling by foot, car, and public transportation, visiting hospitals, poly-clinics, pharmacies, herbalists, churches, schools, and bars during my three research trips to Accra.[18] I talked to people—experts and laypeople alike—about HIV, condoms, health care, and AIDS campaigns. In addition to ethnographic methods and informal interviews, I photographed the streetscape and mapped where AIDS images appeared in space. I also collected relevant media on HIV in Ghana, including newspaper articles, books warning against same-sex attraction sold at grocers, and religious pamphlets passed out in public. These data allowed me to understand the challenges AIDS organizations face in communicating a coherent message about HIV, the institutions that shape people's understanding of HIV, and how Ghanaians' various beliefs and behaviors might undermine AIDS interventions.

To understand the logic and practice of AIDS campaign production and to establish the intended meaning and use of campaign objects, I interviewed staff across the universe of AIDS organizations producing media campaigns in Accra.[19] For the major organizations producing campaigns, I interviewed multiple designers (typically three or four), and when possible I sat in on design meetings. I also interviewed staff at partnered advertising agencies, funding agencies, advisory organizations, government ministries, clinics, religious institutions, and community groups to understand the broader institutional context in which organizations worked.

After organizations launched campaigns into the public sphere, I sought to understand how these objects circulated through the city, where they appeared, and how people interacted with them in situ. I documented their presence throughout the city through photographs and mapping. I observed how people interacted with them as they walked or rode past and interviewed people at campaign sites. I accounted for characteristics of settings, such as how saturated the streetscape around the campaigns was with other advertisements, what kinds of buildings were copresent, and what cultural practices occurred around the object. I noted the condition of billboards and captured changes over time. These observations allowed me to understand how interpretive interactions between people, objects, and settings shaped circulation and meaning making. In turn, I could evaluate whether objects circulated and communicated meaning in line with producers' intentions.

Finally, I needed to measure Ghanaians' reception of AIDS campaigns and to assess whether commonly used symbols resonated with them. To do so, I conducted focus groups with community members, schoolteachers, and HIV-positive Ghanaians. The centerpiece of these focus groups was a poster drawing exercise in which I asked participants to design and draw an AIDS campaign poster for their community. I focus my analysis on these posters and the process of debate and discussion that indicated which symbols provoked consensus or dissent, controversy, or heightened emotions. See the appendix for a more elaborate discussion of my focus groups. These focus groups revealed implicit cultural orientations, when people interpreted symbols in unexpected ways, and how Ghanaians make sense of HIV through the language of available campaigns.

These data and methods make visible patterned ways in which campaigns go awry at each stage of their life course. Public-health research takes a narrower approach to evaluation that is blind to the presence and sources of cultural entropy. Practitioners typically examine the relationship between campaign exposure and a host of outcomes such as campaign recall, HIV-related knowledge, misconceptions, self-reported condom use, and more. What do these evaluations miss? First, these evaluations ignore the design process. Campaign design is not a neutral series of routine steps but a contested process of translation and accommodation. As such, it is crucial to understand how AIDS organizations implement best practices and shepherd audiences, stakeholders, local organizations and funding agencies through the design process. My approach investigates how these efforts shape the campaign's ultimate content, whether best practices of design undermine their own stated goals, and whether design conventions make campaigns more open to disruption.

Second, public-health evaluations of AIDS campaigns underemphasize how people interpret and use campaigns. For a campaign to result in the outcomes that public-health organizations care about, people must see the campaign, interpret its message correctly, be persuaded by that message, and act on that message—if they can afford to and if they remember the campaign when a relevant situation arises. Long-term behavioral change happens only if people believe that making the prescribed change was a good decision and then act to reaffirm that change by consistently behaving in ways that align with the campaign when confronted with the same situation. These important aspects of the communication process are left unconsidered when exposure is the sole measure of a campaign's capacity to engender desired effects. Using broader methods and measures, I consider how exposure is encouraged or inhibited in the first place and how people interpret and use campaigns in practice, and I compare whether people's everyday meanings of campaigns align with an organization's intended message.

Expanding the scope beyond public-health evaluations reveals contention and contingency in the communication process. To capture this, I've created a "social iconography" of AIDS campaigns: a study of the social practices, interactions, and contexts around visual symbols. Time is essential to this analysis because campaigns' meanings are not static. This approach also contrasts with work on the visual culture of AIDS that tends to engage in close readings of images rather than attend to how they are interpreted and used in everyday life.[20] To understand how campaign objects are open to disruption, one must attend to how people interpret and use the campaigns in practice, across an object's life course, rather than conduct a more traditional semiotic analysis of campaigns.

The Argument, in Brief

I begin in chapter 1 by outlining the theory of cultural entropy. As campaign objects move from interaction to interaction—crafted by designers, vetted by opinion leaders and the community, circulated through public space, interpreted and used by the public—they sometimes do the work they were tasked to do and at other times undergo a process of cultural entropy. The energy invested in an object sometimes flows along the intended path, moving people to change their beliefs and behavior in ways aligned with organizational goals (e.g., encouraging condom use or abstinence). Often, though, an object's energy diffuses or diverts along unintended trajectories. Disruption and misinterpretation are always possible, and these alternative paths are built into the interpretive arrangements of people, objects, and settings. This potential instability puts objects at risk for cultural entropy. Organizations can mitigate or forestall entropy to some degree, but they can never entirely eliminate the possibility of entropy because interpretive arrangements never perfectly stabilize.

In light of this reality, I account for instability at every stage of AIDS campaigns' life course. In chapter 2, I map the cultural topography of Accra as it relates to AIDS. In so doing, I show how competing objects on the streetscape and the ambiguities created by competing knowledge domains make it difficult for AIDS organizations to monopolize and control AIDS knowledge. Organizations navigate this challenging terrain using best-practice documents as road maps. AIDS organizations seek to cut through the complexity of the cultural environment by learning about local understandings and everyday practices, harnessing them to craft tailored campaigns, and securing the support of opinion leaders and the community to produce simple, clear, and persuasive AIDS campaigns.

Drawing on a production of culture approach, I examine how institutional practices, contexts, and commitments shape the design of AIDS campaigns.[21] In chapter 3, I analyze best-practice documents and chronicle how best-practice documents undergo their own process of cultural entropy. More than just guidelines instructing organizations how to make successful campaigns, these reports lead AIDS organizations to converge around a set of international standards. In practice, though, AIDS organizations put best-practice documents into practice in divergent ways. Chapter 4 extends this discussion, showing how the production process is shaped by the data used by designers to imagine audiences and by the incorporation of input from cultural ombudsmen, the local authorities who are tasked with shepherding campaigns to the community. Commitments to the best practices of formative research and securing buy-in from community leaders come into conflict, forcing designers to compromise on their principles and resulting in campaigns that sacrifice persuasiveness to satisfy stakeholders.

After organizations settle on a final campaign concept and distribute the message through urban space, AIDS campaign objects lead unexpected lives: billboards fade, posters go missing, bumper stickers travel to other cities with the vehicles to which they are attached. Chapter 5 suggests how the material qualities of the interpretive arrangement encourage cultural entropy through mechanisms of displacement and decay. The meaning of campaigns changes as billboards age and campaign objects move to new settings. These moments subvert campaign visibility and stability.

Chapter 6 describes how Ghanaians' (albeit limited) exposure to the scare tactics of earlier AIDS campaigns determined how they interpreted newer campaigns. With the diffusion of best-practice reports during the late 1990s, AIDS organizations rejected the fear-based campaigns of that decade in favor of positive campaigns that avoided stigmatizing language and images. If these better-resourced, more optimistic campaigns were as persuasive as designers claim, we should see Ghanaians associating HIV with more positive representations, leaving behind the images of illness, skeletons, and coffins that appeared earlier in the epidemic's history. Instead, these older representations led Ghanaians to interpret positive campaigns in unintended ways, sometimes leading them to reject positive messages outright.

I conclude by explaining how cultural entropy systematically undermines the effectiveness of these AIDS campaigns and other modern interventions. I place the various mechanisms of entropy into conversation with one another, showing how they interact to amplify these disruptive effects. I then extend these insights beyond health communication to consider how cultural entropy explains other failures by organizations to use culture instrumentally. Ultimately, cultural entropy offers new ways of thinking about culture that emphasize materiality, interaction, contingency, dynamism, and flow.

Cultural Entropy

Organizations see objects as solutions to a number of problems. Organizations extend their agency and interests through objects, diffusing messages beyond what is possible through face-to-face communication. Objects also appear to stabilize meaning better than trained peer-educators, who might go "off script" when spreading the message. Objects are never off the clock, extending messages through time, even after communications staff have gone home. Using objects, organizations can carefully craft messages they believe will communicate their intended meaning.

Organizations miss how objects are "unruly" (Domínguez Rubio 2014). Although objects stabilize meaning to some degree, objects are inherently open to disruption. Organizations put too much faith in their capacity to craft campaigns that communicate clearly, consistently, and persuasively. Despite organizations' meticulous planning, campaigns misbehave: campaigns communicate unintended meanings, people appropriate campaigns for alternative purposes, objects fall apart or go missing. To successfully impact beliefs and behavior, campaign objects must communicate the intended message to the intended audience, but I find that campaign intentions are systematically disrupted. To explain how this disruption happens, I introduce the concept of *cultural entropy*. Before defining and elaborating this idea, let's examine a few examples that will serve as a foundation for building the framework.

Miscommunication in a Muslim Neighborhood

Family Health International (FHI) staff in Ghana took great care to create a billboard that promoted an HIV prevention strategy that Muslims would support—faithfulness. Working in collaboration with the Muslim Relief

FIGURE 1. Family Health International's Muslim faithfulness billboard near the Nima market in Accra, Ghana

Association of Ghana (MURAG), FHI staff identified images and messages relevant to the experiences and needs of the Muslim community. FHI tailored the billboard for this community by translating a common slogan ("AIDS Is Real") into Hausa ("AIDS Gaskia Ne"), the predominant language among local Muslims (see fig. 1). The billboard also presents the faithfulness message in a way that is inclusive of local sexual practices: the parenthetical "(s)" recognizes that Ghanaian Muslims accept polygamous marriages.[1] In addition, FHI aligned this image with Muslim culture, photographing people in appropriate Muslim dress with a well-known mosque in the background. FHI was careful not to cause offense. While other campaigns depict condoms or flirtatious behavior, sexual content is noticeably absent from this image because depicting sexual activity is taboo in the Muslim community.

FHI directed this message at residents of Nima, one of the poorest slums in Accra and a neighborhood with one of the largest concentrations of Muslims.[2] To ensure that the design was clear and culturally sensitive, designers pretested images with Nima residents and vetted the proposed billboard with the local imam, whose group (initially) approved the image. After assessing the needs of the local community, partnering with a civil society organization to develop an appropriate campaign, pretesting campaign ideas with target audiences, refining ideas to avoid misinterpretation, and getting approval from powerful stakeholders, FHI placed the billboard adjacent to the Nima market, the hub of the neighborhood. By all accounts, FHI met or exceeded international standards of health campaign design.[3] Surprisingly, despite every effort to eliminate misinterpretation by following the best practices of campaign design, the imam and Nima residents ultimately rejected the billboard.

Although the imam had supported the effort when he first approved the image, after the billboard went up he objected to how the image undermined traditional gender norms:

> After the pictures were taken, and everyone had done the pretest, we real-ized we hadn't done pretests with the highest authority within the Muslim community—the Imam. So we had to send the materials to his group to look at. Initially he said the pictures are ok, but then he realized the woman in the picture is telling the man something, which is not normally the case for them and their community. So he would prefer if the man is rather showing or depicting "I am telling you, the woman, something and you should listen."[4]

Contrary to local Muslim mores, FHI's representation of gender dynamics encoded a Western ideal of gender equality held by FHI and other inter-national health nongovernmental organizations (NGOs). In the image, the woman is active and the man is passive. She faces the audience, drawing the attention of both those viewing the billboard and the man in the image, thus giving her authority. Taken with the billboard's text, she appears to instruct her husband about the relationship between faithfulness and AIDS. A woman daring to educate her husband about faithfulness—in public space and under the shadow of a mosque—challenges traditional Muslim gender relations of this community. The billboard's imperfect fit to the local culture disrupts communication of FHI's intended meaning.

Moreover, when I engaged Nima residents walking past this billboard, many indicated that they believed the billboard's message was not intended for them. One woman explained, "Sharia law came first, then AIDS laws . . . I follow Sharia law, I don't go around with lots of men." Another man con-curred, saying, "Already I am faithful to my wives."[5] These residents admitted that others may need to hear the message, but the billboard was redundant for good Muslims like themselves. Local residents did not accept FHI's "defi-nition of the situation" (Thomas 1927; Goffman 1959). The reason to practice faithfulness was not to prevent AIDS, but rather to follow God's will. Sharia law had greater authority to define reality than AIDS organizations. In order to validate their identity as pious Muslims, they had to reject FHI's message.

Another source of unintended interpretations was the material decay of the billboard. FHI installed this billboard before 2003, and it remained in

place until my last visit in March 2008. Over five or more years, harsh environmental conditions weathered this billboard: the image and letters faded,
words peeled off the backing, the billboard was caked in dirt, and the left half
of the billboard was crumpled, partially obscuring the man's image. By 2004,
the funding for FHI's Impact program ended, and the billboard was forgotten. When I asked one resident about the billboard, he remarked, "If they care
about it, they will maintain it—clean it, straighten it out, then repaint it. But
they don't care about it." The lack of maintenance made visible FHI's disappearance, confirming community members' beliefs that government agencies
and NGOs had forgotten them. Material evidence of organizational neglect
detracted from the message about faithfulness.

Why did this billboard fail to communicate its intended message? Health
communicators would attribute these unexpected disruptions to insufficiently
customizing campaigns for the target audience (Backer, Rogers, and Sopory
1992; Nowak and Siska 1995): if only they had pretested the campaign with
more community members, worked *more* closely with the imam, then they
would have identified these problems and changed the image and text to preclude misinterpretations. Another explanation might be that while designers
relied on community involvement, they still imposed their own views (about
gender or polygamy) on the community. Perhaps involving the community
earlier in the process could improve the effectiveness of communication
(Myrick et al. 2005; Wilson and Miller 2003). By allowing communities to
identify their own messages, instead of screening AIDS organization–devised
slogans, NGOs could both improve communication and secure the community's support for the campaign. Before you blame these failures on FHI, let
me tell you another story.

Yes, but Not on My T-Shirt

Known for working closely with Ghanaian communities, Planned Parenthood Association of Ghana (PPAG) placed the community at the center of
the design process. PPAG sought to design an HIV prevention campaign that
encouraged condom use among youth. Through discussions with Ghanaian
youth, PPAG realized that many of them were timid about buying condoms.
If someone saw them purchase a condom, they would be implicated in premarital sex, suggesting a lack of moral character. In collaboration with PPAG,
youth devised several potential messages, including "Don't Be Shy, Use a
Condom." After pretesting these messages, PPAG found that this community
strongly supported the "Don't Be Shy" slogan.

PPAG produced a series of posters and T-shirts with the slogan. When PPAG returned to the community to distribute the materials, many young people refused to accept the T-shirts. According to a PPAG staffer:

> I got this message, "oh, we're getting the t-shirts back." Young people said there was no way they were going to wear those t-shirts in the communities because people would know they were using condoms and stuff. If you're saying don't be shy, that means *they* use condoms. There were probably about 1,500 t-shirts that all came back.[6]

This is surprising for two reasons. First, the community created this message, so why would they reject the T-shirts featuring it? Second, Ghanaians who depend on the used clothing market usually clamor for new, free T-shirts. In theory, abstracted from the public context where the message would eventually be deployed, focus group participants supported condom promotion by PPAG. While Ghanaian youth may agree with the philosophy of the message, and may even use condoms regularly, displaying that message on their chests said more about *them* than it did about promoting condoms. In practice, wearing the T-shirts was tantamount to Hester Prynne wearing a scarlet letter A. If Ghanaian youth advocate condom use, it might "spoil" their identity (Goffman 1963). Wearing the shirt in support of condoms implied commitment to personal condom *use* and therefore promiscuity. More than other channels of health communication such as billboards or radio ads, T-shirts intimately linked the message to an individual's identity. Even though PPAG used design practices that improved its cultural sensitivity, PPAG missed the social consequences of the T-shirt campaign for local youth.

As it did with FHI's billboard in Nima, the field of health communication would attribute the failure of these T-shirts to a careless design process. Whereas in hindsight it is easy to attribute these moments of miscommunication to designers' negligence, my sense is that FHI and PPAG acted in good faith. They diligently followed the steps of good campaign design as laid out by the field of health communication and best-practice documents. They conducted formative research and worked hand in hand with targeted communities to develop what seemed to be culturally sensitive and resonant campaigns. They pretested these campaigns, refining them to ensure that audiences wouldn't misconstrue their message. One must acknowledge that organizations have limits—they lack the resources, time, and people to test all possible iterations in advance. Designers did not find these alternative interpretations during pretesting, so they did not expect to see this variation after the launch. It might still seem like PPAG and FHI could have done *more* to prevent these disruptions. But before you blame PPAG for not conducting enough focus groups or for not asking the right questions, let's examine one more story.

Getting Creative with Condoms

Public-health organizations in Accra (and globally) promote female condoms as a way for women to control fertility and prevent sexually transmitted infections (STIs) such as HIV/AIDS (Kaler 2001; 2004). More often than not, female condoms are promoted through peer education and instructive pamphlets at health clinics and community meetings. During an interview, Grace,[7] the head nurse at an Accra clinic, recounted an unexpected consequence of promoting the female condom. According to Grace, clinic staff noticed a dramatic spike in female condom sales. At the time, clinic staff concluded that their efforts at promoting female condoms had finally paid off. Soon after, a girl came to the clinic asking for a large box of female condoms. Concerned that the girl was too young to be having sex, Grace asked her, "What are you planning to do with these condoms?" The girl replied, "They are not for me, but for my sister." The girl admitted to Grace that her sister turned the condoms into bracelets by removing the latex lining, boiling the plastic rings to stretch them to size, and then dyeing them in bright colors to sell at the market. Later, an older girl came by the clinic with her arm full of these bracelets. Grace reported asking the girl, "How many boyfriends do you have?" The girl answered, "Two." Grace asked if she used protection with these men, to which the girl replied, "Sometimes." Grace became concerned that these girls "would buy the condoms at the clinic in the morning, make bracelets in the afternoon, and then have unprotected sex with boyfriends at night."[8]

From the point of view of clinic staff, they had subsidized, promoted, and distributed female condoms for a singular purpose: so that young women (and men) could avoid contracting HIV and other sexually transmitted diseases. From Grace's perspective, young women who were turning female condoms into jelly bracelets perverted that intention. For enterprising young women, female condoms meant something altogether different: female condoms were raw materials for bracelets, not prophylactic devices.

How could this happen? Why didn't AIDS organizations predict that women would turn condoms into bracelets? Wasn't it obvious? Let's be honest, these questions seem absurd. You might be thinking, "Of course they couldn't predict condom bracelets!" I completely agree. Although this example might seem extreme, I don't see it as any different than blaming FHI and PPAG for their failures. When campaigns don't work according to plan, the field of health communication considers this failure a problem to solve by being more proactive before the campaign's launch. They work to make best practices *better*. Following this instrumental-rational logic, organizations should gather even more data about their audience to develop even better campaigns that speak with even greater cultural sensitivity. Then, they would expand the pretesting of their campaign ideas with additional focus groups to refine and clarify their message (How about five? No, ten! No, twenty!). Organizations could purchase higher-quality marketing data to choose sites for campaigns that reach target audiences more effectively. However, there are rapidly diminishing returns on these investments. The commitment to evidence-based design that informs each of these solutions requires organizations to spend increasing time and money to wipe out the possibility of misinterpretation. As easy as it might be to blame campaign designers for not doing enough, a more fundamental problem exists. Campaigns are disrupted *in spite of* these efforts to align their messages with the audience.

The problem is not with AIDS campaign designers in the field but rather with the instrumental model of culture that undergirds the field of health communication. This model, based in social science research, assumes that AIDS organizations can predictably control how people interpret their campaigns and change their behavior by aligning their message with the culture of the audiences they target through a systematic process of campaign design. This book calls into question this instrumental, audience-focused model. To begin to elaborate the deficiencies of this model, let's unpack the process that led to "condom bracelets."

FROM CONDOM TO BRACELET

The story starts with a young woman visiting a clinic seeking care for an STD or speaking with a nurse during one of the clinic's community interventions. During such a meeting, a nurse discusses the risks of unprotected sex, distributes handfuls of female condoms, and explains how to use the condom effectively. As a female-controlled contraceptive device, the female condom is viewed by public-health organizations around the world and in Ghana as a way to undermine gender inequalities, offering an implicit lesson in feminism. In essence, clinic staff members share a new system of meanings and practices regarding sex and women's empowerment with this young woman.

Opportunities for disruption manifest even at this early stage of the condom promotion process. Women at community meetings who have not experienced an STD may reject the need for condoms outright. Some women may see contraceptive decisions as the responsibility of their partners and reject the empowerment message. Or, the presentation itself might undermine the goal of condom promotion. Many nurses and peer educators have never used a female condom themselves, and their lack of familiarity has been shown to negatively influence clients' likelihood of trying condoms and incorporating them into their sexual practices (Mantell, Scheepers, and Karim 2000).

But let's imagine that the meeting with the clinic staff successfully persuades clients to try the condom. The woman leaves with multiple condoms, a pamphlet (that she may not be literate enough to read), and exposure to new ideas about safe sex practices. If committed to trying the female condom, she may discuss it with her sexual partner or surreptitiously insert it before sex. He may reject the idea when she raises it or react negatively when he notices she's wearing a condom. In response, he might accuse her of not trusting him. He might distrust her and think that she's having sex with other men.[9] These issues are especially salient for young Ghanaian women who engage in "sexual exchange" relationships, where there is a lot at stake in maintaining these relationships that ensure financial stability and status.[10] Married Ghanaian women face similar challenges. Without gender equality and independent access to resources, Ghanaian women often lack the power to insist on or negotiate condom use with partners (Mill and Anarfi 2002). To reaffirm trust between them, she may revert to unprotected sex, placing herself at risk.

Her partner may agree to try the condom, but the material qualities of the condom may also undermine women's successful adoption. Either or both of them might be dissatisfied if the latex diminishes sexual pleasure. Or the awkwardness of inserting a condom during foreplay and the question of whether it is "in right" may ruin the moment. Frustrated by these material impediments, the couple might give up on their intentions to use female condoms.

For these and other reasons, female condom interventions have not been successful (Pool et al. 2000; Mantell et al. 2006). When female condoms fail to do the work designers intended them to do, they become more open to alternative interpretations and uses. Ghanaian women find themselves with leftover condoms that are no longer useful as contraceptive devices. In my experience, Ghanaians rarely throw out anything. Rather, they save objects until they find a use for them, or they circulate objects to others who can put them into service. With "excess" condoms, enterprising Ghanaian women experimented with these remainders and creatively repurposed the condoms for other uses. Converting condoms into bracelets represents just one of many innovative uses Ghanaians identified, others of which failed to continue.

So, why did condom bracelets develop into a robust alternative practice? One obvious reason is that the bracelets had personal value to these women as jewelry. The practice then moved beyond personal adornment to a commodity for sale to a broader public. Once a bracelet market appeared, condoms had an economic value for these enterprising women, incentivizing them to produce more and more bracelets. International public-health organization policies that champion free or subsidized female condoms to prevent HIV facilitated this alternative economic practice, which would not have been possible if the cost of female condoms had been too high to make a profit on the bracelets. Understanding how the condoms became bracelets, then, also requires an ecological view that attends to systemic factors outside the moment of interpretation.

THE INADEQUACIES OF CURRENT THEORY

Social science lacks the tools needed to adequately explain this journey from female condom to jelly bracelet. Disruptions along the path from peer education to market stand are multiple and diverse. Some disruptions are structural, as when gender dynamics lead women to feel they cannot suggest condom use to their partners. Other disruptions are symbolic, as when condoms signify distrust. Others are material, as when a sexual partner feels latex inhibits sensation or when women stretch the rings into bracelets. This book develops a framework that makes visible this variety of disruptions, divergences, and misuses objects confront. This framework facilitates the theorization of generalizable mechanisms that lead to these alternatives. It does so by considering audiences in complex ways, incorporating analysis of reception settings, and examining the agency of objects in shaping meaning and practice. To develop such a framework, I bridge sociological approaches with insights from media studies, anthropology, science and technology studies, and cognitive psychology.

Before I introduce this framework in full, I'd like to suggest why other approaches cannot explain the cases I observed.[11] Social scientists conventionally explain disruptions through the lens of "polyvocality," "multivocality," or "polysemy." These ideas appear most often in work on reception theory and frame analysis. Reception theorists may say objects are "polyvocal," but what they mean is that objects offer a static set of symbols, and people interpret or read those objects differently depending on the cultural capacities of the "interpretive communities" doing the "reading" (Fish 1980). Scholars of reception view audiences as agentic and able to override the intended meaning of objects (Fish 1980; Jauss 1982). This capacity to read alternatives is not unbounded (Lutz and Collins 1993). The object's form and symbolic content together with the audience's knowledge and skills render some interpretations likely and others unlikely (Griswold 1987a). While scholars explicitly

recognize the give-and-take of object and audience, implicitly they emphasize audience-based explanations. They explain different interpretations of
the same object by tracing interpretations back to the cognitive presuppositions that members of the same group or demographic category share: nation,
race, religion, gender, class, political orientation, or other factors.[12] Adopting
this approach, one would expect people with similar cultural dispositions to
interpret the female condom in similar ways. While Ghanaian women share
cultural presuppositions that shape meaning making, this cannot account for
the emergence of the condom bracelet. Had I shown a female condom to a
focus group of impoverished Ghanaian women unfamiliar with the female
condom, I doubt they would have yelled out, "bracelet!"

Other theories of meaning making suggest that an object's meaning is
stable so long as the producer and receiver of the object are aligned.[13] Studies
of framing in the social movement literature and work from the Birmingham
tradition of media studies make comparable claims here: interpretations conform to or diverge from the intended meaning through the mechanism of
alignment or symmetry. The more the frame, the structural position, or the
culture of an object's producer align with the audience doing the interpretation, the more stable the meaning and the more likely that audiences will "decode" the intended message.[14] Misinterpretation, then, appears when object
and audience lack alignment.[15] But many disruptions I witnessed occurred
despite aligned producers and audiences. The AIDS campaign designers I interviewed, mostly Ghanaian rather than foreign-born, based message framing on the experiences and cultural dispositions of local Ghanaians. In addition, most Ghanaians I spoke with *wanted* to know how to prevent AIDS
and trusted these public-health organizations. Disruptions occur even when
interests, dispositions, and meanings are aligned.

One way to improve on existing approaches is to adopt a more complex
view of audiences.[16] Reception theory and frame analysis delimit audiences,
treating people as if their group position or orientations were singular, coherent, and consistent. These approaches cannot account for within-group
or within-individual variation, missing how an audience might interpret the
same object differently over time or interpret that object in multiple ways
simultaneously. Among residents of Nima, some focused on the billboard's
neglected condition, while others dismissed the billboard as redundant with
the higher authority of the Quran. Moreover, the imam saw no problem
with the image at one point but later objected to its representation of gender
norms. The Nima case makes clear that the same person or members of the
same audience group can read multiple interpretations—including intended

and alternative meanings—into the same billboard, something group membership and alignment do not explain or predict.

These theories also miss the important role of bodies. As the "Don't Be Shy" T-shirt example shows, messages worn by people may be interpreted differently than depersonalized messages printed on a poster. People also make meaning through bodily experience—despite being persuaded to wear a condom, the tactile feeling of that condom may undermine future use, depending on the embodied experience of the people involved. An alternative approach would consider audiences' cognitive complexity and bodily capacities as they make meaning across settings and times.

Settings are also undertheorized as a possible path to alternative interpretations and uses.[17] Peer education programs work differently in church halls than they do at the market, and arguments for female condoms that are persuasive in these settings may meet resistance in the bedroom. These settings cognitively cue—or "key," to use Erving Goffman's phrasing—different frames of mind (Goffman 1974). The physical conditions and organization of settings impinge upon objects' interpretation and use within each setting. Harsh conditions and tropical sun degraded the billboard in Nima, influencing local Muslims' interpretations. Whether objects are stationary or mobile also shapes meaning and use.[18] Previous work on polyvocality largely missed these important dimensions. Any framework that aims to theorize how setting-based mechanisms lead to alternative interpretations and uses of objects must attend to the symbolic and physical dimensions of settings.

Alternative approaches also fail to credit objects for their role in polyvocality. Objects therefore appear as a given, a static—though symbolically complex—constraint to meaning making. Attention to the affordances of objects provides an important corrective to this conception of objects. As a relational approach that values the material and symbolic qualities of objects in conjunction with the cognitive and bodily capacities of people in settings, the study of affordances moves beyond the image of audiences as readers who elucidate the symbolic meanings already embedded in an object.[19] The framework I develop in this book uses the lens of affordances rather than polyvocality to go beyond the limitations of semiotic approaches that decode inherent meanings of a text. Attention to affordances makes visible the material and symbolic power of objects above and beyond a semiotic analysis. Taken this way, objects are no longer the static, passive side of meaning making but an active, dynamic cocontributor to the meaning-making process (Latour 1992; Latour 2005; Pickering 1995; Bennett 2009).

Finally, audience-based explanations that privilege disposition and alignment fail to adequately account for change over time. Without a more dynamic framework, these theories draw attention away from the temporal chain of microlevel mechanisms that better explain such cases as the invention of condom bracelets: the materiality of female condoms, the powerful influence of male partners, the practice of subsidizing condom distribution. Iterations of interactions over time, small reinterpretations, and trial and error produce shifts in the meaning and use of the female condom within this community.

Without an account of the chance occurrence, happy accident, or disastrous failure, scholars miss how chains of interactions between people and objects shape and disrupt future interactions. Pragmatism offers an approach to semiotic analysis that focuses precisely on the iterative interactions between objects, people, and settings over time (Peirce 1998; Joas 1996; Emirbayer and Mische 1998; Gross 2009). My framework is informed by pragmatism but differs from symbolic interactionism, another sociological tradition that traces its legacy back to pragmatist sources (Blumer 1969). Symbolic interactionism emphasizes interpersonal, symbolic, and linguistic explanations, missing important material mechanisms. I draw on recent developments in pragmatist theorizing that return to a more robust conception of the way that objects, bodies, and settings interact in the semiotic process. In this way, the framework I propose for explaining the disruptions I witnessed is able to account for the agency of objects, audiences, and settings; account for the symbolic and material qualities of each; and trace the emergence of interpretation and use over time, analyzing how each element works with the others.[20]

Audience-based theories of interpretation are not only within the purview of scholars; such approaches tacitly inform the communication models AIDS campaign designers follow, along with work on the important role of opinion leaders (Katz and Lazarsfeld 2005). These approaches attribute communication failures to a mismatch between campaigns' messages and the target audience's culture. In so doing, the field of health communication misses the larger source of disruption: the dynamic nature of *culture itself*. Rather than seeing culture as something that organizations can direct, constrain, and tame, AIDS campaign designers need a view that recognizes culture as complex, unruly, and unpredictable. Whereas organizations see communication breakdowns as surprising, especially after working for months to refine their message, I've come to expect the unexpected. What campaign designers call failures, I see as the normal, everyday workings of culture and the contingent nature of interpretation. While specific campaign disruptions are hard to predict, these cultural misfires are not random and unexplainable. Rather, disruptions are patterned and widespread, with identifiable mechanisms.

In what follows, I show how attention to *cultural entropy* better explains how these communication disruptions occur, undermining the power of AIDS prevention campaigns. Tracing the process of cultural entropy makes manifest how alternative meanings and uses for objects divert and dissipate belief and behavior away from organizations' intended causal path. In the present framework, these divergences are made possible in the dynamism of *arrangements*—unique instantiations of objects, audiences, and settings.[21] By looking to arrangements, I argue we can better identify and theorize mechanisms of disruption arising from neglect, misinterpretation, and new practices. I then suggest some ways objects resist entropy and some conditions that make objects more or less open to entropy.

What Is Cultural Entropy?

After AIDS campaigns leave the controlled environments of focus groups, advertising agencies, and stakeholder meetings to circulate through public space, people interpret and use campaigns in ways the designers never intended. These disruptions indicate that objects are undergoing a process of cultural entropy. At the level of the object, cultural entropy is the process through which the intended meanings and uses of a cultural object fracture into alternative meanings, new practices, failed interactions, and blatant disregard.[22] The foregoing examples suggest ways campaigns diverge from the meanings and uses organizations intended to communicate: the Nima billboard signifies organizational neglect of the neighborhood, condoms become bracelets, T-shirts carrying a slogan made by the community get rejected by the community. These objects appeared to carry stable meanings when the campaigns launched, but after the objects were made public, those meanings destabilized. By stable, I mean the various people interacting with the object came to a consensus about its meaning and use, engaging in patterned interactions with predictable results.[23] When stability emerges, it requires a great deal of effort to maintain, channeling and coordinating people's action and meaning making. AIDS organizations crafting these campaigns engage in exactly this effort—laboring to get campaign designers, funding agencies, cultural leaders, and communities "on the same page" before the campaign launch. AIDS organizations' commitment to best practices of campaign design, then, is a systematic attempt to resist cultural entropy.

Taken at the system level, cultural entropy—like the thermodynamic principle of entropy—suggests that meaning systems tend toward increasing disorder and instability.[24] Although there might be parts of the system that stabilize, overall, the system moves toward instability: cultural systems are

increasingly diverse and complex, growing more heterogeneous than homo-
geneous. When women use female condoms as prophylactics and fashion,
the bracelet alternative increases heterogeneity in the system; the overall
entropy in the system has increased. When viable alternatives emerge and
spread, others may see new possibilities to use female condoms for still other
purposes, opening up the object to additional creative repurposing. Any appearance of stability is a temporary accomplishment rather than a static and
steady state. Viewed from any one object, there may be a high degree of stability, but when viewed system-wide and over the long term, cultural entropy
predicts that objects tend to destabilize. Individual cultural objects may stabilize and "lose" or resist entropy, but overall the system only gains entropy.

In a given cultural system, more entropy and meaning dissipation could
be viewed as a good thing, encouraging diverse meanings and uses for objects, new ideas, increased creativity, and innovation. For people engaged in
communications projects attempting to use culture instrumentally, though,
acknowledging cultural entropy may lead to fatalism. If most campaigns ultimately succumb to cultural entropy, why attempt to persuade people in the
first place? For that matter, if it is a foregone conclusion, what is the value in
identifying how entropy happens? Here is where it is important to keep the
object and system levels separate. In the short run, for any given object, there
may be a great deal of stability, and campaigns may have powerful effects,
even if objects fall victim to entropy in the long run. That said, cultural entropy suggests that powerful effects are rare and hard-won. For organizations that believe they have design practices that limit misinterpretation and
misuse, cultural entropy helps explain why campaign effects are so hard to
identify and measure—media campaigns have limited effects, in part due to
cultural entropy.

In this book I focus on how cultural entropy happens at the object level,
borrowing language from mechanical and thermodynamic understandings
of entropy in the physical sciences. I find that concepts such as energy, work,
power, and entropy offer productive ways of thinking and theorizing about
cultural objects. The physical sciences define entropy as the dissipation of
energy. As I see it, cultural entropy is also about the dissipation of "energy."[25]
Durkheimians often use the metaphor of energy to describe how objects
motivate behavior (Durkheim 1995; Collins 2004). The heightened emotions
associated with ritual charge symbols (and the objects that embody them)
remind people of their moral commitments to the group. The concept of resonance also implies energy (Schudson 1989; Snow et al. 1986). Just as a plucked
string transfers vibrations to the wooden body of a guitar, resonant cultural
objects transfer energy to the audience in the form of heightened emotions

and new ways of seeing the world.[26] People circulate a resonant object, passing the ideas it makes available on to others, possibly leading to social change.

Thinking *analogically* about the communication of meaning as energy orients us to the flow of objects along pathways of intention, circulation, and resonance, with particular attention to whether objects "energized" to do particular work (i.e., communicate particular meanings, motivate action, or alter behavior) effectively do that work or not. Objects move through chains of interactions transferring "energy" from object to person to object.[27] Depending on how people interpret and use that object, it can motivate people to move along the intended path, divert people along alternative paths, or fail to move people at all. These chains of interactions constitute a "system of action" through which people and organizations deploy specific *intentions* that may or may not result in stability or change.[28] The goal, then, is to assess whether energy transfers along lines of intention, ultimately determining how objects shape belief and action.

AIDS campaign producers imbue campaign objects with just such intention.[29] Campaigns are highly crafted, representing the culmination of resources, coordination, and skill. All this effort results in a campaign object energized with intention—designers' best attempt to make a persuasive message that will align audiences' beliefs and behavior with the organization's interests. This energy is really *potential* energy. Intention, practices of production, invested resources, quality of design, and the object's ultimate symbolic content and material qualities all shape the potential energy of an object. If audiences never interact with an object, its potential energy never turns kinetic. When made kinetic, in interaction with an audience, the "energy" embodied in the object may transfer to that audience in ways that align with or diverge from the organizational intentions. Some people may interpret the object's meaning and use in the ways the organization intended. Better yet, that intended message might resonate with some audience members and motivate them to align their actions accordingly (for the short or long run) and share that object—and its message—with others. Resonant meanings and uses of an object or its message may turn into habit through repeated engagement with "similarly shaped problems."[30]

Campaigns do *cultural work* if they communicate their message and persuade people to align their behavior with the intentions of the designers. For physicists, work is about energy transformation, whether the energy employed (channeled through force) moves a body along a trajectory. Cultural work, as I define it, describes the extent to which an object—made kinetic in interaction—transfers its energy to audiences, leading people to interpret and use the object as intended and shaping their belief and behavior accordingly.[31] *Cultural power*, then, captures how well a cultural object does its intended work.[32] The more powerful a cultural object, the more consistently and rapidly it achieves the intended effect over time and space. Powerful objects, then, reproduce the same intended effects through repeated interactions and across varied settings.

If cultural work and cultural power account for whether and how well objects direct energy, cultural entropy accounts for how energy dissipates and diverts away from those intentions. Organizations energize cultural objects to move people along particular paths—performing specific cultural work— but objects transfer energy imperfectly. The intentions, agency, and effort of organizations embodied in an object can dissipate and divert, pushing people along alternative trajectories, confronting resistance due to inefficiencies in communication or perhaps never becoming kinetic in the first place. The potential energy of an object—the symbolic and material qualities that allow it to communicate the intended message—is bound up with other affordances. As argued in this chapter, all objects inherently carry multiple affordances— intended and unintended—that people can draw out in interaction. As alternative meanings and uses are made kinetic, these alternatives move the object along unintended trajectories. As energy dissipates and diverges from the intended path, the object's capacity to do its intended work diminishes— unless that object is reenergized to defend against profanation or misuse.[33]

Let's pause to clarify: cultural work, power, and entropy should be analyzed relative to the point of view and intentions of the person or organization putting the object to work. That could be the object's producer or someone who has "poached" that object for alternative purposes.[34] The female condom does cultural work for AIDS organizations when women use it as intended to protect themselves from HIV, but it undergoes a process of entropy when women turn condoms into bracelets. The intentions of women making condom bracelets to make a profit are also subject to entropy. Do market shoppers see condom bracelets as bracelets and buy them (cultural work), or do they realize the bracelets are former condoms, view that as disgusting, and spread rumors about unsanitary bracelets (cultural entropy)? Therefore, to study work and entropy, one must have an account of intention to compare to the objects' reception, influence, and impact on audiences.[35] What are their intentions for that object, and does the object realize those intentions or not?

Let us revisit the female condom bracelet example to show the value of this approach. To lower the incidence of new HIV infections, condom makers and AIDS organizations spend resources to design, produce, subsidize, and distribute female condoms. AIDS organizations expect female condoms and peer education intervention to do a great deal of cultural work. Female condoms only protect women against HIV to the degree that they *resonate* with local communities. Female condoms may resonate when introduced during a meeting by a clinic nurse, exciting women who seek a female-controlled solution to an intractable problem: powerlessness to protect themselves from HIV. Motivated by that meeting, then, a woman may take that condom out of the clinical arrangement and bring it to her bedroom with her husband. If the female condom still resonates after she persuades her husband to let her try it, she successfully uses it, and they assess how it affects their sexual pleasure and decide it is not diminished, then the use of the condom may become routine. In this instance the condom accomplished cultural work for the organization, and as this couple uses condoms for this purpose consistently over time and situation, the more powerful that object becomes. The woman may then circulate condoms among her friends with similar needs. If so, the condom gets added energy when she encourages others to try it out, propelling it along the organization's intended path.

However, the resonance of the condom may be disrupted in both the clinical and domestic arrangements, giving rise to entropy. For organizations using culture instrumentally, entropy is often synonymous with failure: the failure of an object to do the cultural work people mobilized it to do. For the designer of the female condom and the organizations that distribute it, when the condom fails to meet the couple's needs and they choose not to use it again, the potential energy of that object is unrealized. The cultural work of the female condom is further disrupted when audiences co-opt female condoms to make bracelets. The condom resonates in a new way and is reenergized with intention as jewelry. Co-opting the condom not only negates the task nurses and peer educators intended for the condom but also creates a new object and practice that can circulate and undermine the original intentions. Instances of entropy diminish the cultural power of an object to shape people's belief and behavior in ways that align with the focal producer's interests.

But entropy may also create new opportunities for cultural power. Misreadings can be just as motivating, persuasive, and powerful as the intended meaning, if not more so. Condom bracelets initiate a new chain of intention, resonance, and circulation. When women reenergize and stabilize the meaning and use of a condom by turning it into a bracelet, they imbue that object with new intention and potential energy. From the perspective of the people doing the repurposing, the condom serves *their* intentions of looking fashionable or making some money on the market.

People often divert the potential energy of a campaign to their own projects, as when Ghanaians use condom ads as home decorations or when social movements in the developed world engage in "culture jamming" to subvert advertising (Klein 1999). It is important to note that entropy does not always render an object powerless, though it does refract energy away from, or deteriorate energy along, the producers' intended path, creating more disorder in the system. By following an object across chains of interactions, we can see when potential energy becomes kinetic and spreads, or dissipates and falters, or gets reenergized for other purposes.[36] Objects have an "unfolding ontology" along "chains of activity."[37] However, cultural entropy happens even within consistent arrangements of the same object, person, and setting. Next, I show that the instability of objects is inherent in arrangements, even when they appear stable. Analyzing arrangements makes visible generalizable mechanisms of entropy at the object level.

THE INSTABILITY OF ARRANGEMENTS

Over their life course, objects fluctuate between stability and instability. AIDS organizations labor to endow campaign objects with stable meanings by following best practices. At the time designers launch a campaign, they feel assured that they have eliminated alternative interpretations and created a campaign that will communicate the intended message.[38] Essentially, the campaign object *is* stable at that moment because designers, community focus groups, and stakeholders agree about its meaning. The winnowing of campaign concepts and their meanings resulting from following the best practices of design give the final campaign objects an appearance of being tested, stable, and "finished" (Becker, Faulkner, and Kirshenblatt-Gimblett 2006). This appearance is both an accomplishment and a facade. Designers trust that their campaigns will predictably communicate the intended meaning because they have vetted them with the community and stakeholders in controlled settings, but this vetting process obscures sources of instability that designers cannot control.

This is not to say that organizations are powerless to stave off some paths to entropy. Recent improvements in campaign design practices (e.g., targeting specific groups, framing messages with local symbols and ways of understanding, and pretesting campaigns) mitigate the chances of misinterpretation somewhat. These efforts might yield better campaigns with short-run effects, certainly better than picking campaign ideas at random. However, these efforts will always be partial and temporary because of cultural entropy. Indeed, organizational best practices typically address only one source of entropy: the lack of alignment between a campaign's symbolic content and an audience's cultural knowledge and cognitive presuppositions. This symbol–cognition link is but one of many factors in an interpretive arrangement that may influence meaning making. Therefore, even if a campaign persuasively aligns a message with an audience, campaign designers cannot stabilize all the aspects of an interpretive arrangement.

As I define it, each interpretive arrangement is a unique instance of people, object, and setting. Arrangements are simultaneously symbolic and material: people are both cognitive and embodied, objects share both symbolic and material qualities, settings are both places that cue expectations and physical arrangements. Each relationship within an arrangement is dynamic and opens objects up to alterative interpretations and uses. AIDS organizations never consider the full complexity of interpretive arrangements or the range of possible interpretations (and disruptions) that every unique arrangement of people, objects, and setting *affords*.[39] Nor could they. There is simply too much complexity at the level of the arrangement for any organization to fully manage.

To further develop these points I introduce the diagram in figure 2, which depicts a basic interpretive arrangement. It includes a person and an object in a setting, recognizes that each has symbolic/cognitive and material/physical dimensions, and illustrates the connections between these elements. As I've argued, best practices of campaign design attempt to control only the symbol–cognition link. Similarly, most research on meaning in cultural sociology also limits analysis to cognition and symbols. This diagram offers an important corrective to these parallel tendencies by drawing analytic attention to the other connections.

First, this diagram shows the complexity of interpretive arrangements and thereby helps us situate vectors for entropy. Previous approaches oversimplify

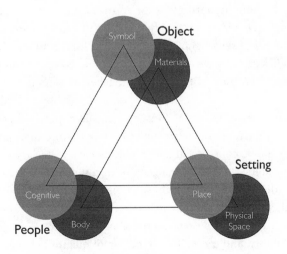

FIGURE 2. Diagram of symbolic and material dimensions of a basic interpretive arrangement

the process of interpretation, treating objects and settings as constants. These other links are often sites of dynamism rather than sources of stability. People embody numerous cognitive and physical capacities. An object's symbolic content connotes multiple meanings, and its material qualities allow for various uses. Places represent diverse groups and activities, and people engage the physical arrangement of space for different purposes. Heterogeneity, then, is built into every arrangement, suggesting what a great cultural accomplishment it is when an interpretive arrangement yields consistent meanings and uses.

The links between these elements are also a source of dynamism. By following the links between these elements, one can trace how these points *influence* and *alter* the others. Additionally, arrangements often have more than one object or person (not depicted), leading to object-to-object or person-to-person interactions that can disrupt the intended meaning of a campaign.[40] When other objects and people are present in an arrangement, the meanings they evoke might bleed into the interpretive process, making some interpretations salient while suppressing others. There is also a temporal element here that makes arrangements dynamic—the person, object, and setting all change over time. The diagram captures a snapshot, but arrangements should be considered as chains of arrangements through time.

Second, this diagram offers a framework for identifying mechanisms of entropy. By directing attention to the links between the elements of the arrangement—how they interface with each other—this diagram orients us to likely areas of disruption that have been undertheorized to this point. In what follows, I show how the links between these elements make visible challenges to stability (and opportunities for entropy) and demonstrate that arrangements are fertile sites for the theorization of mechanisms of cultural entropy. Specifically, I suggest how attention to the links between objects, settings, and bodies make visible generalizable mechanisms, beyond the group membership and cultural alignment approaches of reception and frame theory.

Organizations treat objects as finished and static, precluding their understanding of how these objects create instability. More than just neutral vehicles for symbolic content, campaign objects have material qualities that impinge on the ability of AIDS organizations to communicate their intended message to audiences. The materiality of objects is a central source of this instability. Inherent in, and unique to, every object is a "bundle" of symbolic and material qualities.[41] For instance, a red ribbon has the qualities of redness, lightness, flexibility, and more. This bundling of qualities enables different meanings and uses: people may turn a red ribbon 90 degrees to resemble an ichthus or unpin the ribbon to tie it around a finger as a reminder. This bundling of symbolic and material qualities of objects opens up room for innovation. People may purposively interact with an object because of one quality. As all the other qualities are also copresent, unforeseen alternatives may emerge as the object's other qualities now interact with the new orientations and settings.

Additionally, exposure to the physical environment may alter the material qualities of objects and thereby change their symbolic content (Ingold 2007). As the redness of a red ribbon is made possible through dyes with particular material properties, the meaning of that red ribbon is contingent on the durability of that dye. In fact, more than other colors, red fades rapidly in sunlight; different colors and dyes have material qualities that can react differently to different environments. When red ribbons exposed to sunlight fade to pink, their pinkness symbolizes breast cancer awareness rather than AIDS. In this way, the meaning of an object changes through what I call the mechanism of *decay*. Referring back to figure 2, decay emerges along the links in the arrangement: physical space (sunlight) alters the materiality of the object (color of dye), changing its symbolic content (breast cancer, not AIDS). Identifying decay and other material mechanisms of entropy is vital for organizations seeking to communicate specific meanings. It matters that PPAG *translated* its slogan so it could be worn, not just displayed (same symbolic content, but disruptions occur as the message moved across media), that FHI let the billboard deteriorate (decay), and that the latex of female condoms may reduce sensation during intercourse (material-body interactions trumping cognitive commitments). These material qualities may disrupt, overshadow, or enhance the symbolic content of the intended message even when audiences and objects are aligned.

Settings also have bundled symbolic and material qualities that create instability. Settings are infused with meanings that structure interpretation and action through the cuing of expectations (Gieryn 2000; Babon 2006). Had the Nima billboard been put in front of a mosque instead of a market, local Muslims might have understood it as coming from the imam rather than as a superfluous parallel message. Dirt roads and harsh sunlight damaged FHI's billboard in Nima, opening up FHI to arguments that the disrepair was symbolic of a broader neglect of the neighborhood. The busy nearby market may have distracted audiences from paying attention to the billboard. Additionally, the sign faced southbound traffic, so people who traveled northward past the Nima market and circled south on another street missed the message entirely, rendering the message *imperceptible*. In this sense, how settings structure interaction (traffic patterns) or alter objects (harsh conditions damaging billboards) are mechanisms that influence objects' perceptibility to audiences.

The symbolic meaning of a place and its social arrangement also structure interpretation and action (Goffman 1959; Lofland 1998). Young people may talk about their commitment to condom use in a focus group of peers but experience constraint when faced with wearing it on a T-shirt in front of their parents and neighbors. By making some ways of seeing the world more or less cognitively available, settings influence how people interpret objects. One arrangement of designers, test audiences, and stakeholders may create a campaign that appears stable, but when that campaign object moves to a setting with a different social arrangement, people may interpret or use it in unexpected ways.

I've discussed how audiences create instability based on the cultural presuppositions they bring to the interaction, but bodies, with their material qualities, can also disrupt campaigns. I came to realize the importance of bodies during my first week of fieldwork in Accra. Accra is modern, with Sony stores, high-rise buildings, and five-star casinos. However, Accra is also the capital of a developing country, with all that entails: streets in disrepair, open sewers, human and vehicular traffic. As I walked through the Osu neighborhood looking for AIDS campaigns that first week, I repeatedly twisted my ankle on potholes. To avoid spraining my ankle, I learned to look down while I walked. To navigate Accra without injury, I directed my attention to the people, cars, food stands, goods for sale, open sewers, free-ranging chickens, and potholes that crowd the city rather than the AIDS campaigns I had come to observe.

Having grown up in this setting, citizens of Accra navigate the sidewalk with aplomb. Nonetheless, bodily patterns of movement, the physical arrangement of space, and cultural practices also constrain vision for local Ghanaians. Ghanaians often transport goods on their heads: buckets of water, oranges for sale, or bundled tree limbs. The act of carrying objects on your head demands that you keep your head level and look straight ahead. Turning your head to the right or left to look at a colorful AIDS advertisement could cause you to drop your oranges. Whereas pothole dodging directed my vision downward to the pavement and away from advertising above the horizon line, the visual world to the peripheral left and right is largely unavailable for Ghanaians carrying objects. The physical constraints of carrying goods together with the physical orientation of AIDS media determine, in part, whether AIDS campaigns are perceptible. In this sense physical settings and objects *discipline* bodies, structuring how people can engage the world around them, making the campaign messages AIDS organizations intend them to see more or less perceptible (Foucault 1995).

These examples reveal that every arrangement has some degree of wiggle room, giving objects a multiplicity of "affordances" from which audiences may choose a variety of actions and interpretations. Theoretically, knowing the specifics of the arrangement, one could objectively account for all the possible meanings and uses afforded by an object.[42] In practice, though, this is impossible, and it is what makes disruptions unpredictable and difficult for designers to avoid.[43] It is significant to note that this openness is not random or infinite, but patterned, culturally contingent, and materially limited. While arrangements are inherently open, people cannot interpret or use an object for just anything.[44] Female condoms can be turned into bracelets but not hula hoops. In this sense the physical qualities of the object in interaction with the physicality of the body limit the affordances available. Cultural knowledge also constrains these women: although they may turn condoms into bracelets, they might never think of one of the latex rings as a part for a space shuttle. Despite the lack of perfect determination, there is a strong *partial* determination of meaning.

People often converge around a constellation of affordances when interacting with a cultural object, but consistent arrangements do not lead automatically to stable meanings and uses: cultural reproduction is not a function of arrangements; it is a result of effort and action within arrangements.[45] Establishing stable "frames of order" with long-lasting convergence around the meaning and use of an object is a rather incredible accomplishment made possible in part by robust symbol systems, ideological alignment, rituals, and routines that preclude alternative readings and uses.[46] Stability, when it happens, is not a natural state but hard-won and always at risk. New problems may confront even stable arrangements, altering the choices people make. Whereas people do not make new meanings every time they interact with an object, they do sometimes.[47] The meanings and uses available from a constellation of affordances may be preset, made possible by the unique connections between the people, object, and setting, but *which specific affordances and how people select them* is not wholly predetermined by the arrangement. If the possible meanings and uses of an object people can "articulate" are only partially constrained by the arrangement, then alternatives, creativity, and innovation are always possible.[48]

As soon as one acknowledges that interpretive arrangements are not determinative of meaning—offering only the raw materials of meaning making—we can treat arrangements as sites and sources of creativity that are always open to change.[49] The meanings and uses people select for objects from the set afforded by any unique arrangement emerge in action. Creativity, in my account, is when people see and pursue new lines of action, selecting unanticipated affordances made possible by an arrangement (i.e., those unintended or nonroutine meanings and uses inherent in every arrangement) as part of that path.[50] Considering arrangements in all their material and symbolic complexity helps us understand how people in stable arrangements with objects can initiate new understandings and uses.

OPENNESS AND RESISTANCE TO CULTURAL ENTROPY

Although all communication is open to disruption, objects are more open to entropy than face-to-face communication is. Communicating through cultural objects is always imperfect because representations are never perfect reproductions of the original idea.[51] During person-to-person interactions, people can manage the impressions they give off (Goffman 1959). Seeing a listener's face scrunch up suggests that he or she has misinterpreted, or at least dislikes, what was said. In response, the speaker can clarify his or her intended meaning by restating the point or trying a different tack. Unlike the complex and emergent "impression management" in person-to-person interactions, object-to-person interactions are more open to disruption because a billboard can't "save face" when its audience misinterprets the message (Goffman 1959). Ephemeral face-to-face conversations seem to work well enough most of the time, but the longer life span of most objects and their inability to adjust makes them open to increased interactions and opportunities for disruption.

No cultural object perfectly encapsulates or communicates intended meaning, and all cultural objects distort the ideas they are meant to represent (Becker 2007). One small misinterpretation or creative appropriation may seem insignificant, but it conceals an array of possible disruptions. Once alternative meanings and uses emerge, they can spread through a community to compete with, or even overtake, the intended meaning. Given this understanding, a study of entropy should account for factors that increase objects' openness and resistance to entropy, identify predictable general patterns of entropy, and consider the rate, scale, and degree of entropy.

All objects are open to cultural entropy, and in the long term all objects likely undergo entropy (both cultural and physical). In the short term, objects vary on their degree of openness to entropy. Objects designed to communicate meaning are characteristically more open to entropy, whereas technical objects tend to be less open to entropy. Technical objects include tools, technologies designed for singular purposes and small communities of specialists, or gadgets that operate in the background like Latour's door closer.[52] Such objects are often grounded in tacit knowledge that discourages conscious reflection. As long as they are durable, perform the work they were designed for, and operate in their intended settings, such objects resist entropy. We consciously consider such objects only when they break down or fail to do the work we ask of them, at which point people replace, tinker, or innovate (Pickering 1995). Once technologies stabilize, they become resistant to entropy, at least for a time (Pinch and Bijker 2012). Microscopes in a biologist's lab or machines on the factory floor are unlikely to be understood in new and creative ways, unless something in the arrangement changes. Compared to technical objects, cultural objects are much more difficult to stabilize and protect from entropy.

Assuming the object isn't already institutionalized, then the larger the audience, the more an object diffuses, and the longer it exists, the higher the likelihood of widespread entropy (Colyvas and Jonsson 2011). As Umberto Eco has suggested, "the aberrant decoding *is the rule in the mass media*" (2003, 5, emphasis in the original). Over the life course of an object, entropy often wins: objects fall apart or get thrown away, the social world shifts so it is no longer relevant, audiences' cultures change such that objects seem out of fashion. Resistance to entropy is not just rare; it takes a great deal of work to maintain, usually through the stabilizing mechanisms of routine and ritual.

Iconic objects include national flags, religious totems, and commemorative sites that carry condensed, deeply held, stable, and widely shared meanings (Wagner-Pacific and Schwartz 1991; Armstrong and Crage 2006; Bartmański and Alexander 2012). As such, iconic objects are resistant to entropy because the rituals within which their iconicity is embedded protect and correct alternative uses. Such objects of ritual are prototypically Durkheimian, symbolically embedded with social feelings and moral codes, established and reinforced through collective acts of ritual.[53] Rituals charge up symbolic objects with significance and emotional energy, giving people confidence and a sense of agency to act in alignment with the shared beliefs embedded in the object. Objects gain power when they are embedded within ritual. Rituals stabilize the meaning of the object for its audience and reaffirm their commitment to it.[54] American flags, with their corresponding anthems, pledges, and rules for folding and retiring, energize people with feelings of national connection and stabilize the meanings of "America," providing a social use context where deviations are observable and social sanctioning is encouraged. When people contest the intended meaning of the American flag by burning it in protest, the process of cultural entropy can often reinforce its ritual power—leading other groups of Americans to attempt to slow down this perceived dissipation of the meaning of a sacred symbol by attempting to "reenergize" it with the original meaning preferred by state elites (e.g., embedding the flag back into rituals of patriotism and nationalism). However, what cannot be undone is the fact that the overall entropy in the cultural system has increased as the flag is now *both* a symbol of oppression, imperialism, and immorality (to some groups) and a symbol of pride and moral superiority (to others).

Ritual is not the only way to stabilize objects, however. Routine is another way in which objects stabilize. Meanings and uses of objects narrow when they become habitual and automatic, appearing natural.[55] In such moments, people engage objects in unconscious and unreflexive ways. People tend not to actively interpret an object that is embedded in routine, so long as it exists in its typical setting with people who regularly engage it. The meaning of such objects is singular, instantaneous, and linked to prescribed action. Stop signs on traffic corners may be just as powerful as flags or religious symbols in their ability to shape action. Objects, then, do not need to be deeply held or rich with meaning to have powerful effects (Swidler 1995). When meaning and action around an object stabilize into routine, especially when these arrangements are institutionally supported, objects can powerfully shape action.[56] Though some degree of routinization protects objects from entropy, highly routinized objects are paradoxically reopened to challenge and appropriation. Stop signs are an attractive target for meaning subversion precisely because their symbolism is so taken for granted. Movements co-opt stop signs, adding stickers to the bottom of the sign to transform the taken-for-granted traffic injunction into an eye-catching and thought-provoking "STOP Animal Cruelty" or "STOP AIDS." Stop signs are such powerful objects that even in these potentially entropic moments when people appropriate the sign to communicate other messages, the stop sign still serves its intended purpose. This is a case in which cultural entropy does not reduce the object's capacity to do the cultural work intended by the state's interest in controlling traffic.

Objects that are not embedded in ritual or routine, such as AIDS campaigns, are relatively more open to entropy. Unlike culturally powerful objects that stabilize meaning and action in routine and ritual, AIDS campaigns introduce novel ideas and practices through unfamiliar objects in mundane and varying settings. AIDS campaigns rely on best practices of design to stabilize meaning, as if the object itself could be so well designed—so clear and powerful—to prevent misinterpretation. Rather than identify ways to create ritual around AIDS campaigns, AIDS organizations often extract culturally significant symbols from situated ritual and combine them with new messages. Designers hope to borrow symbols' residual energy, repurposed for the project of persuading changes in sexual behavior, as when religious images are appropriated to speak about AIDS. In effect, these AIDS campaigns make the error of privileging codes over ritual. They find images and text that are culturally resonant by pretesting campaigns with focus groups, but they fail to embed these symbols and text in the rituals and settings that give them power in the first place.

This practice of "de-fusing" symbols from their ritual setting undermines their stability and capacity to energize.[57] FHI's choice to depict a couple talking in front of the mosque is just such a moment. The religious image did not infuse the billboard with power but instead undermined FHI's legitimacy by reminding community members of religious authority. Moreover, every act of "de-fusing" creates more system-level entropy, through "low entropy borrowing."[58] The practice of borrowing stable symbols made powerful in ritual and putting them to various alternative uses can destabilize those symbols. "De-fusing" makes alternative understandings of symbols more available, potentially undermining the stability of a symbol in its ritual setting or making further appropriation more likely by showing how that symbol can be borrowed for other purposes. As symbols "de-fuse" from their ritual contexts, more segmentation and differentiation emerges (Alexander 2004). Even as entropy seems to decrease at the object level as new objects stabilize through ritual or routine, entropy increases in the system because borrowing symbols causes meanings and uses to multiply.

Not only do organizations attempt to use powerful icons to enhance the power of their campaigns, organizations attempt to anchor campaigns in target audiences' everyday lives. They do so by working within local ways of seeing and integrating campaigns into routine community practices. They believe doing so will increase their campaigns' visibility and convince audiences that the changes in sexual behavior they advocate are attainable. As the examples in this chapter show, getting teenagers to wear T-shirts is harder than it sounds, and subsidizing female condoms has unintended consequences. As I show later, Ghanaians establish their own routine uses for campaign objects that defy organizations' intentions. In the abstract, incorporating campaigns into everyday routines seems like a good strategy, but organizations miss how difficult it is to integrate their unfamiliar campaigns into familiar routines.

The point I want to make here is how difficult it is to keep an object stabilized and energized to do cultural work. It is rare to find cultural objects that resist cultural entropy. AIDS campaigns produced for mass consumption are vulnerable to entropy because they lack established rituals and routine. Entropy is likely when multiple iterations of the same "object" circulate among audiences in their varied and particular situations. When audiences lack the commitment to an object that comes from moral obligation or routine use, objects become open to reflection or the "trying on" of different interpretations.[59] When an object enters people's everyday situations without the stabilizing power of ritual or routine, they can read that object with skepticism, devise alternative interpretations, or put the object to alternative purposes.

In this sense, cultural entropy varies by time and familiarity. Stability is a result of coordination across an arrangement: people, objects, and settings working together to produce consistent meaning making. Instability is the norm in interactions with new objects and novel situations. People "try on" different meanings and uses because *the* meaning and use have not been established. Over time, through continued interactions with the object and other people, some meanings and uses for the object are construed as more appropriate, stabilizing interpretation and action in collective agreement.[60] It becomes more difficult to consider alternatives after objects are embedded in ritual and routine. Habitual interpretation discourages creative or alternative meanings and uses, and ritual uses of objects focus attention and thought on ritualized meanings, bound up in group bonds and moral commitment (Langer 2014). In these situations, the object means what it *means*.

To summarize, even if consensus emerges, alternative affordances are always available, and the object's potential meanings and uses await activation. Material qualities of objects change over time, altering their capacity to do the work they were intended to do and opening up new paths of interpretation and action. People may adopt new ways of seeing the world and bring these new lenses to the arrangement, or bodies may age and become unable to interact with objects as they used to, thus changing objects' meaning. Settings take on new associations and change people's understandings of the rituals in which they engage.

Assuming static arrangements free from exogenous disruption, I suggest that objects tend to be most open to entropy early and late in their life course, if they achieve stability initially. Durable objects paradoxically tend toward entropy because their long lives offer increased opportunities for endogenous instability. This tendency toward entropy is especially true if the object is never incorporated into routine or ritual. In this sense, durable and ephemeral cultural objects may be equally open to entropy, just in different ways. For these reasons, attending to the life course of an object is necessary to account for changes to the rate, scale, and degree of cultural entropy.

The qualities of an arrangement can contribute to an object's openness to entropy even when an arrangement is consistent over time. A more complex arrangement offers more paths along which the meaning of an object may be disrupted. When an arrangement includes a diverse audience and a great number and variety of objects, more potential uses for the space exist, and meaning and practice are difficult to stabilize. The introduction of just one new object or person into a stable arrangement can alter the available affordances and disrupt routine and ritual.

Conditions exogenous to an arrangement can also put an arrangement into disequilibrium. Ecological shifts, such as changes in the availability of an object, may change the meaning and value of the object, independent of internal changes to the arrangement. Rare objects that become widely available no longer seem precious, and thus they open up to alternative uses. Additionally, the field of objects outside the arrangement may shape how objects inside the arrangement are understood. Objects that attempt to change established symbolic systems and cultural practices are more likely to be ignored, face active resistance, or be read through the lens of the stable meanings supported by the field. In this way, previous campaigns can undermine current campaigns by shaping the audience's interpretive lens.

Seen from the perspective of AIDS campaign designers, entropy only matters in as much as it impacts their campaign's effectiveness. Some instances of entropy severely undermine producers' interests and intentions, whereas others are less significant. If a member of the campaign's target audience never interacts with the message, then that is a major failure. On the other hand, some disruptions seem minor, as when a target audience makes a minor misinterpretation but still gets the gist of the campaign. Although cultural entropy may be widespread, it may not always subvert campaign goals. For that matter, as I will show, some misinterpretations and misuses of campaign objects may in fact meet campaign goals, just not along the path the producers imagined. In analyzing the effects of cultural entropy, one must assess how devastating the disruptions are to the campaign goals.

The Path Forward

As the three examples in this chapter showed, AIDS organizations invested in billboards, T-shirts, and female condoms as ways to extend their reach, communicating health messages and protective sexual practices through objects. Objects are not neutral carriers of an organization's agency and intention; they afford multiple meanings and uses. Given the symbolic and material complexity of unique arrangements, Ghanaians interpreted and used these objects in ways that organizations never even considered. These alternatives emerged despite organizations' diligent attempts to narrow meaning and enhance the power of campaigns. When people select interpretations and lines of action from these unintended affordances, the object undergoes a process of cultural entropy: the energies invested in that object are dispersed and diverted from its intended path. AIDS campaigns undergo cultural entropy at every stage of their life course.

For organizations using culture instrumentally, this is a cautionary tale. Organizations have improved their ability to control meaning, but they cannot totally resist entropy. The complexity of the social world, organizations' limited capacity to read and respond to that world, the diverse affordances of interpretive arrangements, and the creativity and commitments of people going about their daily lives all siphon energy off these projects. Campaigns face an uphill battle without the energizing forces of routine and ritual or the ability to manage interpretive arrangements, making them more likely to fail than succeed. Cultural entropy, then, reveals why the efforts of campaign designers so rarely yield tangible results.

The Cultural Topography of Accra

When I arrived to start my research in Ghana, I needed someone who could set up focus group interviews for me. I found a woman in my neighborhood who was perfect for the job. She was friendly and well connected so she could easily recruit respondents. Additionally, she had a degree from the University of Ghana, Legon, had taken a class on HIV, and volunteered at a local HIV testing clinic. Not long after we started working together, we conducted a focus group with members of her church. One man from her church discussed their pastor's ability to cure people of HIV:

> The pastor was ministering and saying there's somebody here with an HIV virus. He [had gone] to the clinic and he was tested and the doctor told him that he has AIDS. [The pastor said] the lord is prepared to heal him. That person must come forward. And he came out of the crowd and he was prayed for. The pastor told him, after seven days, go for another checkup and bring me the results. He came and the result was negative.[1]

Much to my surprise, my assistant then spoke up to confirm this account, saying "Yes, he calls them out to cure them."[2] When I followed up with her later, she made clear her belief that certain prophets, including her pastor and another man she'd heard of, could heal people through God's grace.[3] Despite being well versed in the medical science of AIDS, having counseled people at HIV testing clinics and articulated to me that no drug could cure AIDS, her public-health expertise did not contradict the reality that her pastor could heal people who had the disease.[4]

Despite near universal awareness of AIDS, Ghanaians have diverse conceptions of the disease.[5] These various understandings are bolstered by the local cultural environment. For instance, the belief that AIDS is caused by witchcraft originates in long-standing local understandings of disease. Some diseases have spiritual causes and therefore demand spiritual purification to heal (B. Meyer 1999). Many Ghanaians don't believe a healthy person can have HIV. The visual landscape encourages Ghanaians' disbelief by emphasizing visible symptoms of illness and the association of mosquitos with disease. Independent doctors and healers often display hand-painted signs that graphically depict the symptoms they treat, such as diarrhea or genital sores. In addition, antimalaria campaigns present images of mosquitos as harbingers of disease when promoting mosquito nets and coils, leading Ghanaians to conflate malaria with other infections, including HIV.

Over and over again throughout my time in Ghana I met people who held contradictory beliefs about AIDS without any hint of cognitive dissonance. One cab driver I spoke with claimed that most of the time you could prevent HIV through condom use but that witches had cursed some people with AIDS through supernatural means. Another man I met at a bar told me that condoms could prevent the transmission of HIV in principle, but you couldn't trust them because Americans conspired to exterminate Africans by infesting condoms with AIDS "worms." Some beliefs—for example, the ideas that AIDS is curable, supernatural, or a bioweapon—undermine public-health interventions supporting HIV prevention, testing, and care. They may give people false hope that a nonmedical cure is possible or promote a sense that condoms are not worth it because one can contract HIV anyway through witchcraft or schemes by foreign governments.

The cultural topography of Accra supports multiple, contradictory understandings of AIDS that lead to confusion about the disease and undermine how people interpret AIDS media campaigns. As with any complex urban environment, there is noise in the system. AIDS organizations attempt to reduce this noise by using AIDS media campaigns to establish order in communities' shared understandings of the disease. Media campaigns encourage beliefs and practices that protect people from HIV, attempting to discredit myths with the authority of medical science. Health organizations have an uphill battle, though, as medical science is not considered the only source of authoritative knowledge.

AIDS organizations view religious leaders, herbalists, local rumor, and the news media as sources of misinformation. These competing domains of knowledge create ambiguity by offering alternative perspectives and sources of legitimacy. In addition, the visual landscape of the city and local knowledge of AIDS landmarks bolster these competing ideas and facilitate the spread of stigma. In what follows, I account for these competing sources of authority and changing patterns of knowledge circulation that can cause official AIDS messages to succumb to cultural entropy. Mapping this rocky terrain makes visible the obstacles AIDS campaign designers must overcome as they design media they hope will terraform the cultural environment.

An Ambiguous Cultural Environment

Near the entrance to Korle Bu Teaching Hospital, where most HIV-positive residents of Accra receive their antiretroviral therapy (ART), is a hand-painted sign with bold red lettering. It proclaims: "HIV/AIDS! HIV/AIDS!! HIV/AIDS has got a Natural cure. Some patients results have proved NEGA-TIVE" (fig. 3). This sign is right outside the entrance, and people traveling in and out of the hospital can't miss it. Its presence confronts people living with HIV with a competing understanding of the disease. Inside the walled campus of Korle Bu, doctors claim that AIDS has no cure and that ART can only suppress the virus. Outside in the public sphere, people living with HIV regularly confront claims that AIDS is curable.

These competing claims are grounded in commitments to alternative forms of knowledge and practice, one being the rhetoric of scientific evidence. This billboard directs people to a doctor, Dr. Amoakoh, "the WORLD'S

FIGURE 3. Advertisement for an HIV/AIDS "natural cure," outside the entrance to Korle Bu hospital in Accra, Ghana

No 1 AIDS CURER." On his website, which is now defunct, he posted evidence of his curative ability through photographs of lab results labeled "Negative for HIV Antibodies," according to the Public Health and Reference Laboratory of the Ministry of Health. "Cured" is written by hand on each result, along with another handwritten note that directs people to the clinic where the evidence of "positive" results is located. If these HIV-negative test results came from formerly HIV-positive people, the results might shake medical science to the core. However, the website lacked evidence that these results came from people infected with HIV. The danger here is that including overwhelming evidence of negative results from official lab reports lends the legitimating weight of medical research to his claims.

I found another sign advertising AIDS treatment (fig. 4) outside of a medical laboratory, also near the Korle Bu hospital campus. The hand-painted sign borrows language from billboards that Family Health International (FHI) developed with the National Fire Service, stating "HIV/AIDS IS PREVENTABLE, JUST AS FIRE IS," and advertises "FREE HIV/AIDS AND TB VOLUNTARY COUNSELLING, TESTING AND TREATMENT." The building's facade is covered with "Don't turn your back on AIDS. STOP AIDS. Make the Promise" posters produced by the Joint United Nations Programme on HIV/AIDS (UNAIDS), lending the establishment additional legitimacy as a site for HIV

FIGURE 4. Sign outside a medical laboratory in Accra, Ghana, advertising HIV/AIDS treatment and testing services

testing and treatment. I went inside to ask about the posters and a soft-spoken man greeted me. I introduced myself as a researcher studying AIDS campaigns and inquired about the activities of the laboratory. "So you do VCT [voluntary counseling and testing] and HIV treatment here?" I asked. "Yes," he said, "we do VCT and treat patients." I replied, "Oh, so you administer antiretrovirals?" He responded by saying no, that he'd developed his own medicine.[6]

He went to his cabinet and pulled out a spiral-bound report. The front page described the HIV prevention activities in which the laboratory engaged, displaying photos of groups with whom the laboratory worked, including fishermen and hairdressers. The report described that he had administered his medicine to nineteen HIV-positive patients. The next twenty pages presented the blood work (over time) for these patients, tracking the health improvements while on the medication. As I went through the results, he pointed out changes in his patients' T cell count.[7] As I continued to flip through the notebook, he went to a cabinet behind me and pulled out a bottle of his medicine—CML Interferom.

The bottle was plastic and room temperature. Adhered to the bottle was a white piece of paper too big for the bottle with some printed material. In the bottle was a thin, orange-colored, semitransparent liquid. The instructions were to mix a spoonful of the medicine with some honey and hot water and take once a day. I didn't recognize any of the ingredients listed on the label, though some, such as "liminium," appeared to be Latin, lending the list the appearance of scientific credibility. I asked whether these were the Latin names of the ingredients, and he replied that they were the "botanical names." "Oh," I said, "What are the plants' everyday names?" He answered that he was "not releasing them yet."

He said that when people come to him for testing and ultimately test as HIV positive, he sends them to Korle Bu for ART. But in addition to the ART they receive at Korle Bu, and for those people who aren't eligible or can't afford ART, he gives them this medicine.[8] He claimed it acts as an "immuno-booster." He said a young man from Bolgatonga came in and his numbers (I didn't catch what numbers they were) went up from 3.6 to 6.0 with the use of his medicine. The medication seemed to take effect within a month. He suggested his medicine was a "supplement." He never used the word "cure," but he suggested that people got better while using his medication.

At that point he went back to his cabinet, returning with a letter from one of his patients. The first day she came into his laboratory, he reported, she could barely walk the one hundred meters from the local tro-tro (private minibus shared taxi) stop to his offices and needed to sit down three times along the way. She was frail and sickly but had a CD4 count that left her ineligible for ART.[9] He gave me a copy of the letter, which he received in advance of her initial visit. It reads:

> Dear Sir,
>   I was tested HIV/AIDS positive in 2004 after the death of my husband who died of AIDS in 2003. His first wife also died ill of AIDS earlier before I married him. I have been suffering from several illness yet the hospital here refused to give me ART except vitamin tablets. I want to Komfo Anokye hospital in Kumasi two times but they also refused me treatment of ART. They told me that my CD4 was above 200. I am a hairdresser and I make good money at the Bolga market. Gossipers have spread news that I have AIDS so all customers have stopped coming to me. The stigma in Bolga is too much. Unfortunately my aunties and cousins have ejected me from our family house and advised my 12 year old soon not to come close to me. The church gives the AIDS and old people in the church 100,000 cedis each every month. I got ill of headache, running stomach, swollen stomach, vomiting and difficulty with breathing and could not walk by myself. I did not sleep at night my friend gave me one bottle of your medicine CML Interferom and after few days all the diseases went away. So I need more of your medicine but I have not come to the south before. We shall make SUSU in order to send of us to Accra to see you for more CML Interferom. I now ride my bilycle also sleep well at nigth. Members of the yinepanga AIDS Association meet the Bishop Secretariet. We are more than 100 members form paga naurouge and Bolga area. There are only 3 men among us. The rest are women. There is too much stigma and gossip in this area, so as soon as any man is counseled and his positive status declared to him he goes home to commit suicide by hanging or drink rat medicine. They kill themselves, because they could not stand the discrimination. Last year over 70 men commited suicide after being declared HIV positive.
>   Good Bye God will Blees you.[10]

This letter provides insight into why CML Interferom might be a desirable option, despite the increased availability of ART at places such as Korle Bu. This woman found CML Interferom through informal sources, not through a visit to the laboratory. Many of the people living with HIV whom I've met described how the power of stigma keeps people from seeking treatment at established sites. According to HIV-positive Ghanaians I spoke with, being seen entering the fever unit at Korle Bu—where people receive their ART—is enough to mark you as HIV positive. As this woman's report of suicides suggests, the fear of being exposed keeps people from publicly revealing their HIV-positive status. If this fear keeps people from seeking treatment, this makes the informal circulation of CML Interferom an attractive alternative to ART.

The cases of Dr. Amoakoh and the Director of this medical laboratory epitomize Ghanaian herbalists' practice of using medical science to support claims they can treat HIV. This practice can be traced back to the story of Nana Drobo, an herbalist whose claims of having found a cure for HIV captured national (and potentially international) attention in 1992 and 1993. Reportedly, French and Japanese researchers took serious interest in Nana Drobo's cure (Awusabo-Asare and Anarfi 1997). Radio programs at the time perpetuated Nana Drobo's claims, which a number of Ghanaians believed (Barnett, de Koning, and Francis 1995). The Nana Drobo story has circulated among the public for years since. In 2007, while I was at a formal banquet for an industry and trade association (unrelated to my research), I spoke with two Ghanaian businessmen, who when learning of my research asked if I had heard of Nana Drobo. When I admitted I hadn't, they described his discovery of an AIDS cure and his suspicious death. They claimed that official sources reported that he died of a self-inflicted gunshot wound but asked, "If it was a suicide, why did they find two bullet wounds?"—inferring that he was killed for his knowledge of a cure.[11] These long-circulated rumors led many Ghanaians I spoke with to believe a cure for AIDS existed and could be found again among local herbalists.[12]

In 2006, the Food and Drugs Board (FDB) of the Ghanaian government, working with the National Media Commission, imposed a temporary ban on the advertisement of herbal medicine on the radio. The FDB had a growing concern that herbalists' advertisements often overstated the efficacy of these medications. Without evidence supporting herbalists' claims that their medicines had the reported effects (without hazardous side effects), the FDB feared for public health: "They are making pronouncements on the efficacy of some drugs to the public without taking into consideration the danger public health is exposed to" (Ghana News Agency 2006). Whereas it is easy to ban these advertisements on the radio, it proves more difficult to eradicate signs that promote cures throughout the streetscape.

Throughout Accra pharmacies would advertise a Chinese herbal drug called "The Recharger," an oral liquid made from the male silkworm moth (fig. 5). When I was in Accra, it was the most commonly displayed advertisement at pharmacies. The advertisement does not state the drug's purpose or effects, but the bottom of the sign depicts a red ribbon and the statement "AIDS IS REAL, USE A CONDOM." The ambiguity of the sign might lead some people to assume that "The Recharger" could prevent, treat, or cure AIDS. Pharmacies in Ghana operate as central sites in the circulation of medical knowledge. As drugs are available without a prescription, Ghanaians who can't afford a trip to the hospital often go straight to the pharmacist.

FIGURE 5. A signboard outside a pharmacy in Accra, Ghana, using a red ribbon to advertise "The Recharger" herbal enhancer

"The Recharger" gains legitimacy when promoted by pharmacies and sold by formally trained and certified pharmacists rather than "quack" doctors or herbalists. Although "The Recharger" is intended as a supplement to enhance men's sexual performance, the ambiguity of this sign leaves it open to interpretation as a legitimate AIDS drug.

Sites of medical knowledge such as herbalists, medical laboratories, and pharmacies circulate ambiguous and unverified information about the medicine they distribute to Ghanaians seeking treatment for AIDS. Certainly, some herbalists selling these drugs are taking advantage of desperate people for their own financial gain. Others—such as the man I met at the medical laboratory, who seemed earnest in his intentions—seek to help people with

AIDS by using their botanical and medical knowledge to develop their own drugs. Still other cases, such as pharmacies selling products with misleading advertisements, may unknowingly encourage confusion out of carelessness rather than malicious intent. Bolstered by rumor and the appearance of medical approval, the therapeutic and curative claims made through these alternative health care sites made available unsanctioned drugs for people seeking to treat and prevent HIV. For Ghanaians motivated by the threat of stigma, the expense of seeking care, and distrust of Western medicine, these alternatives are viable—and in some cases preferable—options. The popularity of the Nana Drobo story suggests just how attractive the belief in a homegrown cure is for Ghanaians, possibly driven by anticolonial tendencies. Even though most Ghanaians aren't looking for AIDS drugs, the visibility of these alternatives makes available parallel meaning systems that undermine the claims made by public-health organizations. They make real a fundamental question: Is AIDS curable, or not?

Established Institutions Supporting Illegitimate Claims

Thus far, I've described how medical understandings of AIDS are contradicted or undermined from everyday conversations and interaction with the streetscape: rumors of a cure, stories of religious healing, and signs made by entrepreneurial local healers. In this section, I discuss how established institutions such as news media, churches, schools, and hospitals lend credibility to such claims and complicate the public health project of disseminating medically legitimate understandings of HIV/AIDS.

NEWS MEDIA

The Ghanaian news media also lend credence and visibility to claims that recent discoveries can cure AIDS. In an interview with a staff member at the Ghana AIDS Commission (GAC), I learned of a recent case of the news media spreading rumors of a cure.

> I was interviewed one day by the *Mirror*. [The reporter] said this man Gary Davis came in from South Africa and said he could cure AIDS by using gold mixed with some other, and asked what the [Ghana AIDS] Commission would do. So I said, "Well, we have institutions that have been put into place to take care of these things. If the man has a claim he should go to them to look at it further, test toxicities and all." The next day was a front page story in the *Graphic*, it said "Hope for HIV/AIDS patients: Gold serum proves effective." Effective! The man hadn't gone through the protocols yet! When people

are down, anything that offers hope, they take it. Care should have been taken.
[After hearing this news] a friend of mine called and he said, "My friend, I can
now take off my condom!" That is what he told me![13]

Circulating claims of newfound AIDS cures through major daily newspapers
not only give false hope to Ghanaians living with HIV but also give HIV-
negative people justifications for being more reckless. If there is a cure, why
should people wear condoms anymore?

GAC coordinates and verifies AIDS media campaigns to ensure that messages align with the national behavior change communication (BCC) strategy, but it has little power to regulate AIDS news coverage. GAC recognizes
the challenges newspapers pose when they circulate stigmatizing images and
misinformation to the public. GAC's strategy has been to use workshops to
teach reporters how to cover AIDS in a positive manner that supports GAC's
prevention and antistigma efforts. Much to GAC's chagrin, these workshops
have had little impact:

> We had a workshop for the media. We took them through how they should
> report HIV/AIDS issues. For instance, we announced how [HIV/AIDS] is kill-
> ing more women, girls. This came out today. Look at the images they used!
> [He holds up a newspaper covering the announcement, which used a sickly,
> gaunt AIDS patient as its image.] You want to talk about what Ghana has
> done, but these are the images that we have. You stigmatize the news already.
> I would have liked a feature story on somebody who has fought AIDS and do
> a good story on that person and then link it to Worlds AIDS Day. That is posi-
> tive news. But when you show people at the last stage, the news is stigmatized
> already. Why are we working in different directions?"[14]

The news media in Ghana are uneven in their journalistic standards.[15] Most
newspapers include a mix of serious journalism and sensationalist tabloid-
style pieces. I've seen the same paper cover HIV/AIDS with respect one week,
only to publish an inflammatory, stigmatizing story the next.

RELIGION

Newspapers are not the only institutional source of authority that complicates prevention efforts. While some religious leaders work with AIDS organizations to protect their congregations from HIV, other leaders make public
claims that diverge from standard medical knowledge, many of which are
stigmatizing. A staff member at one AIDS organization discussed how difficulties arise when respected religious leaders undermine efforts to spread
consistent, public health–informed messages:

You spoke about the fact that everyone knows about HIV. But what is the quality of that knowledge? For instance, my grandmother knows there's something called AIDS but does she still believe it is a punishment from God? Does she still believe somebody is suffering because his grandfather angered the gods and the gods are paying back the family? There was a front-page story in the *Graphic*, a pastor declared that if anybody died of HIV, it [sic] was definitely not supposed to be buried in a cemetery. If my grandmother thinks HIV is punishment from the gods, not that HIV is caused through 1, 2, 3, 4, 5, it's coming from source credibility, coming from somebody she reveres, somebody she holds up.[16]

Ghanaians are fervently religious.[17] Backed by community reverence, some religious leaders make non-biomedical understandings of AIDS viable, undermining public-health organizations' attempts to disseminate medically informed knowledge. Recent research suggests how religious leaders' claims about AIDS and approach to prevention can powerfully shape how people understand the disease.[18]

How do religious claims undermine health-based AIDS interventions? One man recounted for me his pastor's claim that AIDS is caused by the "devil entering your body." I've heard of leaders from traditional Ghanaian religions stating that HIV is a punishment from the gods for an ancestor's wickedness, or that AIDS is caused by a jealousy curse. When I ask people who attribute AIDS to supernatural causes if they've heard that HIV is spread through sex, they often conflate causes, seeing sex as the path through which the devil enters the body.[19] Those who believe AIDS has supernatural causes seek spiritual cures, rendering public-health solutions inadequate. These beliefs create a market for spiritual cures, leading pastors to treat HIV through faith healing, which in turn creates new obstacles to prevention. All that AIDS organizations can do in the face of these claims is repeat over and over again that AIDS is a disease transmitted through bodily fluids, not spiritual means, though many staff fear they may be losing the battle to these local interpretations.

Another interpretation of AIDS that many religious leaders share is AIDS's origin in sin, especially promiscuous sexual activity. From this point of view, AIDS is a righteous punishment for engaging in sinful behavior. Immorality, then, drives the spread of the disease. Many AIDS organizations believe that religious leaders are the primary source of stigma around HIV. Specifically, the belief that people infected with HIV have sinned against God drives widespread stigmatizing behavior (Mbonu, van den Borne, and De Vries 2009). Stigma in Ghana is high as the majority of Ghanaians are intolerant of people living with HIV.[20] While religious leaders may view the practice of stigmatizing promiscuity as a core strategy for protecting their congregations from HIV, AIDS organizations' staff members adopt a different view. Beyond the ways stigma leads to the mistreatment of people living with HIV (or those suspected of being infected), AIDS organization staff members recognize that stigma reduces the number of people seeking such medical services as HIV testing and undermines treatment efforts (Ghana AIDS Commission 2005a; Gerbert et al. 1991; Kelly et al. 1987). Research has shown that moralizing the disease may put people at a greater risk for contracting HIV (Smith 2004). Paradoxically, Christians who believe HIV is the consequence of the sin of promiscuity have been shown to adopt "moral partnerships" that resemble serial monogamy, but they discourage condom use to show mutual commitment. When partnerships are less than monogamous, it increases the risk of HIV transmission.

While some religious leaders create problems for AIDS organizations, many others become partners in prevention. On balance, religious leaders in Ghana have done a great deal of good in an effort to reduce HIV prevalence. In particular, the Presbyterian Church of Ghana has a positive reputation among AIDS organizations for its grassroots HIV prevention activities. Additionally, the local religious groups working with AIDS organizations I visited dismissed the association of AIDS with devils and witchcraft, instead describing HIV as a disease and not a curse. Despite these partnerships, AIDS organizations believe religious leaders complicate their AIDS interventions. Many AIDS campaign staff members believed they could not challenge moral claims made by religious leaders, as such challenges would undermine their legitimacy among congregants.

Under these conditions, organizations would partner with religious communities but alter their messages to avoid contradicting the moral authority of religious leaders. AIDS educators eliminated talk of condoms and explicit sexual practices from their church- and mosque-based interventions, emphasizing abstinence and faithfulness instead. Rather than contradict medical approaches for promoting prevention, AIDS educators working in churches engaged in sins of omission. AIDS educators justified this radical departure from their "ideal" informational session in two ways. First, making these compromises kept religious leaders happy and aligned with their interests. Even though AIDS campaign staff believed that the abstinence-only message was incomplete, they also believed that religious leaders were less likely to spread (what they viewed as) misinformation if they felt aligned with AIDS campaign staff. Second, AIDS organizations anticipated that as religious leaders were exposed to their interventions, they would become more comfortable with discussions about AIDS. In time, they believed religious leaders would become more willing to address taboo topics, but the staff members I spoke with admitted that this strategy had failed to convince many pastors and imams to permit discussions of condoms. The structure of these partnerships may explain why Ghanaian Christians know a lot about AIDS but have low rates of condom use.[21]

SCHOOLS

Schools are also imperfect sites for disseminating comprehensive AIDS knowledge. Like religious leaders, teachers advocate abstinence at the expense of other AIDS prevention strategies. Teachers I spoke with said they thought that discussing condoms encouraged premarital sexual activity. Although an abstinence-centered approach enjoys broad support because it is politically uncontroversial, statistics reveal that abstinence is already widely practiced among Ghanaian youth. According to the Ghana Demographic Health Survey, the average age of first sex for women is 18.2 years, and for men it is 20.2 years, and this average has been stable over time.[22] As staff at USAID in Accra said to me, Ghana's age of sexual debut is among the highest in the world, so there is "nowhere to go with those numbers." Many AIDS organization staff members said they believed that proabstinence campaigns would have little to no impact on increasing abstinence or in reducing HIV prevalence. Ghanaian AIDS campaign staff members who believed they could "move" the numbers for condom use said they felt stymied by the abstinence-only restrictions at most schools.

Furthermore, AIDS education in schools is ad hoc. Although the Ghana Education Service organized AIDS prevention training for teachers, few of the teachers I met had attended. Those who did attend reported feeling uncomfortable running programs at their schools on their own. Instead, teachers preferred visits from outside experts who could provide AIDS education for students through assemblies.[23] These assemblies were often presentations from AIDS nongovernmental organizations (NGOs) or testimonials from associations of people living with HIV. Bringing in outside sources required effort on the part of overwhelmed teachers, so the schools I visited laid in wait for AIDS experts to approach them about presentations. Most of the schools I visited had not had an AIDS presentation in years.

What little AIDS education happens in schools appears either through the initiative of individual teachers or through educational materials such as posters, AIDS storybooks, or "The AIDS Game" and group activities such as the "Journey of Hope" left over from past visits by AIDS campaigns or circulated by the Ghana AIDS Commission.[24] These sources present their own challenges: the AIDS education materials teachers showed me were out-of-date or not targeted at youth. Additionally, many of these materials sit in the library and require student initiation: students must give up their study time to play "The AIDS Game" or read "Tales of AIDS."

HOSPITALS AND CLINICS

If the news media, religious leaders, and schools disrupt the flow of public-health communication, surely legitimate sites of health information—hospitals, polyclinics, and voluntary counseling and testing centers—must facilitate the dissemination of biomedically informed AIDS information. Not so: stigmatizing interventions, staff, and settings undermine treatment and the communication of AIDS prevention information even in these sites.

The most detailed HIV/AIDS education in Ghana is available to clients of HIV voluntary counseling and testing (VCT) centers and sexual health clinics. Before and after test results, nurses educate clients on sexually transmitted infection (STI) prevention and management, with particular attention to HIV/AIDS. At these clinics in Ghana, nurses use the one-two punch of first showing an "STI flip-book" and then giving verbal education on prevention and care, using a pamphlet and reinforcing the message with a condom demonstration.[25] This approach is not unique to VCT and sexual health centers. HIV/AIDS peer educators also adopt these methods when meeting groups of commercial sex workers, men who have sex with men, and uniformed services personnel such as the Ghanaian military. Although VCT centers and peer-education interventions provide Ghanaians with more detailed knowledge than media campaigns do—along with the opportunity to ask clarifying questions—these approaches reach very few people.[26]

High levels of stigma prevent many people from seeking care at these clinics. Many people would never enter clinics where VCT or STI treatment are available because of the stigma they might face if people saw them and assumed they were HIV positive or promiscuous. Similarly, to be seen entering the fever unit at the Korle Bu Teaching Hospital (the center for infectious diseases but also where ART is administered) marks one as an "AIDS patient." To avoid stigma, many people refused to seek official medical services at sites associated with AIDS, which in turn pushed some of those people away from HIV/AIDS prevention advice and care at legitimate clinics and hospitals and toward alternative sources such as traditional healers. Ironically, many health workers spread stigma. In my conversations with Ghanaians living with HIV, they recounted stories of fearful nurses dropping medication into their hands to avoid touching them.

An Entropic Terrain

The cultural environment of Accra renders major facts about AIDS ambiguous and encourages stigma. An invisible disease becomes visible when newspapers depict people living with AIDS on their deathbeds and clinics show images that conflate sexually transmitted infections with HIV. Religious leaders and medical staff stigmatize in their sermons and behavior. AIDS "cures" abound, advertised by local herbalists and pharmacies, preached by religious leaders, and promoted by the news media. Couching their products in the discourse of science and evidence, herbalists and pharmacies blur the lines between modern and traditional medicine, straddling both domains of authority. Competing messages from different domains of authority confuse local communities. These blended understandings make it easier for people to forgo condoms or ART and increase their risk of infection or death. Although the communities I engaged with expressed a trust in modern medical sources for their information about AIDS, most Ghanaians don't know someone with HIV to verify this information.[27] The presence of viable alternatives enables Ghanaians to choose between official and lay understandings when it suits their interests.[28]

AIDS organizations have a great deal to manage and overcome when designing campaigns. This is true for any organization seeking to engender widespread changes in belief and behavior in a city as large and complex as Accra. While Accra's cultural terrain is distinct, the diversity of cultures and settings that compose most modern cities renders urban centers hotbeds of entropy. Objects and meanings flow through urban settings in unpredictable ways, meeting new audiences in unfamiliar arrangements that make serendipitous encounters and innovation possible (Hannerz 1992). Whereas cities are motors of cultural entropy, explaining the specifics of how the cultural and visual landscape encourages entropy requires the mapping of each city's unique topography. Such a survey of the cultural environment makes visible how cultural landmarks, obstacles, eddies, and well-worn paths of travel shape the circulation of ideas.

Critical media scholars often attribute too much power to well-funded media operations, assuming that organizations can reshape these cultural landscapes by imposing ideas on publics (Adorno 2001; Herman and Chomsky 2002; Rushkoff 1999). Certainly, AIDS organizations can buy more media space than other actors can in this cultural environment, making their images and narratives more available to audiences through the "mediascape" (Appadurai 1996). Although this is true, this "propagandist" bias misses the complicated constraints information flows face.[29] We do not live in a Habermasian ideal where information is exchanged freely through the public sphere and people make choices based on logic and the best information available (Habermas 1991). Although AIDS campaigns can buy more ad space, print more bumper stickers, and produce more television commercials, rival visual cultures undermine these powerful NGOs by confirming what people want to believe. The lack of municipal regulation over the visual environment means that people can put up their own signs, and the lack of drug regulations permits unconfirmed claims making about AIDS treatments. When communication spaces operate outside of a regulated market, AIDS organizations cannot monopolize the landscape by buying up space.

The local cultural environment creates entropy in the system by creating obstacles and alternative paths of travel. Religious beliefs about condoms and promiscuity inhibit AIDS organizations' capacity to borrow the power of religious authority. An herbalist with few resources can undermine official sites for treatment with a strategically placed hand-painted signboard. Sensationalist news stories that display images of weak and skeletal people dying of AIDS make the disease visible and encourage the stigmatization of thin people who may be HIV-negative. Despite the power of NGOs, the complex cultural environment of Accra encourages the alternative interpretations and the avoidance of official AIDS interventions. Yet although AIDS organizations cannot control or marginalize these alternative sources of information, they can try to overshadow them. Next, I discuss the logic of AIDS campaign production and the routines organizations put in place to enhance the effectiveness of their messages.

3

"Best" Practices

AIDS organizations view the multiple, often ambiguous meanings of AIDS circulating through the public sphere as an obstacle to reducing the incidence of new infections, getting people tested, and offering adequate care. Without a cure, a vaccine, or an inclination toward totalitarian sexual policing, democratic societies must persuade the population to change its sexual practices to align with public-health goals. The primary way AIDS organizations do so is through media campaigns that communicate the "right" meanings of AIDS and encourage people to adopt protective sexual practices: don't have sex with multiple partners, do put on a condom, don't engage in premarital sex, do remain abstinent. Ultimately, if these campaigns are done well, AIDS organizations believe the campaigns will reduce the incidence of new HIV infections. AIDS organizations across the globe have embraced standardized behavior change communication (BCC) strategies to suppress the spread of HIV.

As AIDS media campaigns proliferated and spread globally throughout the 1990s, development and aid agencies believed that early campaigns lacked focus and needed a coordinated approach (Epstein 2007, 167). Early campaigns were often thrown together by local organizations with little, if any, training in health communication. After local organizations were supplemented by global health organizations, new international standards began to spread, along with a commitment to the "mechanical objectivity" of quantification and adherence to explicit guidelines required by aid agencies needing the legitimacy of accountability (Porter 1995; Merry 2011; Timmermans and Kolker 2004; Espeland and Stevens 2008). By the early part of the first decade of the twenty-first century, organizations in Accra had adopted systematic evidence-based approaches to design that purported to demonstrate effectiveness.

The pressure of this new "audit culture" created problems for AIDS organizations: proving campaign effectiveness was, and is, elusive (Strathern
2000). As I will discuss in this chapter, organizations had difficulty discerning
the effects of AIDS media campaigns because available data were low resolution. How, then, do AIDS campaigns prove their worth to funding agencies when evaluation data are fraught with problems? AIDS organizations
and funding agencies focused organizational attention on the design process
rather than on evaluating campaign effectiveness. This overinvestment in best
practices created opportunities for cultural entropy.

Difficulties in Demonstrating Campaign Effects

Media effects are difficult to measure, even in environments with good measures of media exposure and outcomes (Katz 2001; Schudson 1986; Schudson
1995). Demonstrating the effectiveness of HIV/AIDS communication in the
developing world is even more difficult. Even if HIV prevalence and incidence decline at the national or regional level, it is impossible to conclude that
AIDS media campaigns were the definitive cause, let alone isolate the effects
of a single campaign in a field of many campaigns. Other changes might also
suppress HIV transmission, such as the availability and subsidy of condoms,
new community interventions aimed at commercial sex workers, the growth
of voluntary counseling and testing (VCT) centers, or changes in the political
will of governmental, religious, or traditional leaders. It is exceedingly difficult to convincingly demonstrate a causal relationship between a media campaign and trends in prevalence.

As such, organizations often focus on shifts in individual-level behaviors,
such as abstinence or condom use—outcomes that AIDS campaigns actually encourage. However, studies that include direct observations of sexual
behavior are *exceedingly* rare (Egger et al. 2000). Organizations therefore rely
on self-reports as a proxy for behavior, but such data are vulnerable to multiple types of measurement error, including self-report bias, forgetfulness, and
social desirability. These studies can exaggerate actual levels of condom usage,
abstinence, and partner reduction, casting doubt on campaigns' claims of success (Catania et al. 1990).

In addition to the lack of good outcome measures, the institutional field
within which AIDS organizations operate is complicated by competing efforts
by other organizations. What is reported as a direct effect of a campaign (i.e.,
see condom ad, put on condom) may in fact be an accumulation of multiple,
indirect effects, leaving the degree of influence of any one campaign a black
box. Funding and coordinating agencies acknowledge these difficulties and

have started to accept indirect evidence that suggests overall progress. One agency staffer put it this way:

> Before any action is taken, you need a baseline. What is the level of knowledge of people? What are the attitudes towards people with HIV? The Demographic Health Survey was done in 2003. There will be a survey again in 2008 when the campaign is over. Then you can compare 2003 and 2008, is there a difference? Of course, these things take time. You can't make a huge impact with one input. But at least you get a feel if things are moving.[1]

In getting "a feel" from national surveys, funding agencies vaguely measure a variety of influences on AIDS prevention knowledge and behavior. As long as progress is made, they can argue that the interventions they've funded have increased knowledge, lowered stigma, or reduced HIV prevalence. These measures don't give funding agencies a sense of the effectiveness of specific interventions or organizations.

The designers I spoke with talked about the pressure to show success, and some argued it was unfair to require evidence of effectiveness in such a short time.

> We have a set of indicators that we have to move. That's how we are measuring the effectiveness of our campaign. Sometimes I think that is a little unfair. It is a lot to expect of a communications campaign that, you know, runs for six months or eight months. It's something clients always demanded of us. You know, "Show us the impact of this campaign." And we've put things together. And it was kind of bogus. I mean, it's really hard to measure the exact impact of communications because there are so many other factors.[2]

Designers recognize that measuring the impact of their campaigns is next to impossible, expressing deep reservations and skepticism about evaluation. At the same time, they tacitly accept the need to "perform" evaluation to bolster their legitimacy. The evidence may be "bogus," but they do it anyway. As another campaign designer told me:

> Things aren't measured. We don't really know what is effective. But there is a way to work the numbers, and that is the whole system of development. If you don't do well, you won't get funded.[3]

Many AIDS campaign designers in Ghana know the question of effectiveness is unsatisfactorily answered, but they accept that they need evidence of success to show funding agencies so that they can secure funding. "Working the numbers" is just one strategy for managing this tension between uncertainty and legitimacy.

Organizations often rely on thin measures of media exposure, such as "reach and recall" studies to account for success. These techniques evaluate how many people have seen or heard the campaign or how well they recall it. As one designer suggested, they collect "quick and dirty data":

> We do a lot of quick and dirty data, what we do is something we call dipsticks, dipstick surveys. The marketing people give out questionnaires on a monthly or bimonthly basis whereby each employee in the organization, on the way home, over the weekend, they're supposed to fill them out . . . it is just to find out what people think about a new campaign.[4]

Like a dipstick in engine oil, these surveys give organizations a quick, general measure of the level of the campaign: how many people have seen it, what do they remember of the advertising, what do they think of it. Because campaigns have high visibility, dipstick surveys allow organizations to claim success. Dipstick surveys are a weak measure of campaign exposure, not a robust measure of campaign effectiveness. They offer a thin indication of how many people the campaign *could* affect, but because the results are based on convenience samples, these data are not generalizable. Additionally, these measures ignore important questions about the quality of exposure. Recall does not measure whether people interpreted the campaign message in line with the designers' intentions or whether those who saw the campaign altered their behavior.

When organizations lack the ability to evaluate the effectiveness of their campaigns, organizations collected thin, surface-level data that could bolster their claims of progress, avoided evaluation by (conveniently) running over budget, or cut out systematic evaluation altogether. In the absence of good data on what works, organizations producing health communication campaigns often suppressed the importance of evaluating "success" by raising the importance of the design process. Correspondingly, funding agencies have come to value accountability more than success. When I asked a staff member at a major funding agency about the contingent relationship between "campaign performance" and funding, my respondent focused on measures of progress rather than measures of outcomes:

> We work out benchmarks, targets to meet. Some targets are purely qualitative measures of progress, say, develop a national campaign by the third quarter of 2006. We have adopted a modern management style. We leave them to do their work as long as they are responsible.[5]

Organizations that demonstrate good faith attempts to meet campaign design benchmarks are judged "responsible." Rather than insist on direct and robust measures of campaign effectiveness, funders focus on good progress and designing campaigns the "right" way. This compromise (i.e., direct measures of progress with indirect measures of outcomes) has become the norm for agencies and organizations.

Given this ambiguous and uncertain environment, designers *invest in making the design process as rigorous as possible.* Internationally circulated "best practices" documents provide agencies with rigorous standards for AIDS campaign design. These documents encouraged widespread institutional commitment to these practices and created standards for "good" campaign design, leading to convergence in the field of health communication. Doing campaign design well confers legitimacy upon organizations, even if they can't demonstrate positive results. If the designers I spoke with were skeptical about the value of evaluation, they expressed devotion to the best practices of design.

Best Practices

Throughout the 1990s, most health campaigns in Ghana had not adopted systematic, evidence-based approaches to design. Local organizations without training in communications or public health produced AIDS media campaigns in a haphazard fashion. Despite their good intentions, organizations sometimes made campaigns that spread misinformation and stigma, basing campaign ideas on instinct rather than evidence. Organizations rarely worked together in this early era, flooding the public sphere with contradictory messages. After years of these unsystematic campaigns, health communication professionals advised that haphazardly thrown-together campaigns could not effectively shape belief and behavior; they needed a more rational approach.

By my first visit to Ghana in 2003, every internationally funded organization producing AIDS campaigns had adopted these best practices: crafting messages based on formative research conducted in communities, pretesting concepts with audiences to ensure clear and culturally resonant messages, and securing buy-in from local stakeholders. Organizations were collaborating, coordinated by international stakeholders such as the Joint United Nations Programme on HIV/AIDS (UNAIDS), funding agencies such as the United States Agency for International Development (USAID), and state secretariats such as the Ghana AIDS Commission (GAC). How did AIDS organizations in Ghana move from a decade of uncoordinated, unsystematic campaigns to campaigns produced through a rigorous, evidence-based process that coordinated a wide array of stakeholders?

The answer to this puzzle became clear when I started noticing best-practice reports throughout AIDS campaign offices. I found best-practice collections in stacks on designers' desks, arrayed on bookcases, and resting on coffee tables in the lobbies of AIDS organizations. These reports were always at hand. Additionally, national-level policy documents reference these reports early and often, suggesting just how central the reports are to their thinking. Ghana AIDS Commission's "National Integrated IEC/BCC Strategic Framework 2006–2010," which outlines Ghana's AIDS communication strategy, references best-practice documents from such international agencies as Family Health International (FHI), the World Health Organization (WHO), and the United Nations Population Fund (UNFPA). Starting in earnest in the late 1990s, organizations including UNAIDS, WHO, and FHI produced best-practice reports that outlined how best to implement HIV/AIDS public-health interventions.[6] Since the rise in publication and diffusion of best practice reports, the field has undergone a sea change (Atkin and Freimuth 2001). Through the global dissemination of hundreds of best-practice reports, the field of health communication established design conventions, diffused those conventions through the field, and secured widespread, if not universal, adherence to these practices across the globe.[7]

These reports abstract from the experiences of local practitioners those practices that seemed to "work." Based on case studies of interventions across the globe, these reports modeled how organizations *should* intervene (and when it comes to lessons learned, how *not* to intervene). According to the UNAIDS website:

> The **Best Practice Collection** . . . provides information about what has worked in specific settings, for the benefit of others facing similar challenges and fills a gap in key policy and programmatic areas by providing technical and strategic guidance as well as state-of-the-art knowledge on prevention, care and impact alleviation in multiple settings.[8]

In many respects this is a noble effort. Rather than having each organization reinvent the wheel of AIDS prevention and care, these international agencies serve as clearinghouses for "state-of-the-art" approaches that can achieve results across a variety of settings. Free and available online, these reports lower the barriers to entry into AIDS intervention activities. For states, organizations, and communities engaged in HIV prevention and care, these best-practice documents offer road maps to guide the design of interventions, enabling the organizations to predict and respond to problems before they happen.

Best-practice reports gave funding agencies and local AIDS organizations new sources of organizational legitimacy (J. Meyer and Rowan 1977). Funding agencies now had a new tool for surveillance and an important measure of accountability. For practitioners, best practices offered standards with reasonable expectations that AIDS organizations on the ground could achieve. Best practices made what was once an obscure, haphazard, and locally variable design process into something routine, legible, and quantifiable. Legitimacy, then, depended on an organization's capacity to do two things: (1) collect data and anchor campaigns on this evidence, and (2) work with local stakeholders throughout the design process and secure their support for the campaign.

Labeling these procedures *best* practices in effect reifies them. Best practices shifted from being guidelines to being hard-and-fast rules deemed necessary to produce "successful" campaigns and to demonstrate progress and legitimacy. In this sense, best-practice documents offered local organizations more than just a way to demonstrate competence to funders. Deploying the rhetoric of "best" imparts a sense of confidence by suggesting that these practices have competed against other practices and come out on top. This notion gives campaign designers a false impression that the field of public health has rigorously field-tested these practices. Ironically, the "successful" case studies from which these best practices emerge face the same problems in measuring outcomes as any campaign. Best-practice reports necessarily exaggerate success and rarely articulate the obstacles organizations might face when adopting these practices.

AIDS campaign designers have internalized a deep commitment to these practices (Sauder and Espeland 2009). Rather than a burden, designers view these practices as the only reasonable way to produce campaigns. From their point of view, to make a successful campaign requires a substantial investment of time and resources to refine the design, strip out alternative interpretations, and secure a coalition of supporters. To do otherwise, to rush a campaign or throw something together without working with the target audience, would waste resources. As I describe subsequently, the AIDS campaign designers I spoke with vigorously defended the two central tenets of good design as espoused by best-practice documents: a commitment to *formative research* that grounds the campaign design process in the culture of the target audience, and an obligation to secure *buy-in* from local stakeholders that support the campaign and help staunch the circulation of alternative messages. Designers follow best practices on faith, albeit faith backed by the institutional field. They want to believe these practices work, and in the absence of evidence, their commitments to these best practices become religious.

Formative Research

Evidence-based interventions are the gold standard in medicine and public health. By valorizing formative research, best-practice documents align with this dedication to evidence. Operating under the belief that "audience-oriented" campaigns are more effective, these documents advocate that organizations learn as much as they can about their audience and develop campaigns with this audience in mind (Nowack and Siska 1995). The more they can cater campaign messages to the culture of their target audience, the more confident they can be that the messages are clear and resonant. Designers believe that understanding the worldview of their target audience will help them develop convincing campaigns. To this end, organizations create a profile of their audience by conducting formative research: research used to improve campaign messages before the campaign launch (Atkin and Freimuth 2001; Palmer 1981).

Formative research encompasses two distinct stages of the campaign design process. First, organizations engage in "preproduction research" whereby they collect data on characteristics of their audience that might inform message production and medium selection (Palmer 1981). Organizations use these data to create a "brief" that imagines their audience. This brief describes what their audience knows, believes, and aspires to be, audience habits and sexual practices, and audience attitudes and preferences. The brief then identifies strategies for how to reach the target audience and persuade its members to change certain beliefs and behaviors. Organizations then use this brief to design a series of mock-up campaign ideas through their partnership with a creative team at an advertising agency.

When designers have generated what they believe to be one or more workable campaign ideas, they move to the "pretesting," or "production testing," phase of formative research (Palmer 1981). In pretesting, organizations try out campaign ideas with a sample from their target audience. Pretesting helps designers determine which campaign ideas will be most persuasive, how an audience might misinterpret a message, and whether the proposed messages are culturally sensitive. Based on these pilot studies, designers refine campaign messages and images, ultimately submitting the final campaign ideas for review by expert consultants, collaborating organizations, and community leaders. When they are satisfied that they have a persuasive campaign, the designers move forward into the production and distribution of the final campaign.

Formative research gives designers confidence that they have made campaign materials that work. Trying out campaign ideas with the target audience and then adjusting campaigns based on their responses appears to narrow and stabilize the meaning of the campaign. Designers have adopted a series of techniques to ensure that they communicate the intended campaign messages. For example, one designer told me that when pretesting posters with focus groups, the slogan is hidden to make sure the campaign message and image are aligned.

> After a lot of brainstorming, we came up with this slogan: "If your gift is for sex, keep it." What kind of picture should this [slogan] go with? What kind of gift are you talking about? There are so many gifts. At first we used just some gift box; somebody just handing over a gift. Then after about two years, we went back. That message was still good, [but] the youth in the community were saying that the gift is more to do with money. You always give money. So during the next campaign . . . we didn't use boxes, we used money, that somebody is giving out money to the person. Whilst taking the shot, there happened to be a taxicab parked behind.
>
> When we did the pretesting, we covered the words [and showed] only the picture. [Focus group participants] were saying: "Oh, that man is a cab driver who is giving money to the lady." Some other people said, "Oh, he's trying to bribe the lady." Others will say, "No, it's the—it's the cab driver who's giving the woman the change." So we just realized then that the cab [in the background] was creating a problem. So we just went into Photoshop, took the cab out, got a different group, just show this to them and it just came out: "Oh the guy is trying bribe the girl. The guy is trying to give money to the girl." So then it came out very well. Taking the taxi out was just enough to change everything.[9]

PPAG staff members found that people misinterpreted the image because of a taxicab in the background. The woman in the revised image was perceived as getting a bribe, or receiving change, but not being propositioned for sex. Pretesting revealed this misinterpretation and enabled the organization to further revise the image. This process of refining campaign materials through formative research persuades organization staff members that they have done all they can to ensure their campaigns will work.

Organizations like this new commitment to evidence-based design. Viewing communication as a proven science with routine procedures and predictable results gives designers confidence and lends legitimacy to their work. Such legitimacy is important for designers, who believe their status is threatened. Some designers I spoke with lamented how "everyone" feels like they are an "expert in communication," without realizing the work and skill that go into it:

> Some people who are doing stigma programming are actually developing stigmatizing behaviors because of the way they do it. A lot of prevention stuff that people do, they show that the woman is the factor, the sex worker, perpetuates stigma. Or there is some stuff on the Ghana AIDS Commission website, "Let's Kick AIDS out of Ghana." It's a very stigmatizing message. It's really hard to

get people to see that there's a systematic way to do communication. Everyone's an expert in communication.[10]

Distinguishing their approach from campaigns that failed to pretest and missed the stigmatizing misinterpretations of campaign messages lends these designers the appearance of legitimacy. Such objective evidence is essential for weakly positioned bureaucratic actors who need to defend their positions to funding agencies and local stakeholders (Porter 1995). The more the health communicators can rely on such expert skills as data collection and analysis, the better they can counter lay opinions by referring to data. Collecting pretest data allows designers to convince others that their campaigns will work. The external pressure to produce evidence-based campaigns and an internal commitment to bringing scientific practices to bear on campaign design engender a conviction that incorporating research into design is the one true path to success.

Campaigns based on formative research probably outperform campaigns that do not pretest or customize messages for target audiences. That being said, funding agencies and designers place too much faith in the power of data to create effective campaigns. Without viable measures of campaign effectiveness, organizations and funding agencies cannot weigh the costs and benefits of collecting data and tethering campaign messages to that data. Because demonstrating the relative effectiveness of campaigns based on formative research is difficult, designers' faith in formative research is unshaken. Formative research has become an unquestioned good, a tool to achieve a more perfect campaign. As I discuss later, this faith in formative research leaves designers blind to the inherent biases in formative research and to the ways those biases shape the kind and quality of AIDS campaigns.

Buy-In and the Multisectoral Approach

In addition to formative research, best-practice reports urge a *multisectoral* approach to campaign development that incorporates local actors (e.g., relevant state agencies, religious and traditional leadership, other nongovernmental organizations, and the health sector) into the design process. Integrating these many stakeholders into design process is intended to ensure that relevant parties are on the same page as to the meaning and goals of a campaign. As one best-practice report argued, "Mass media efforts would be more effective if they were reinforced with consistent messages from other sources and supported by services that enabled young people to act on the messages" (Makinawa and O'Grady 2001, 29). By bringing other organizations on board early in the process of campaign design, the field of local actors can come to a single, unified message that all of them support, both ideologically and institutionally. In addition, involving stakeholders in the process helps secure buy-in. The more stakeholders feel ownership of the campaign, the more committed they will be after the launch.

Best-practice documents call on organizations to provide *technical leadership*, which entails the coordination and management of various partner agencies. These lead organizations work with research firms to conduct formative research on the target audience; partner with advertising agencies; and manage the process of design, distribution, and evaluation. Most important to establishing multisectoral support, lead organizations seek out and incorporate the voices of respected local experts who can speak on behalf of the target audience. Best-practice documents encourage lead organizations to "assume a mediating role among organizations or individuals with different opinions or approaches [and assert that] the involvement of a few highly respected local experts facilitated this decision-making process" (Makinawa and O'Grady 2001, 31).

Best-practice documents suggest that multisectoral participation eliminates competing messages in the public sphere. Organizations in Ghana identify the lack of coordination as a problem to solve. As one designer suggested:

> If we do a little piece here, a little piece here and there's different messages and they're conflicting, then you don't have any impact at all—that's what's happening in HIV from the beginning. You have different donors coming out: "I'm going to do a campaign on this," "I'm going to do this," "I'm going to do that." You end up with confusion in the field.[11]

Designers committed to best practices argue that different organizations doing different campaigns with different messages makes for "confusion in the field." Campaigns working on their own don't have the checks and balances, or the institutional support, that other organizations and cultural groups can bring. By coordinating efforts across organizations and interest groups, and by offering expertise in communications, AIDS campaign designers in Ghana now seek to align stakeholders around a single campaign strategy:

> You really have to bring everyone together. We're one player, if we were to just launch a campaign, it would be a waste of money, unless you got all the partners together to do it and it took us this year and I don't think we wasted any time. I mean, we met every month and slowly everyone is brought into this concept but it took time to do it. I don't think people understand that it takes time to bring coalitions together. If everyone buys into the messages and the materials and there's one message going out, if they integrate it into the

way they do their stuff, that's fine. It's making certain you haven't forgotten anyone because there's a lot of constituents out there. . . . You don't want [a situation] where everyone wants to go off and do their own thing. The herding cats part is to get everyone to agree, yeah, let's do it together. Actually if we do it together, we'll have an impact. If we don't do it together, we won't have an impact. I think people are slowly buying into that concept that if there's one message distributed through every single network and channels stimulating community dialogue and discussion, then we can see a difference.[12]

Advocates of multisectoral participation, like this designer, see it as essential to making persuasive campaigns. Designers believe that building coalitions and securing buy-in eliminates disordered and distorted messages from the public sphere.

Advocating commitment to multisectoral participation is one thing. Successfully putting it into practice is another thing altogether. Best practice reports depict a world where diverse experts and local leaders work together and designers seamlessly integrate everyone's contributions. Yet best-practice documents rarely discuss the inescapable challenges of managing the divergent interests. Best-practice reports don't make suggestions for how to handle competing voices, implying that once lead organizations get everyone in the same room together, they will collaborate to produce an effective campaign. Managing the differing opinions of diverse local experts and then incorporating those ideas without alienating any experts or groups that invested time into the process is a delicate and difficult task, one that takes a great deal of time, as the designer I quoted suggested. These challenges posed real problems for designers in Ghana. Though best-practice documents and designers agree that a unified voice is an unquestioned good, having so many voices in the room affects the kind of campaign that is produced. As I discuss later, too many cooks can spoil the soup.

Cultural Entropy through Convergence

International AIDS organizations hoped that best-practice documents would coordinate the behavior of AIDS campaign designers globally and systematize design practices in the service of making more-effective AIDS campaigns. Though it appears as though the best-practice documents have stabilized the field, leading organizations to converge the practices of formative research and securing buy-in, this convergence can undermine the goal of making persuasive campaigns that are sensitive to local culture. Like AIDS campaigns, best-practice documents confront cultural entropy. The intended outcomes that best practices were meant to engender are ultimately disrupted.

The *organizational convergence* around best-practice documents leads to the cultural entropy in three ways. First, in addition to creating convergence around locally sensitive best practices, these documents also encourage convergence around locally insensitive campaign templates. When borrowing these generic models, campaigns fail to fully incorporate local culture, and then best practices become performances of legitimacy. Second, to secure future funding, organizations must demonstrate their capacity to follow best practices. Innovative and controversial campaigns, though potentially powerful, carry more risk and leave them open to criticism. This commitment to following best practices restricts designers' creativity, discouraging risky campaigns in favor of safer, more mainstream campaigns that may not be as resonant. Third, field-wide support for investing in best practices of campaign design gives designers false confidence that their campaigns will work. When resources are diverted to design, at the expense of campaign evaluation, designers miss how people misinterpret campaigns after the launch. These blind spots create further opportunities for entropy over the life course of campaigns.

CIRCULATING TEMPLATES, NOT JUST PRACTICES

One best-practice report recounts the development of an AIDS prevention TV spot called "Fiesta" aimed at youth in the Dominican Republic. A survey revealed that young people had minimal sex education, low HIV-risk perception, an aversion to using condoms, initiated sexual activity at an early age, and engaged in sex with multiple partners. A common strategy for health communicators is to increase individuals' risk perception to encourage changes in sexual behavior. By adopting the commonplace trope that you can't identify someone living with HIV by sight, the ad challenged young people's feelings of invulnerability:

> ["Fiesta"] showed young people dancing, talking and looking for partners in a situation where intimacy, alcohol and lack of parental supervision all played a part in placing them at risk. This spot used a questioning approach, challenging the widely held misperception that a person with HIV/AIDS can be identified by his or her appearance. "You can't guess who has AIDS," it concluded. (Mendrano and De Lister 2001, 34)

Though "Fiesta" was designed for Dominican youth, the "Fiesta" campaign sounds shockingly familiar to a Ghanaian campaign. The Ghanaian TV ad, produced by the recent national antistigma campaign, opens with a similar party scene. The band is playing, and people are dancing and drinking. The narrator introduces us to Kwesi and Kojo. "Kwesi is a 34 year-old accountant. Kwesi is hard working and likes to work on his car. Meet Kojo, a 36 year-old pharmacist. Kojo likes fufu and loves to play football on Sundays." Both Kwesi and Kojo look healthy, both are enjoying the party, shaking hands, hugging friends. At the end of the spot, the narrator reveals that Kojo is HIV positive, making the case that HIV is not visible to the naked eye and challenging Ghanaians by asking, "Who are you to judge?"[13]

If best practices are meant to create campaigns customized to local culture, why do these campaigns look so similar? Shouldn't campaigns in the Dominican Republic look very different from campaigns in Ghana? More than just distributing technical steps of good campaign design, best-practice reports also circulate ideal types, or templates, of AIDS campaigns. Best-practice documents propagate "success cases," putting specific campaigns on a pedestal and leading to instances of isomorphism. Even if organizations collect formative research, designers can import these insights into ready-made templates. I gather that much of this process is subconscious. Ghanaian designers claim that their campaigns are "unique" and "unlike any other."

Despite these claims, examples of borrowing abound. When I asked one JHU staff member from the Johns Hopkins University School for Public Health (JHU) whether JHU based the "Stop AIDS Love Life" campaign on other campaigns in other countries, he replied, "In fact, I must say that 'Stop AIDS Love Life' is totally original to Ghana."[14] Despite these claims, the language of "love life" was not unique to Ghana. One of South Africa's most visible campaigns was the "loveLife" campaign, directed by the Henry J. Kaiser Family Foundation. Started in 1999, just a year before Ghana's "Stop AIDS Love Life" campaign, "loveLife" garnered international attention, making it available to imitate. Like "Stop AIDS Love Life" in Ghana, "loveLife" was that country's most ambitious national campaign. Similarities continue, as both campaigns secured the support of political and religious leaders, and they promoted AIDS prevention through a positive, hip approach (Epstein 2007, 128).

In addition, AIDS campaigns in Ghana—including "Stop AIDS Love Life"—incorporated the "ABCs of HIV prevention" approach that originated in Uganda during the 1990s. This approach, which encouraged people to abstain, be faithful, and use condoms to avoid contracting HIV, was touted throughout the international public-health community as a crucial factor in Uganda's successful drop in HIV prevalence (Hogle 2002; Cohen 2003; Singh, Darroch, and Bankole 2003). In the years since, the ABC approach has diffused throughout streetscapes across English-speaking sub-Saharan Africa

(Cohen 2003). Despite claims of success, a number of scholars have identified alternative explanations for the Ugandan "success story," suggesting that the ABC campaign does not adequately account for the positive change (Allen and Heald 2004; Heald 2002; Oster 2012b; Swidler 2009). The global convergence around the ABC strategy has faced criticism for using a generic, individual-level approach that leaves populations such as married women in traditional societies especially vulnerable—abstinence and condoms are out of the question, and although they may remain faithful to their husbands, their husbands may not stay faithful to them (Akeroyd 2004; Smith 2007).

Drawing on campaign templates that circulate through best-practice reports opens campaigns up to entropy in two ways. First, blindly borrowing templates from apparent success cases does not necessarily lead to success in all contexts. When campaigns move from one arrangement to another, they become increasingly open to entropy. As critics have argued, the ABCs may only work in situations where women have more equal partnerships with their husbands. Positive campaigns that rely on hip aesthetics or representations of parties may work better in countries with greater economic development. As I discuss later, red ribbons mean something different to local Ghanaians than they do to the international organizations that circulate them. Precommitting to a template because it worked elsewhere, whether conscious or not, opens those campaigns up to unforeseen misinterpretations.

Second, the availability of preexisting campaign templates constrains the set of possible campaign ideas some organizations consider at the local level. If the goal of best-practice reports is to give organizations the tools to create locally sensitive campaigns, they undermine these intentions by making certain templates more available. For all the efforts of AIDS organizations in Ghana to tailor campaigns to the local cultural context, knowing that "best practice" campaigns have had success leads organizations to gravitate toward campaigns that resemble previous successes.

I do not mean to suggest that organizations are unwilling or unable to make a good faith effort at incorporating data, nor do I mean to suggest that formative research has minimal influence on the ultimate campaign. As I discuss in the next chapter, the kinds of formative research that organizations conduct have real effects on the kinds of campaigns produced. That said, in some instances, formative research reveals just enough information to support a designer's inclination to put ready-made messages and templates into action. On such occasions, formative research is centrally about the performance of legitimacy rather than incorporating local knowledge to better reach and communicate to target audiences.

HOW BEST PRACTICES RESTRICT
CREATIVITY AND INNOVATION

Adherence to best practices leaves campaigns susceptible to other unintended consequences; namely, risk aversion and an inability to innovate. Like Max Weber's "iron cage," after organizations adopted these instrumental-rational practices, designers became more constrained by them (Weber 1992, 181). Basing campaigns on best practices restricts the range of possible campaign ideas. The demand to ground campaigns in data limited designers' creativity. "Outside the box" ideas that received polarizing responses in pretesting are ruled out because they are difficult to defend with data, despite the fact that polarizing responses might promote productive engagement in the public sphere. Securing buy-in from a range of cultural and political stakeholders often required willingness to compromise, which eliminated riskier, potentially more resonant imagery.

For instance, one of the riskiest campaigns that made it into Accra's public sphere was a billboard that wrote out "Use a Condom" with sexually explicit stick figures reenacting the Kama Sutra (fig. 6). A designer at the advertising agency Origin8 pitched the concept, but Ghana Social Marketing Foundation (GMSF) dismissed it as too risky. Toward the end of the project, after the organization had invested the bulk of its resources in a different campaign strategy, there were some additional funds to spend. The designer pitched it again. GSMF decided to take a chance, despite evidence of its polarizing nature, putting up two billboards in Accra. The designer recalled:

> We put up a billboard saying, "Use a condom." There's an article in the newspaper, *The Graphic*, on it. It downright condemned it. We've learned that whenever we've received criticism the product does remarkably well. It does better because more people to pay attention to what we're saying. And, there's a certain level of hypocrisy in Ghanaian society. They know it, they do it, they like it, but they don't want to talk about it. Eventually, it becomes acceptable, but, initially, you have one or two outbursts. People saying, "That's not right, take it off," but after a while it's like, "Well, you know, you don't talk about this in public" . . . for instance, the one in *The Graphic* who [said] "you're supposed to be telling people to use condoms, not to have better sex." Who told you that was better sex? The message is "Use a condom." How it says that is entirely up to you.[15]

Taking a chance on this billboard might have paid off. Though there is no proof, this designer suggests that condoms started selling better because of the controversy around the billboard. Whether the ad increased condom sales or not, putting up a provocative billboard got people to discuss condoms and

FIGURE 6. Ghana Social Marketing Foundation's "Use a Condom" stick figure billboard advertisement on Ring Road East in Accra

publish critiques in the *Daily Graphic*. The ad forced Ghanaians to confront suppressed issues of sexuality and condoms. Even if it was controversial, the designer believed the debates it evoked pushed people toward accepting condoms.

That this billboard had a positive effect on the public does not mean it reflected well on the organization. I asked the designer about who criticized the "Use a Condom" billboard. He first pointed to Ghanaian individuals, but then launched into a longer discussion about criticisms from other NGOs and the competition for funding:

> Some of those criticisms are competitor-based, from other NGOs who are competing with GSMF. A competitor would want to make the campaign look bad. I think the competition is between the NGOs and their bid for funding. They have an objective, which is to educate people on HIV, get people to use condoms and stuff like that. As NGOs, they need to fight for budgets from bigger NGOs. There's a lot of competition on what to do with their strategies. [Other NGOs] might want to make the campaign or the output from that NGO look bad.[16]

The decision to put out this controversial image at the last minute without adequate best-practice evidence left GSMF open to criticism. Other NGOs desperate for funding have an interest in labeling such moments as errors in

judgment, highlighting the ways such a campaign fails to follow standard design practices. When I asked GSMF staff members about the controversy, they
laughed off the consequences of this billboard controversy. Despite their good
humor, this experience might lead them to be more risk averse in the future,
pushing them to commit to more conservative campaigns. Even though
riskier campaigns might have the desired effect of changing sexual behavior
or improving condom sales, designers might discount such approaches if it
makes it harder for them to secure funding in the future.[17]

FALSE CONFIDENCE IN BEST PRACTICES AND INABILITY TO ADAPT AFTER THE LAUNCH

Designers often expressed their belief that these newly adopted design practices would ensure clear communication by customizing their messages to
the needs of local communities and heading off alternative interpretations.
As in the case of the "If Your Gift is for Sex, Keep It" campaign of the Planned
Parenthood Association of Ghana (PPAG), designers repeatedly described to
me the lengths they went to in order to strip campaign objects of alternative
meanings. They see the benefits of such best practices as pretesting. After the
arduous process of conducting a needs assessment, researching their audience, and then crafting, testing, and distributing a campaign, designers feel as
though they've done everything possible to make a clear and resonant campaign and they have evidence to back that up. Designers found it hard to
imagine how audiences could misinterpret their campaigns after they had
invested so much "sweat equity" into the campaign, working with communities for months to develop campaigns and narrowing their message through
an iterative process of pretesting. Their emotional commitment to the process
and the ultimate campaign gave them a false confidence that their campaign
would work as intended. Without good measures of the desired effects of their
campaigns, AIDS organizations in Ghana gave full-throated support for best
practices of campaign design. Although this false confidence is understand-
able, their trust in and convergence around best practices created cultural and
contextual blind spots that opened them up to widespread cultural entropy.

These blind spots emerge when organizations direct more time and resources toward campaign design while diverting resources away from following campaigns after the launch. Adhering to best practices imparts a sense
of control, and designers refuse to take seriously the possibility that their
campaigns might not communicate what they intend. If organizations evaluated their campaigns after the launch as rigorously as they invested in the
design phase, they would see the cultural entropy I witnessed again and again.

Even if campaigns cannot adequately measure the sexual health outcomes of their messages, they could take my approach and evaluate whether they have communicated their intended meanings. Instead, organizations prefer to trust the design process rather than face the reality of cultural entropy and possible threats to their legitimacy. None of the organizations I spoke with described using methods to assess meaning making after campaigns went public. Designers likely prefer to remain blissfully ignorant—that way they can report positive progress back to funding agencies. Even if organizations did do enough evaluation to realize there is a problem, their overinvestment in the design process leaves them with few resources to remedy the situation.

Organizational commitment to design undermines campaign effectiveness.[18] Creating one behemoth, inflexible campaign that all organizations support, even if designers tailor and refine the campaign message for local populations, makes campaigns more open to cultural entropy. Campaigns inevitably move to new arrangements that designers cannot predict—and for which they cannot prepare. The greater the number of organizations involved, the greater divergence in these arrangements, and the greater likelihood of entropic meanings and uses. When several organizations support one message, rather than each making a unique campaign, the costs are considerably higher when a campaign flops. When massive campaigns succumb to cultural entropy, years of research and resources are wasted. Additionally, if all campaigns experience cultural entropy to some extent, organizations have a more difficult time course-correcting titanic campaigns after the launch than smaller, nimble ones. By placing all their eggs in the basket of one campaign, so as to avoid sending mixed messages into the public sphere, organizations create more opportunities for mixed *reception* without recourse to identify misinterpretations or manage those impressions.

Cultural Entropy through Divergence

Organizational convergence around best practices obscures moments of unintended divergence and differentiation: how organizations put best practices *into practice*. As I've argued in this chapter, cultural entropy often appears whenever arrangements shift. In the case of best practices, different designers in different local contexts interpret and implement best practices differently. Every shift in arrangement opens up opportunities for divergence. Despite widespread commitment to best practices, there is still enough "wiggle room" to corrupt the intended responses to the best-practice documents. In this way, the *organizational divergence* in best-practice implementation reveals mechanisms of cultural entropy.

In the next chapter, I account for variation in *how organizations use evidence*. Whereas all AIDS organizations in Ghana make evidence-based campaigns, what data they collect and how they use that data varies dramatically, ultimately yielding distinctive styles of campaigns. In addition, commitment to securing multisectoral involvement, through mechanisms of *compromise* and *conflict*, leads designers to invest in campaigns they do not believe in. In this sense, commitment to best practices exposed organizations to unforeseen deviations that undermined the intended outcomes of best practices. When designers use best practices differently, it leads to unexpected variation in the kinds of campaigns produced and creates tension when the strategies suggested by evidence run counter to the strategies backed by stakeholders. Opportunities for entropy abound within and between best practices.

The appearance of entropy in spite of stable, field-wide convergence is a product of the best-practice case studies themselves. What best-practice reports include is at best only a partial representation of the constellation of factors that contributed to the observed success. Success is attributed to the practices, rather than to the particular arrangement of practices, audiences, and contexts. Unfortunately, what goes unsaid in these reports is just as important as what is said. When best-practice reports summarize a success case, important information from the lived experience of designers and the institutional environment gets lost in translation (Becker 2007). Then, when designers shift these practices to new contexts, such transpositions are vulnerable to misinterpretation, misapplication, and unintended consequences (Sewell 1992). These unpredicted enactments of practices produced through interactions with local institutions and culture then produce cultural entropy.

Imagined Audiences and Cultural Ombudsmen

Best-practice documents embody the intentions of global AIDS organizations. These intentions are twofold: first, that AIDS organizations designing campaigns will converge around commitment to these design practices of formative research and securing buy-in, and second, that following these practices will lead to more culturally sensitive campaigns and increased commitment from community leadership, resulting in the desired behavioral changes. Best-practice documents have fulfilled the first intention by converging the field of AIDS communication around formative research and buy-in. The designers in Ghana are best-practice disciples, convinced that following best practices results in effective campaigns. Surprisingly, best practices fall victim to cultural entropy even when designers are committed. When best practices are put *into practice*—into new arrangements of organizational actors and settings—each organization enacts them differently due to the idiosyncratic constellations of audiences and stakeholders that designers confront. Best practices do not simplify or contain the messiness of the world but paper over and obscure this complexity.

Formative Research

Campaign designers have come to believe that the better they know their audience, the better they can design campaigns that persuade. Like other organizations that use culture instrumentally, AIDS campaign designers use the data they collect to *imagine* their target audience. Designers craft campaigns based on how they imagine their audience would respond, and then they test their accuracy by pretesting campaign content. While organizations universally adopted the practice of collecting data throughout the design process, *what kinds* of data they collected and *how* they collected it varied a great deal.

Organizations differentiate themselves by the kind of data they collect, often as a way to compete for funding opportunities. The kind and quality of data shape how producers imagine their target audience, structuring the form and content of the ultimate campaigns in ways that designers fail to recognize. Specifically, survey data reveal abstract *categories* of behavior and identity that lead designers to represent ideal versions of these categories. Focus groups reveal stories grounded in the everyday experiences of Ghanaians that lead designers to develop *narrative* campaigns. These variations yielded unintended consequences, in some cases subverting best practices' intent by creating campaigns that lack cultural relevance.

THE IMPORTANCE OF RESEARCH

When asked, "What makes your approach different from other organizations designing AIDS campaigns?" almost every AIDS organization responded with the same answer—"research." The common refrain of "research" across organizations indicates just how effective the circulation of best-practice documents has been in organizing the design practices of AIDS organizations. Collecting evidence is considered an unquestionable good by organizations in Ghana, funding agencies, and the public-health community globally. Tellingly, they did not say "our campaigns work." Without solid evidence that campaigns *are* working, AIDS organizations shift their attention to collecting data that suggest what campaign ideas *will* work. Unlike evaluation research, formative research tends to produce clear findings, in part because it is descriptive rather than causal. Identifying the community-level obstacles to condom use, or which campaign idea Ghanaians prefer, is concrete. It is much more difficult to prove whether exposure to a campaign changed sexual behavior.

AIDS organizations operate in a competitive environment. By aligning organizations across the field, best-practice documents created new spaces and opportunities for divergence. Funding for AIDS campaigns is competitive, and organizations bidding on contracts look to differentiate themselves not by the commitment to research that they all share but by the *kinds* of data they collect. This explains the ironic finding that designers assert that their campaigns are *distinctive* for the same reason.

Different approaches to health communication value different kinds of formative research. Social marketing, based on market-based models of communication, tends to rely on commercial marketing tools—for example, detailed market segment surveys. Community-based approaches tend to define research as "getting to know" the community. Different theories of health behavior lead to different communication strategies that require the measurement of different levels of analysis (e.g., individual versus community), and different behavioral predictors (e.g., knowledge, attitudes, practices, cognitive presuppositions).[1] In my experience, the kinds of formative research organizations in Ghana deployed vary a great deal at the local level. How did AIDS organizations vary in their approach to formative research, and to what effect?

ORGANIZATIONAL DIFFERENCES
IN FORMATIVE RESEARCH

To suggest the range of formative research practices adopted by AIDS organizations in Ghana, I will compare two major national-level campaigns: the "Stop AIDS Love Life" campaign implemented by a partnership between Johns Hopkins University School for Public Health (JHU) and the Ghana Social Marketing Foundation (GSMF) and the recent anti-stigma campaign produced by the Ghana Sustainable Change Project (GSCP).[2] These campaigns were the first two well-funded, national-level campaigns driven by a commitment to evidence-based design. This comparison is useful because these organizations share important similarities. Both campaigns were funded by the United States Agency for International Development (USAID), and both campaigns used the advertising firm of Saatchi and Saatchi/Origin8 for technical design. Holding funding agencies and ad agencies constant makes visible how different research strategies can yield disparate campaigns.

JHU/GSMF's social marketing approach relied on Knowledge, Attitude, and Practice (KAP) surveys and market research on people's desires and aspirations.

TERENCE E. MCDONNELL: How does your approach differ from other HIV prevention and condom campaigns?

GSMF STAFFER: Research, and the research is relevant.

TEM: So you do more research, different research?

GSMF STAFFER: You want to do knowledge and attitudinal research. . . . Just like in the commercial sector they do a habits and attitudes study. We are looking to change behavior and until people have changed behavior, we haven't succeeded. It is like having a heat-seeking missile—get targeted. Find out what do people want or think about this, and then we can proceed. So once we know that we can respond to the concerns, then we know we are almost there. Once you respond to those concerns you begin to see change in behaviors. And that base study, you repeat it at the end to see if there has been any change.[3]

In their view, campaigns should target people's concerns and attitudes because changing these factors will change behavior. GSMF designers trust in a direct relationship between attitudes and concerns, and behavior, where people are rational actors who make choices to maximize the likelihood of achieving their goals. GSMF designers believe that survey research, modeled on marketing tools from the commercial sector, offers the best way to understand the public's attitudes and concerns. Survey research anchors the design process for GSMF and serves as the foundation for imagining its audience.

GSCP takes a different approach, viewing people as fundamentally emotional beings who make decisions in non-rational ways. During an interview, an employee of GSCP described their approach to campaign design this way:

> We're doing something very evidenced-based. We're looking at the research that's already out there, and then doing formative research. We get people to think from the heart and not the head. And I know, because we've been working in capacity-building in institutes here, that this evidence based approach isn't being taught anywhere in Ghana.
>
> The paradigm of "information provision," which is how the Health Promotion Unit at the Ministry of Health is set up, is to get people health information. But that's not going to change any behaviors. You really have to think about the emotional issues, and how people make decisions. So our communication messages are aimed at that.[4]

GSCP staff members make clear how GSCP is distinct from other organizations, such as the Ministry of Health. Other organizations see the circulation of health information as enough to change behavior: as long as people have good, trustworthy information about how to protect themselves from disease, they'll adopt protective sexual practices. The goal, then, is simply to disperse good information into the public sphere. By contrast, GSCP staff members believe decisions about health behavior are driven by emotions, not rationality. As such, GSCP engages in qualitative, focus group research to reveal the content of people's "heart," not what is in their "head."

Although best-practice documents demand that organizations base campaigns on evidence, they tend to be agnostic when it comes to advocating which kind of data organizations should use. This lack of direction gives organizations great latitude to choose evidence that works best given their organizational position and philosophy. Variation in the kinds, qualities, and uses of formative research has real consequences. I find the kind and quality of formative research shapes the formal styles of the campaigns in unforeseen ways. Survey data and focus groups produce different kinds of knowledge. These data, then, determine the portraits organizations can paint of their audiences, ultimately structuring the kinds of campaigns they design. The point I want to press here is that the technology of data collection *makes* the audience just as much as (or more than) real Ghanaians do. Designers cater campaigns to these imagined audiences, but designers render those audiences in more or less complex ways depending on how their data-gathering method has shaped what they know. Different imagined audiences, created by different kinds of data, demand different styles of response. Quantitative survey data produce categorical knowledge and categorical campaign styles, while more qualitative data produce narrative knowledge and narrative campaign styles. I will now take each organization in turn, discussing how its methods of data collection and communication philosophies lead to distinct patterns in the styles of campaigns they produce.

THE CATEGORICAL STYLE: FROM NUMBERS TO PICTURES

GSMF centers its formative research on KAP surveys, which it believes make Ghanaians' attitudes about AIDS and condoms visible:

> You have to find out what the people know about the particular behavior, their attitudes, and their practices, so we do a KAP study. That forms the basis of our campaign design. There isn't a cookie cutter approach. Each campaign is different. For example, you are doing a condom campaign. Do people know about condoms? Sure they do. But what are their attitudes about condoms? Some think it promotes promiscuity, and so you need to take all those attitudes into consideration, and find out which one [matters]. If you hit, you'll get the best result. *Because attitudes actually beget behavior.*[5]

Here, GSMF staff members address their design philosophy. While every campaign (read: audience) is different, they adopt a single approach to understanding those audiences—KAP surveys. For GSMF, "attitudes beget behavior." As long as GSMF can identify a local audience's attitudes about AIDS or condom use, it can design a campaign that attempts to change those attitudes in ways that encourage behaviors that will prevent HIV. KAP surveys are the tool that makes this possible for GSMF.

GSMF's core activity is the social marketing of a variety of condom brands. Historically, GSMF has marketed the Protector, Panther, Champion, Bazooka, and Aganzi brands among different segments of the population, usually along class lines. Alongside KAP surveys, GSMF conducts "living standards" surveys to measure class status through consumption patterns, which GSMF staffers argue offer a better measure of economic behavior than traditional measures of socioeconomic status do. As one GSMF staffer told me, "In the West, education, job, compensation, quality of residence all correlate around income and consumption habits. In Africa these measures are meaningless."[6] In Africa, socioeconomic status is "speculative," but living standards provide "fine classification" on a 1–18 scale. This quantification is valuable to an organization such as GSMF because, as one staff member argued, "if you have a rich cattle rancher, he may still have never used a WC [water closet; i.e., flush toilet] before, so there is no sense in selling him toilet bowl cleaner."[7] KAP and living standard surveys provide organizations with a "snapshot" of an audience's reported pattern of AIDS-related attitudes, knowledge, and practices. GSMF, whose mission includes a mandate to market condoms in an effort to prevent AIDS, uses these data to assess which audiences use condoms and which do not, to explain variations in condom use and nonuse, and to identify whether people use condoms to prevent AIDS or pregnancy, the consistency of condom use, preferred brands, where people purchase condoms, and more.

Internationally, purveyors of social marketing and experts in public-health communication extol the virtues of KAP surveys for giving organizations an idea of where and how they should concentrate their efforts. Nonetheless, KAP surveys have been criticized by social scientists (Akeroyd 2004; Schoepf 2004). These scholars argue that the coupling of attitudes and behavior is considerably looser than advocates of KAP surveys would like to believe. In particular, they claim that using KAP surveys in local communities to obtain information for campaign design is reductive. As scholars have argued, KAP surveys ignore social factors:

> KAP surveys of AIDS knowledge . . . acted as though increased information would be sufficient to change complexly determined actions and as though individuals could exercise control over the social and cultural constraints to prevention. They focused on individuals in special "risk groups" and their "high risk behaviors," rather than on processes of economic empowerment and sociocultural change. (Schoepf 2004, 17)

Some go further, arguing that KAP surveys lead to campaign strategies that focus on individual choices rather than such broader social patterns as gender relations. Rather than capture the complexity of social life, an intervention based on the KAP survey approach adopts

> an individualistic perspective and emphasizes the protection of self, not of others. Messages such as the ABC refrain—"Abstain!," "Be Faithful!," "Use

Condoms!" reinforce this. However, many individuals, and especially young women, may be powerless to control the sexual behaviors of their partners or are unable, for reasons of economics or customary norms for example, to resist engaging in sexual interactions even though these might put them at risk of infection. (Akeroyd 2004, 90)

In many ways, these observations about the reductive effects of KAP surveys ring true for the incorporation of survey data into campaign design at GSMF.

Consider the following excerpt from my interviews with JHU and GSMF staff about the origins of the "Stop AIDS Love Life" campaign. Notice how a youth survey produced the need to direct a campaign at young people, and how survey questions about personal risk and condom use drove their campaign strategy.

> Our research showed young people were more concerned with social risk than personal risk, so it was an attempt to help them get a stronger grasp on their own perceptions of personal risk. Condom prevalence was very low, or 13%, among young people. It was thought that a program targeted toward promoting the perception of young people in relation to the growing HIV/AIDS situation in their country would be very useful. Realizing also that the infection is geared more toward young people than other segments of the population. So "Stop AIDS Love Life" was created as a generic campaign. The first phase of the campaign was a program directed toward young people 18 to 24 years. They were the primary object. The larger population of adults becomes the secondary population.[8]

JHU/GSMF interpreted these data as evidence that young people had unrealistic perceptions of their risk of contracting HIV, giving prominence to concerns about their social status among peers rather than their individual health. Condom use was low, and Ghanaians lacked social support for condom use. These data established the central goals for "Stop AIDS Love Life": increase individuals' risk perception as a way to encourage their condom use.

Adopting the language of "choice" was paramount to the JHU/GSMF strategy, continuing the theme of their previous family planning campaign "Life Choices. It's Your Life. It's Your Choice." "Stop AIDS Love Life. The Choice is in Your Hands" was the full slogan for their AIDS campaign and was usually placed in context with the "ABCs" of AIDS prevention: "Abstain, Be Faithful, Condom Use." This rhetoric of "choice" deployed by JHU/GSMF throughout their history of campaign design reveals their view of their audience as rational individuals with the agency to make choices that protect their health, independent of social and cultural constraints. When discussing how research translates into a campaign, one GSMF staff member remarked:

You want people to use condoms, have safe sex. Those are your target behaviors. So look into the data. What are the inhibitors to adopting those behaviors? Now some are flimsy, so what are the deep-seated inhibitors? Next, we sit with the agency and design a campaign to respond to that. [Our] study found young people are concerned with pregnancy and the effects on their school . . . everyone is oriented towards achieving a dream. The strategic framework is you "choose your future." Nobody chooses it for you. Your actions or your inactions can take you to your future, or off your target. So the choice is with you. There are several behaviors could either help or take us of the track. If you have unsafe sex you probably wouldn't get your future. If we can get you to begin to think about having safe sex and protecting yourself, there is a good chance it will extend into those other sectors of your life because there is no point in you taking my message if your behaviors in other sectors are just going to negate your future.[9]

GSMF believes it can use media campaigns to reason with people, defining condoms as a social good that rational individuals recognize as a path to achieving their goals. Once the argument is made clear to them, they have the "choice" to enact that behavior of using condoms. This imagined audience is produced by GMSF's use of KAP survey data, reinforcing its preconceived notions of how people behave. As its primary source of information about its audience, these data revealed particular facts about the population that JHU/GSMF could attempt to counter. The survey demonstrated that Ghanaians rarely use condoms, so the solution is to promote condom use. JHU/GSMF found that young people are concerned with pregnancy and school success, so they use these future goals to incentivize condom use.

Because these surveys yield static statistics, as opposed to deeper connections between meaning and action, KAP survey data rarely reveal the social and structural constraints placed on individuals when it comes to sexual behavior. For instance, based on KAP survey data, GSMF realized that most people cared more about avoiding pregnancy than about avoiding AIDS. In response to these data it chose the tagline "Choose your Future, Use a Condom."

We found that among young people, especially the young men, pregnancy is a bigger fear than disease. Because you are young, you are in school, so somebody is looking after you, so if you impregnate somebody, the social sanctions of pregnancy are heavy. Sometimes the boy could be thrown out of the house. The research [showed] that that is the biggest fear, so it is always at the back of their mind. When they are engaging in sex, they protect themselves because it is not just a question of "Oh disease, oh I don't think this lady will be a problem," but she could get pregnant. On the social side, you could lose your education. She'll lose hers, and you could lose yours, and so on. You bring untold problems to your family and it's a consequence you have to deal with. Now that in and of itself could be a drawback for people, either for them to have safe sex or to abstain altogether. . . . So we craft the campaign based on that theme. Your future depends on your choices that you make. Whether your education progresses or retrogresses, it depends [on] the choices you make. Whether you are healthy or unhealthy depends on the choices you make.[10]

To communicate core campaign concepts, taglines stem directly from data. When KAP survey data revealed that men were emasculated by condom use, they came up with "Champion Condoms, Wo Ye Metcho," ("Champion Condoms, They Are Strong/Macho"). When GMSF found that professional drivers were engaging in unprotected sex with commercial sex workers, it developed the "Drive Protected" campaign. When wealthier Ghanaians reported a greater interest in sexual performance than a fear of HIV infection or pregnancy, GSMF developed the Aganzi Wildfire performance condom with the tagline "Go Wild."

GSMF develops campaign images based on these tagline concepts. Images from GSMF campaign materials have a number of shared attributes. First, many of the GSMF campaigns do not depict people, or they show only a disembodied body part. The "Drive Protected" campaign depicts a cartoon of a tro-tro wrapped in a condom (fig. 7). "Stop AIDS Love Life," which GSMF designed in association with JHU, depicts a cartoon hand signaling "stop" while shattering through glass (fig. 8). This, GSMF staff members say, is meant to represent the campaign "shattering the silence" about AIDS. The "Champion Condoms" image depicts a flexed muscular arm (fig. 9). "Wo Ye Metcho" means "They Are Strong," and the image makes a link between masculine strength and strong condoms. Aganzi Wildfire condoms, the new upscale, for-profit brand introduced by GSMF, shows an empty, disheveled postcoital bedroom. Aganzi trades on sex appeal and bravado but depicts the remnants of a sexual encounter rather than a more narrative representation (fig. 10).

When GSMF does depict people, it does so in reductive ways. One Aganzi ad depicts a woman with her head back in erotic pleasure alongside the tagline "Aganzi: Unleash the burning passion within you" (fig. 11). Although this image is one of GSMF's few HIV print advertisements that depicts an actual woman, there is little communicated about who this woman "is," only what she is "doing." Men are the target consumer for condoms, and this is especially true for the Aganzi condom. The woman in the image is objectified, and the photo is presented from the perspective of the "male gaze" (Mulvey 1975).

FIGURE 7. Tro-tro (private minibus shared taxi) displaying a Ghana Social Marketing Foundation "Drive Protected" sticker

FIGURE 8. Johns Hopkins University's "Stop AIDS Love Life" campaign billboard advertisement on Labadi Road in Accra, Ghana

FIGURE 9. Ghana Social Marketing Foundation's Champion Condoms bus shelter advertisement on Ring Road East in Accra

After GSMF surveys revealed that the target men wanted to satisfy women, their data suggested to them that the perfect response was to put a "satisfied woman" in the ad.

Data limit the kinds of "knowledge gaps" that GSMF can identify, and the campaigns GSMF develops are similarly constrained by these data. As these examples demonstrate, KAP survey data reveal only particular kinds of knowledge about a target audience, what I call categorical knowledge. GSMF's surveys summarize and collapse a great deal of information into categories. Audiences *are* or *are not* condom users, or abstinent, or faithful at the level of the population. The task, then, is to show audiences these categories and to persuade them to move from one category to another. As I have shown in the

FIGURE 10. Ghana Social Marketing Foundation's "Aganzi: Go Wild" print advertisement

images from GSMF advertisements, reducing people into categories based on KAP surveys leads to simple taglines, and simple taglines require denotative symbols as representations (Barthes 1975). The result is a series of abstracted images: body parts, depersonified images, and logos.

GSMF's "Use a Condom" billboard also takes this categorical approach (see figure 6). The image makes a clear statement: use a condom. Beyond this direct recommendation to the audience is the fact that the letters spelling out the text are made up of stick figures. Upon examination, these stick figures are gendered (some have penises, others have breasts) and are displayed in a variety of sexual positions. The figures represent abstract categories of male/ female, heterosexual/homosexual. The interactions between these figures are static, without narrative direction or a sequence through past or future time. The interactions depicted in one letter do not sequentially relate to what is depicted in the next letter. The image does not actively tell a story; categorical knowledge leads designers to produce categorical campaign styles. Unlike the narrative campaign styles I discuss in the next section, in which audiences can see detailed social relations between the people depicted, these images empty out the content of the relationships and characters depicted.

Organizations such as GSMF that imagine audiences as categories produce *simpler* and more *abstract* campaigns. The campaigns are simpler in that they depict people as depersonalized, labeled by categories that summarize rather than elaborate. They are abstract in that they create clear boundaries

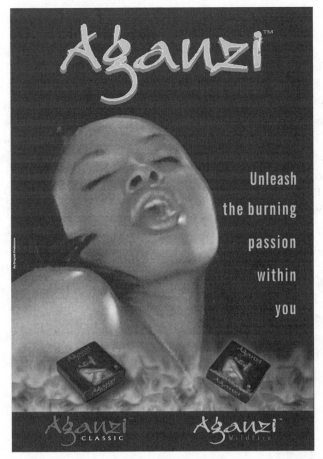

FIGURE 11. Ghana Social Marketing Foundation's "Aganzi: Unleash the Burning Passion" print advertisement

between categories decontextualized from the messiness of everyday lived experience. Categorical campaigns also depict *stasis*, rather than change. People are what they are, and do what they do, based on the categories they occupy.

This approach is also less culturally sensitive. Predetermining the categories that matter in advance, rather than using categories that emerge from the data, the KAP survey format affirms the categories that public-health practitioners view as important. Thus, what designers can learn about their audience is always mediated by the designers' prior ignorance of that same audience. It is like the blind man holding onto the tail of an elephant who attempts to know its true nature by asking, "How venomous are you?" and "How long are your fangs?" If GSMF's data lead to these patterns in knowledge and campaigns, how does GSCP's formative research shape its campaigns?

THE NARRATIVE STYLE: TELLING STORIES

The organization that put the most emphasis on focus group data was the Ghana Sustainable Change Project (GSCP). Unlike the categorical style of GSMF, GSCP designers' use of focus groups allows them to imagine a target audience of people with complex, contradictory motives, tensions, and emotions often expressed through their stories and experiences. These narratives are unruly and messy, difficult to categorize into preexisting epidemiological classifications. Although the GSCP designers still seek patterns in the data, these narratives resist simplification and abstraction.

USAID gave GSCP two AIDS communication-related mandates. First, GSCP offered AIDS communication support to Strengthening HIV/AIDS Response Partnerships (SHARP), another USAID-funded organization that works with commercial sex workers and men who have sex with men. Second, GSCP served as the secretariat for the production of a national antistigma campaign, leading diverse stakeholders through the design process, securing buy-in, and coordinating the campaign rollout. Ultimately, the campaign developed a mass media campaign and workshops for antistigma training and sought to mobilize local organizations (faith-based, nongovernmental organizations [NGOs], traditional organizations, and others). Throughout these projects, GSCP relied on focus groups to understand how commercial sex workers, men who have sex with men, and everyday Ghanaians made sense of HIV/AIDS. GSCP argued that using focus groups allowed it to access the emotional associations people have with the disease. Understanding these emotions gave the designers insight into what messages and communication strategies would motivate people to change their behavior.

This close attention to emotional, relational, and motivational factors is clear in the GSCP's marketing of condoms to commercial sex workers. Consider the stark difference between the condom campaigns of GSMF and the GSCP condom campaign aimed at commercial sex workers. "I Am Someone's Hope" was produced by GSCP in 2008 and distributed throughout sexual health clinics, in bars that support sex work, and via peer education in poster and pamphlet formats (fig. 12). This poster is typical of what I classify as having narrative elements. While the tagline and associated text—"I Am Someone's Hope: Always use a condom, even with your regular boyfriend, to protect yourself from HIV and STI"—is not particularly narrative, the images associated with it present a carefully constructed narrative.

The image makes clear to the Ghanaian audience that the "main character" is a sex worker: she has dyed hair and a nose stud, and she is wearing an "immodest" dress that reveals her shoulders. That is not all that is revealed about

FIGURE 12. Ghana Sustainable Change Project/SHARP's "I Am Someone's Hope" print advertisement

her "character," however. She is also a mother who cares for a young daughter, a role she plays alongside—but independent from—her sex work. We can observe from her smile that she takes great joy in motherhood. The poster displays her in a third role, as the girlfriend of the young man depicted in the bubble illustrations presented at the bottom of the poster. HIV puts these roles into conflict. Contracting HIV and other sexually transmitted infections (STIs) would undermine her capacity to raise her daughter. In the long term, contracting HIV and dying an early death would leave her child orphaned. In the short term, contracting an STI that manifests visually would reduce her ability to keep clients. Since she is "someone's hope" and her daughter relies on her life and livelihood for economic and emotional support, contracting HIV or other STIs undermines her ability to parent her child.

According to GSCP staff working with the commercial sex worker community, many commercial sex workers in Ghana use condoms with their clients but not when having sex with their regular boyfriends. By not wearing condoms with their boyfriends, commercial sex workers establish trust and distinguish between client and nonclient sexual activity. This poster makes clear how caving to a boyfriend's refusal to wear condoms might *also* place her life—and her role as mother and provider—at risk by bringing HIV or an STI into the relationship. Through the series of images depicted here, the poster offers resolution to this conflict through an unfolding narrative. In the first bubble, she holds firm by refusing unsafe sex with her boyfriend. In the second bubble, he rethinks his position on condom use. By the third bubble, he has come around and agrees to use condoms when having sex with his girlfriend, who is also a sex worker, mother, and daughter.

This poster *tells a story* through a number of narrative conventions. First, it develops character by depicting multiple identities in tension with each other. We learn a great deal about this character just by what she wears and with whom she interacts, but we also see the pressures she faces as her various roles come into conflict. Second, it depicts events over time through the use of sequential bubbles. Third, this image develops narrative tension. These narrative elements enable GSCP to honor the complex social world that commercial sex workers have to navigate. Condom use is not simply an individual choice isolated from social pressures but a complex decision-making process embedded in social obligation and rife with meaning. To wear a condom often communicates a lack of trust in your partner, and commercial sex workers typically forgo condom use with their boyfriends to distinguish their romantic relationships from relationships with clients. GSCP understood the complexity of the meaning of condoms and the difficult situations that commercial sex workers face because of the stories they heard in focus groups and through working with commercial sex workers. GSCP also recognized this practice of non–condom use with boyfriends as a risky practice. This poster incorporated the stories GSCP heard from sex workers about the need to cultivate trust in their personal romantic relationships, the difficulty in bringing up condom use with boyfriends, the risks of disease and the need to provide for family, and attempts to forge a narrative path that sex workers and their boyfriends can follow.

GSCP also brought this approach to its development of a national anti-stigma campaign. Staff attributed diminished success in such areas as testing and care to the high stigma associated with having HIV in Ghana (Luginaah, Yiridoe, and Taabazuing 2005). GSCP's focus groups with Ghanaians sought to understand the sources of and reasons for stigmatizing behavior by Ghanaians, with special attention to the emotional underpinnings of stigma.

GSCP staff members believe that "straightforward questions usually result in straightforward lies" because focus group participants want to give the "right" answer, or the answer participants believe the researchers were "looking for." Instead, GSCP employed a number of nontraditional focus group techniques such as emotion cards and word balloons to get at what one designer called the "authentic" emotions under the surface, and to encourage people to open up about stigma. GSCP staffers took one technique from advertising research, not from best-practice reports, because they believed it would give them a better image of their audience. GSCP presented focus group participants with a drawing of a person with empty dialogue balloons originating from the mouth, head, and heart. They then asked focus group participants what they might say when learning someone was HIV positive, compared to what they might think, or what they might feel. GSCP sought to tease apart differences between outward and internal emotional states, making visible distinct internal conflicts about stigma that they could leverage toward behavior change in their campaign.

When participants' external and internal emotional states appeared unaligned, GSCP staff believed this signaled an "emotional pulse point." Emotional pulse points, GSCP believes, drive behavior:

> Quantitative research doesn't get to emotional pulse points . . . quantitative techniques are used to measure effectiveness, baseline, midline, endline surveys. Quantitative research shouldn't drive communications campaigns since they can't get at emotion.
>
> If in communication you can solve conflicts for people, that is the best situation ever. Providing for kids is an issue, and then introducing family planning as a solution, a man will be much less likely to feel threatened and more likely to go out and change behavior. When external conflicts come up it's a good place to sit back, let emotions fly, and see what comes out. Conflict came up in our stigma focus groups. They'll say PLWA [people living with AIDS] need compassion, but their initial reaction to PLWA are anger, disgust. So that is the core level, deeper. They know the right answer but feel at another level. A lot of health campaigns don't hit a pulse point. They give logical reasons or information but don't hit a pulse point. Logical reasons don't change behavior.[11]

GSCP uses pulse points to refine its campaign concepts. GSCP saw how Ghanaians recognized their own hypocrisy. Ghanaians understood that their actions were not any more moral than those of people living with HIV, but they still stigmatized others to protect their own identity as moral. In response, designers developed campaign concepts centered on this pulse point of *recognition*, in an attempt to turn stigma on its head. To counteract stigma, GSCP proposed campaigns that would stigmatize stigmatizing behavior. GSCP wanted its communications to emphasize that stigmatizing people living with HIV will lead a person to "be *recognized* as an immoral, ignorant, or worse." To address the complexity of these pulse points, they created more narratively complex campaigns than campaigns made by organizations using survey data.

Designers at GSCP developed three concepts for the national antistigma campaign. Informally, they referred to these concepts as the "ridiculous," "comparison," and "religious" campaigns. Exploiting the pulse point of recognition, each concept leads audiences to reflect on the immorality of stigmatizing behavior. In effect, the ads attempt to help people recognize stigmatizing people living with HIV as immoral and show HIV-negative Ghanaians that their communities would view them as *less* virtuous, rather than more, if they were to stigmatize.

The "ridiculous" approach was designed to make stigmatizing behavior seem absurd by depicting people going to great lengths to avoid people living with HIV. One mock-up depicts a man serving another man (presumably HIV positive) a meal on a shovel. The man extends his arms out as far as possible to create the maximum distance between himself and the man with HIV. Unspoken, but implied in the mock-up, is that this stigmatizing behavior is driven by an irrational fear of infection that leads the uninfected man to act in ridiculous ways. By depicting the actions of the HIV-negative man as ridiculous while the HIV-positive man appears normal, GSCP hoped audiences would empathize with the man living with HIV and look upon the man holding the shovel with derision. The idea is summed up with the text, "Who are you to judge? You are showing your ignorance to treat people with HIV different." Another version of the tagline appealed to the audience's desire to be respected as forward looking by their peers, imploring audiences, "Don't think backwards. It is backward to treat people living with HIV different."

Other versions of this campaign concept work similarly: each image displays the active mistreatment of another person, using relatable and morally inflected characters in familiar settings. Each concept makes acts of stigma appear both ridiculous and dishonorable by telling a story. Like many narratives, it contains a moral, a lesson to be learned. While most mock-ups for the "ridiculous" concept adopted a single-panel approach, GSCP put together one design that took the narrative forward, showing the positive consequences of overcoming stigma. In this design, the scene of the man using the shovel was followed by an image of a family in close contact, raising glasses together at an outdoor picnic. Rather than ending with an act of stigmatization, this version shows family life in a poststigma world, celebrating time together with family without fear or harm. The text changes here: "Move from ignorance to respect," calling on audiences to move beyond stigma.

GSCP's formative research also indicated that Ghanaians believed they could be promiscuous, as long as they did not get caught. To get caught was to get HIV, which indicated one's deviance and immorality. As such, GSCP wanted to show two people who were essentially equivalent in their practices, with one HIV positive and the other HIV negative. The "comparison" mock-up depicts two men, standing back to back, both looking at the audience. A character profile accompanies each man's image. One man is a "Medical Doctor, Has two girlfriends, Youth President at church, Is HIV-positive." The other is an "Accountant, Has three girlfriends, Likes partying and going to nightclubs, Is HIV-negative." The large text at the bottom of the design displays the campaign slogan, "Who are you to judge?" An alternative design, using women, makes ambiguous which of the women is living with HIV. "One of these women is HIV+. Who are you to judge?" implies that these two women are morally equivalent, similar in character to the audience, and yet one contracted HIV. Rather than using abstractions, GSCP grounded these character comparisons in familiar behaviors that many Ghanaians share.

GSCP understood that religious beliefs and the desire to be moral motivated much of the stigmatizing behavior. To illuminate this view as hypocritical, one mock-up drew on religious authority to undermine stigma. The "religious" concept used Christian and Muslim rhetoric to argue against stigmatizing. The Christian mock-up depicts a statue of Jesus and references Matthew 25 and Jesus's Parable of the Judgment. In this parable, Jesus tells the blessed they will inherit the kingdom because "whatever you did for one of these least brothers of mine, you did for me." Treating others with love and respect, even the least of us, is a core Christian value, and one that parallels the antistigma agenda. GSCP reminds Christian Ghanaians of this story with the following text: "'In as much as you have done it to one of them, you have done it to me.' He didn't judge, so why should you? Judging people with HIV isn't Christian." The mock-up aimed at Muslim Ghanaians makes a similar move by quoting from the Quran (31:18). The image depicts a crescent and star, with the following text: "'And do not turn your face away from people in contempt . . .' He didn't judge, so why should you? Judging people with HIV isn't Allah's will."

Unlike the abstract campaigns produced by GSMF, these mock-ups rely on narrative elements to create tension in the audience. The various contexts in which people stigmatize, the logics of when people choose to use condoms or feel they cannot even suggest it, do not cleanly resolve into easily representable ideas. To honor the complexity of the imagined audience their data generated, organizations in Ghana that work closely with communities or use focus groups produce campaigns with a *narrative* style. Narrative campaigns

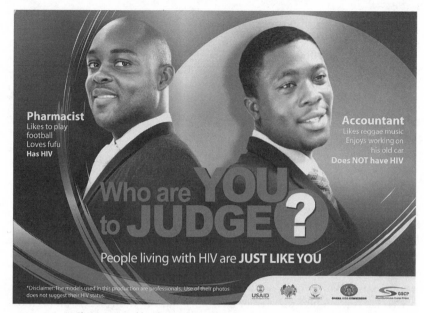

FIGURE 13. Ghana Sustainable Change Project's national antistigma campaign "Who Are You to Judge?" comparison print advertisement

ground representations of people in character, showing intersecting identities rather than depicting people simply as a category. Narrative campaigns portray unfolding events over time, along with social interactions, processes, and change. While narrative campaigns certainly rely on categories to communicate meaning, they go beyond simple expressions of category.

Comparing two campaigns using the generic "comparison" form makes clear the distinction between categorical and narrative campaigns. Consider GSCP's final "comparison" advertisement (fig. 13) for the national antistigma campaign and a similar "comparison" made for GSMF's "Choose Your Future" campaign. Like the mock-ups discussed earlier, the final GSCP image compares two character sketches. These character sketches attempt to honor the complex issue of stigma by showing audiences they can't predict who will get HIV and who will not. GSCP designed the character sketches to be relatable, so Ghanaians can see themselves in the characters' preferences and practices and then realize they should not stigmatize people living with HIV because they could succumb to the same fate.

By contrast, the KAP-driven GSMF advertisement gives the audience much less detail in favor of presenting digestible categories. Like the GSCP ad, it compares two men, both in plain T-shirts: one man frowns, slumped over, and holds his head up with his fist; the other smiles ecstatically, has his shoulders back, and appears confident. In the middle is a picture of a rolled condom. The ad states, "CHOOSE YOUR FUTURE, USE A CONDOM." Over the first man it reads, "I DIDN'T . . ." and over the second, "I DID . . ." Compared to GCSP's ad, GSMF presents people *empty* of character. Audiences can only recognize the two men in the GSMF ad as happy or sad, and as a condom user or not. By depersonalizing these men, they are reduced to symbols denoting categories of happiness or sadness. These men simply, cleanly, and prototypically present categories of emotion. While the slogan encourages Ghanaians to "Choose Your Future," that future is unarticulated. The image does not address how using a condom (or not) might make people happy or sad, or lead to consequences like HIV or pregnancy. The elements in this image offer categories that privilege a clear message rather than a complex narrative.

Narrative and categorical styles vary in the characteristics they exhibit. First, they vary by how explicitly "peopled" they are. GSMF's categorical style creates iconic images that symbolize core campaign ideas: a flexed muscular arm to connote strength and masculinity; a pair of holding hands to represent compassion and care; a woman with her head back in ecstasy to depict sexual pleasure, performance, and sexiness. Categorical styles use figures or cartoons, show body parts disconnected from whole bodies, or deploy abstract symbols such as red ribbons. When this categorical style depicts people, they are presented as symbols for abstract concepts. Most narrative styles use photo-realistic representations of people interacting, embedded in social contexts. There are often multiple images of the same people, suggesting change over time.

Second, the two styles differ on the specificity of content that can be read into the campaign. "I Am Someone's Hope" provides details about the three people featured: their roles, emotions, professions, relationships, gender, race, age, and more. In contrast, GSMF's "Use a Condom" stick figures present significantly less social context. The figures are gendered and their sexual proclivities are visible, but beyond that, the audience must read additional detail or narrative into the ad. Categorical campaigns tend to universalize—even people outside of Ghana can understand what is happening in the stick figure image or that a flexed arm is meant to communicate masculinity. One could export many of GSMF's campaigns to other countries without fear of confusing local populations because the categories are transposable and devoid of much culturally specific content. Narrative campaigns are more likely to customize to the local context. Outside of Africa, people would miss much of the intended meaning. Namely, they wouldn't recognize the "I Am Someone's

Hope" campaign as aimed at sex workers, whereas Ghanaians easily recognize the cues. Narrative campaigns, then, appear more sensitive to the local cultural milieu.

Third, narrative images show or imply action and interaction over time, whereas abstracted images often depict one-shot moments dissociated from a chain of events. While one-shot images like the Aganzi poster of the post-coital bedroom (figure 10) can lead the audience to imagine a narrative, the image itself does not guide audiences through a story. How and when those footprints got on the wall is left to the unpredictable dirty minds of varied audiences. More important, how the Aganzi condom fits into the narrative is even less clear. Narrative campaigns, on the other hand, walk audiences through a process, holding the audience's hand as the campaign depicts— through character and plot—the behavioral change that health communicators want audiences to make.

To sum up, narrative and categorical campaigns differ by the amount and kind of work they expect the audience to do (Becker 2007). Narrative campaigns depict richly developed characters drawn from the particular local sociocultural contexts, embedded in stories that privilege interaction and change over time. In narrative campaigns, the "events seem to speak themselves" (White 1987, 3). When campaigns take a narrative approach, they control and constrain people's reading such that meanings are made *for* audiences. Categorical campaigns, with their underdeveloped characters; abstract, generalized content; and one-shot content, do discursive work that does not "impose upon the speaker" (White 1987, 2). They provide more interpretive space for audiences to engage, potentially leaving the message more open to alternative readings.

CULTURAL ENTROPY THROUGH FORMATIVE RESEARCH

What is at stake in this variation between categorical and narrative campaigns? It suggests that best-practice documents' mandate to develop evidence-based campaigns undergoes cultural entropy. While authors of best-practice reports elevate evidence-driven campaigns to the status of a sacred credo, they neglect to consider how different kinds of data collected might pattern campaigns in unseen and unintended ways. Convergence around best practices creates opportunities for divergence that undermine the intentions of those practices. Despite a shared commitment to evidence, organizations claim that what makes them distinctive is the kind and quality of the evidence they collect. In an uncertain funding environment, organizations need to make themselves distinct from the competition. Driven by this need to differentiate, the convergence around best practices established an arena for competition among AIDS organizations designing campaigns. Divergences in data collection practices lead to different campaigns styles that are more or less sensitive to the local context and that may be more or less persuasive.[12] If the intended outcome of conducting formative research is to design more culturally sensitive campaigns, then the use of KAP surveys and the resulting categorical campaigns undermine this goal. In effect, best practices undergo entropy.

Basing campaigns on formative research is not sufficient for producing culturally sensitive campaigns. Categorical campaigns collect a great deal of data, but their methods reify the categories organizations believe to be relevant. Despite going through the effort of collecting data on the target audience, new, locally specific categories rarely emerge from KAP surveys and market research. In this way, categorical campaigns draw on and speak to the same categories as do AIDS campaigns in other countries (e.g., youth, people who engage in unsafe sex) and do so in ways that make campaigns seem generic and disconnected from local populations.

Basing campaigns on evidence gives designers confidence that they have crafted campaigns that meet their audiences' needs. Yet how well they can meet those needs depends on their capacity to imagine that audience. Without disconfirming evidence, designers have no reason to believe their data misrepresents their audience, which presents an additional source of entropy for categorical campaigns: Designers have no reason to correct course because their target audience is contained within an imagined world they fabricated based on the data they collected. Preproduction research reveals what audience needs organizations are obliged to meet. When pretesting the mock-ups designed to address those needs, community focus groups choose between the options the organization presents to them—options already constrained by the preproduction data. If the preproduction data fail to give organizations a representative image of their audience, the campaign designers will lack the knowledge necessary to ground campaign ideas in the lived experience of local communities and completely miss the problems inherent in their imagined audience. Organizations, then, cannot anticipate the ways audiences may misinterpret, reject, or ignore campaigns after their release, leaving campaigns more open to cultural entropy later on.

Best-practice documents present evidence-based design and secure multisectoral support as if they were aligned, that following this linear path improves campaign effectiveness. I find that these best practices are often at odds with each other. Meeting the demands of both best practices can create conflict, forcing compromises that undermine the intentions of the best-practice reports and the goals of the campaigns.

Cultural Ombudsmen

In a mock-up of its iconic yellow "Stop AIDS Love Life" print advertisements, JHU depicted a hand held up to signal "stop" and symbolically shattering glass as if it was "shattering the silence" (fig. 8). Unbeknownst to its designers, JHU had made a major faux pas. As reported by a staff member from the Ghana AIDS Commission (GAC) who was involved in advising the design phase of the "Stop AIDS Love Life" campaign, a traditional Ghanaian chief noticed the ad had depicted a left hand instead of a right:

> We realized that it was the left hand that was used instead of the right. In Ghana, you're disrespectful if you use your left or if you wave at somebody with your left hand. You know how this came out? It was actually the Chief who brought it to our attention. He told us, listen you're using the wrong hand here. These are graphics, so we have to change to right-handed. The kind of people you involve in your pretesting tell you the kind of things you need to do next time, or the failures or the limitations of the campaign that you've done.[13]

In Ghanaian (and other African) cultures, it is considered offensive to use one's left hand when greeting, passing objects between people, or signaling someone.[14] When the chief, a paragon of tradition and respected local leader, observed that JHU depicted the use of a left hand "shattering" rather than the right, he caught a major error. The chief contended that this image, if it were to reach the public, would cause great offense. This error was simple to correct, but without the local expertise of the cultural ombudsman to identify it, JHU could have spent a great deal of money on a campaign that might have undermined its legitimacy as a source of AIDS knowledge.

In the ideal world imagined by best-practice reports, this is how incorporating stakeholders should work. In the absence of advisers with a deep knowledge of local culture, evidence-based campaigns might still cause offense. Vetting campaigns through these representatives offers an additional check, helping to avoid controversies that might derail the campaign once public. Catching such cultural errors, designers believe, ensures cultural sensitivity and prevents misinterpretations before they happen. Integrating chiefs, religious leaders, government representatives, and other experts has become a central tenet of the design process in Ghana. By incorporating these leaders, designers refine their message, commit varied stakeholders to a single message, and engender a sense of ownership and commitment from those involved. This way, when an AIDS organization launches the campaign, it has a ready-made network of influential Ghanaians who stand behind the campaign and shepherd the message to the community.

These local experts and community leaders mediate between the needs of the organization and the public interest, especially regarding tradition and local cultural knowledge and practice. I call these stakeholders *cultural ombudsmen*. Like public advocates for governments or newspapers, cultural ombudsmen represent the interests of the public to these organizations. While they have insider status, they also have a great degree of independence from the day-to-day workings of the organization. Organizations take care to select ombudsmen who represent a variety of categories, such as religious leaders, traditional leaders, government officials, civil society groups, politicians, and administrators from other HIV/AIDS-related NGOs. Cultural ombudsmen are usually elites, often prestigious "big men," who speak for and defend the interests of the communities they represent.[15] These stakeholders play a different role than "the community" or "the target audience." When organizations develop campaigns in tandem with the community or use formative research to imagine target audiences, designers use the information they glean from communities in an advisory manner. Cultural ombudsmen, on the other hand, do more than help designers talk out ideas. They have insider status and veto power. These cultural ombudsmen are distinct from Ghanaians working within AIDS organizations.[16] Ghanaian staff may have organizational authority but lack the cultural authority of the ombudsmen.

Beyond their capacity as cultural advisers, ombudsmen offer organizations something just as important as getting the right message: access into communities after the launch of the campaign. For campaign activities that require peer education or community interaction, partnering with a powerfully positioned cultural leader can facilitate an organization's access to that community (i.e., a congregation). Almost every organization I spoke with relied on these leaders to return to their communities and encourage local Ghanaians to use their materials. In this sense, "buy-in" is not simply about getting Ghanaian leaders in line around a single message. It is also about seeking help from these cultural ombudsmen in mounting AIDS prevention efforts at the community level.

Sometimes vetting campaign ideas with ombudsmen works as intended, as the JHU example showed, but my data suggest that involving community leaders just as often complicates campaign design and selection. Recall the case of the billboard designed to encourage faithfulness among Muslims (fig. 1). In that instance, the imam first approved, and then rejected, the campaign for its portrayal of Western gender norms. What an ombudsman viewed as culturally sensitive one day became controversial the next. Ombudsmen sometimes back a campaign throughout the design process but then disappear when the campaign is launched if it no longer serves their purposes. Additionally,

stakeholders use their moral and cultural authority to exert pressure on designers and force compromise. Ombudsmen sometimes push designers away
from campaigns for the most vulnerable populations, leading them to diverge
from more targeted audiences or campaign concepts backed by evidence. To
show how cultural ombudsmen can complicate the design process and undermine the intended outcomes of securing multisectoral support, I take up the
story of GSCP's national antistigma campaign design process.

SECURING BUY-IN

GSCP had a strong commitment to cultivating buy-in from cultural ombudsmen. During the production of the national antistigma campaign, GSCP
opened every meeting I attended with a discussion designed to get everyone
on board with the campaign. They showed a busy PowerPoint slide depicting twenty-one logos of organizations connected to the campaign and then
pressed meeting participants to make sure their organization's logo was on
the slide. This was a not-so-subtle attempt to secure, at least symbolically, support for the campaign. Viewed neutrally, this collection of logos recognizes
the contributions these organizations have made to the campaign. Seen more
strategically, acquiring a logo is a contract of sorts. It links each organization
to the fate of the campaign, and GSCP staff hoped it would encourage further
commitment after the campaign's release. More cynically, this list of partners could diffuse blame away from GSCP if the campaign raised controversy.
Once an organization's logo was on that slide, that stakeholder organizations
had a diminished capacity to criticize the ultimate campaign.

Working with these cultural ombudsmen can prove to be a tricky endeavor. While designers recognize the importance of getting opinion leaders
on their side, once ombudsmen engage in the design process, they also have
the capacity to derail the work designers have already put into developing a
campaign. On the one hand, designers try to temper the power of these cultural ombudsmen because they do not want to go back to the drawing board
at the whim of an influential adviser. On the other hand, organizations don't
want to lose these leaders' commitment to the cause by alienating them.

Delicately, GSCP sought to minimize the power of cultural ombudsmen
through a number of techniques. First, it brought ombudsmen into the design
process late in the game. GSCP staff thought that if ombudsmen contributed
ideas early on, they might be disappointed when their campaign idea did
not end up as the ultimate campaign message. GSCP feared that ombudsmen could take such rejection personally and refuse future involvement with
the campaign. Designers I spoke with also reported that having "too many

cooks in the kitchen" early in the process causes a loss of focus and inevitable delays. Instead, GSCP invited ombudsmen into the process after mock-ups were designed. This timing forced ombudsmen to work within the core campaign ideas that GSCP designers developed based on the formative research process.

Second, GSCP sought to mitigate the chances that cultural ombudsmen would derail the design process by backing up their concepts with the authority of formative research. Designers believed that ombudsmen often overstep their expertise, either making claims about the culture of Ghanaian communities based on personal assumptions rather than actual knowledge, or giving communications strategy advice when they had no experience developing media campaigns. Formative research can temper what designers viewed as off-the-wall or uninformed contributions from ombudsmen. Armed with a body of competing knowledge based in the legitimacy of empiricism and scientific methods, designers could counter ombudsmen's gut reactions and speculation. Given their focus group pretest results, GSCP staff felt confident bringing in ombudsmen to discuss potential campaign strategies:

> At that point we have a big meeting with stakeholders to go through the strategy, the concepts that came out of it, and the pretest results. That is a great opportunity to have the stakeholders make decisions on which [campaign] they want to go with. We always pretest before presenting the ideas to the stakeholders, otherwise we have stakeholders coming up with their own ideas— and they are not creative people—or saying, "Oh, this one is no good." But they are not the target audience. So we say, "That is really interesting, if you were our target audience, we wouldn't use this one, but our target audience is commercial sex workers." So it is really important to pretest before going into these meetings with stakeholders because that is who you really care about what they think, the people that you are targeting.[17]

Communication specialists at GSCP and many other AIDS organizations in Ghana are often Americans and Europeans working alongside Ghanaian specialists. As foreigners, they are powerless to respond to ombudsmen's claims about how Ghanaians would respond to a campaign. That is, unless they have access to an even more legitimate source of knowledge: members of the target audience. This practice elegantly deflects the sticky issue of Western expert knowledge trumping local Ghanaian culture by assigning authority to the target audience members themselves.

Based on these practices, AIDS organizations primarily use stakeholder meetings to develop relationships with cultural ombudsmen and secure their support. While designers want help from ombudsmen in catching unforeseen cultural insensitivities and in selecting from the campaign ideas driven by the formative research, there is a sense from designers that incorporating ombudsmen into the process is more to get them invested than it is to improve the campaign. Despite this recognition, GSCP designers often expressed frustration after these meetings:

> People feel like developing communication materials is simple. There might be one person at these meetings that understands communication. Most of their comments weren't helpful. They don't understand that these are concepts, not final products. The stakeholders were hung up on minor details . . . whether Jesus' arms should be outstretched, or wordsmithing. These meetings are meant to help stakeholders feel part of the process. We use the meetings to bring people along, to get them invested in the materials, but they are not making a serious contribution to the process. It should be the target audience that informs design, not stakeholders.[18]

Design staff work to minimize the contribution of these cultural ombudsmen because their comments can distract from the task at hand or undermine their campaign design expertise. Designers view the presence of ombudsmen as necessary to ensure their support for the campaign after its launch but often deem their involvement in design "not helpful." For instance, another designer described the stakeholders' meeting as about building credibility. GSCP placed "big people" in the Ghanaian AIDS world at the center of the meeting to give its activities credibility. More than just getting them invested and aligned with a campaign, the presence of powerful ombudsmen made GSCP's activities legitimate.

CULTURAL OMBUDSMEN'S VETO POWER

When developing the national antistigma campaign, GSCP took an evidence-based approach that informed the development of three culturally sensitive campaign ideas: "ridiculous," "religious," and "comparison." Designers pretested each of these ideas in focus groups to assess which campaign concept was most likely to reduce stigmatizing behavior. Of the three campaign ideas, the "ridiculous" campaign was the unanimous favorite among focus group respondents and, for that matter, the designers. According to the pretest report, the "ridiculous" campaign provoked strong emotional responses from respondents, especially after seeing the man being fed with a shovel:

> The participants in all groups identified well with [ridiculous] as a concept . . . the pictures in this concept affected their emotions very much. Though the participants showed much emotion towards each version of this [concept],

comments were mostly directed at the one with food on a shovel. One person confessed that he did that to a relative who was [living with HIV] because at that time he did not know much about the modes of transmission. In each of the focus group discussions one person visibly shed tears. He said he felt it was ridiculous for any person to stigmatize or discriminate so.

They expressed amazement, sadness, shock, feeling bad, confusion, and sorrow at the *"inhuman"* treatment. Some were disturbed by the poster and blurted out:

"He is a human being not a pig."

"You know, I am a farmer and this is how we feed the female pig who is very wild."

"Confused. Why should we treat each other like that?"

Another sat humped and heaving a sigh responded,

"I'm thinking deeply toward a solution to show concern for PLWHAs [people living with HIV/AIDS], to inform those who stigmatize."

Another in a very reflective mood said,

"I used to think that I should send PLWHAs away from me before seeing this. But this is telling me I should not judge."

In all groups, the "ridiculous" concept with someone being given food on a shovel was unanimously chosen. The following reasons were given for this choice:

"It touches our heart most."

"You don't need an explanation or take a long while to read the statements before getting the message."

"With the shovel immediately you see it you know what is about."

"Even a child can see what is all about"

Why not the religious concept?

Participants gave the following reasons for not choosing this concept:

The reasoning in the groups was the images of the religious concepts are seen almost everywhere and most people at a glance will immediately conceive it as something to do with the religious people (Christian and Moslem).

Why not the comparison concept?

One has to pause and read everything before you can get the message.

It doesn't evoke as much emotions as the others. (Ghana Sustainable Change Project 2006)

While the other two campaigns had some support from pretesting, it was clear from conversations with GSCP staff that they preferred moving forward with the "ridiculous" campaign. Despite this preference for the "ridiculous" concept, the national antistigma campaign design team ultimately dropped the "ridiculous" idea and went forward with the "religious" and "comparison" concepts instead. What happened that GSCP moved away from the campaign most supported by evidence? This is especially surprising because this report gave designers clear data to support the "ridiculous" concept when going into their meeting with stakeholders.

In the case of the "ridiculous" campaign, the *veto power* of cultural ombudsmen came to the fore. Some ombudsmen observed that local audiences might interpret the behavior depicted in the campaign literally. That is, they expressed concern that audiences might interpret the campaign as prescriptive, encouraging Ghanaians to keep their distance from people living with HIV and to feed HIV-positive family members with a shovel, turning an anti-stigma ad into a stigmatization instruction manual. Ombudsmen argued that most Ghanaians would not identify the behavior as negative or absurd or ridiculous because they lacked the subtlety and experience to interpret it as ironic. Believing Ghanaians were unable to grasp the irony that GSCP intended, they argued that Ghanaians would view this campaign as an invitation to stigmatize.

In response, GSCP staff members argued on behalf of the "ridiculous" concept. They reminded stakeholders that everyday Ghanaians in focus groups had no trouble interpreting the campaign idea as it was intended. Representatives from NAP+, the Ghana Network of Persons Living with HIV/ AIDS, then responded with their concerns. They argued that if this campaign led to the further stigmatization of even one person living with HIV, then the "ridiculous" campaign was a nonstarter. Although representatives of NAP+ were not the target audience for this campaign, their livelihoods depended upon effectively reducing stigma through this campaign. NAP+ and the broader community of people living with HIV had the most to lose should the campaign backfire. This fact gave these cultural ombudsmen the moral authority to override the evidence-based authority of GSCP designers.

This notion that the "ridiculous" concept was open to an interpretation completely opposite of its intentions may have its origins in the visual execution of the mock-ups.[19] From early on GSCP staff understood the difficulty of pulling off the "ridiculous" concept. One GSCP designer claimed that the first mock-ups produced by its advertising agency, Origin8, depicted the HIV-positive characters as "pathetic." The images showed people with dour faces and body language that suggested they were depressed. GSCP was concerned that this depiction might lead to further stigmatizing of people with HIV, so it had Origin8 reshoot the images. GSCP found these new images to be an improvement but not yet in the zone of what GSCP thought of as acceptable. Again GSCP asked the agency to reshoot the concept, this time without depicting faces. The new mock-ups arrived just before a stakeholder meeting. When the GSCP staff members looked at the images, they said, "We can't show these today," and "I thought we weren't going to show faces . . . we asked them not to show faces, but they're showing faces."[20] These failed attempts at representing the concept suggest that creative staffers at the advertising agency may have unconsciously held stigmatizing and stereotypical ideas about how HIV-positive people feel because these ideas continued to appear in the mock-up images despite complaints from GSCP. The inability to communicate the intended irony may have pushed the ombudsmen away from the concept, despite evidence of the dramatic impact the "ridiculous" concept had on focus group participants. With these pressures, GSCP and the consortium of stakeholders went with the safer, less-controversial "religion" and "comparison" concepts.

In effect, GSCP's commitment to evidence-based campaigns conflicted with its commitment to designing campaigns with multisectoral support. Unlike the ideal vision conveyed by best-practice reports, in which each step of the process works seamlessly with the others without contradiction, vetting campaigns with stakeholders undermined the organization's commitment to evidence-based campaign design. Had GSCP rebuffed the cultural ombudsmen and gone ahead with the "ridiculous" campaign, it would have lost the support of a wide range of stakeholders and undermined its legitimacy in the field. But, GSCP believed it would have been more effective had it gotten the imagery right. Instead, going with the "religious" and "comparison" campaigns undermined the hard work and momentum of designers passionate about the "ridiculous" concept. They understood why they had to give up the "ridiculous" approach, but informal discussions with GSCP staff members suggested they felt deflated and less confident about the other approaches.

THE CULTURAL OMBUDSMAN AS GATEKEEPER

GSCP moved forward with production of the "religious" and "comparison" campaign strategies. Designers expressed hope for the "religious" strategy because GSCP was creating "Who Are You to Judge?" workshops and manuals for religious communities. By consulting with the religious leadership as they created workshop materials, GSCP designers thought religious leaders would both recognize the importance of reducing stigma and commit to using these materials in their congregations. These beliefs went hand in hand with the sustainability mission of the Ghana Sustainable Change Project. After GSCP provided these materials to religious leaders and their churches and mosques, these religious communities could conduct antistigma workshops into the future. With commitment from religious communities, the campaign could continue to have positive effects long after the GSCP funds ran out.

GSCP wanted to establish continuity with the previous national antistigma campaign. After achieving the massive visibility of the "Stop AIDS Love Life" AIDS awareness and prevention campaign in Ghana, staff from JHU/GSMF turned their attention to the issue of stigma. In an attempt to counter stigma, JHU/GSMF designers developed the "Reach Out, Show Compassion" campaign, even though the timing of this new campaign was not ideal: the five-year USAID contract that funded the AIDS prevention activities of JHU/GSMF was about to run out in 2003. In an effort to ensure the sustainability of their efforts, JHU/GSMF worked closely with local religious leaders, involving Ghanaian religious leaders in the design process. If JHU/GSMF could get religious leaders to buy in, these leaders would continue to disseminate the antistigma message to their communities even if JHU/GSMF lost their USAID funding. JHU/GSMF ultimately lost the bid (that would renew their funding from USAID), and the contract went to GSCP.

The religious leaders JHU chose to work with were powerful and publicly recognizable religious figures. The "Reach Out, Show Compassion" campaign included TV advertisements with appearances from these partnered religious leaders, depicting them discussing the problems with stigma. They also developed "Show Compassion" training manuals that could be distributed to local churches so as to educate the laity about HIV/AIDS and to reduce stigma. According to GSMF officials, many of the churches that received these materials never opened them:

> "Reach Out" wasn't as successful as we wanted. The Compassion campaign took a little twist. The Compassion campaign was run in such a way that the churches and the Ministry of Health were supposed to take it over and run with the campaign. And unfortunately, it didn't happen that way. Maybe if GSMF and JHU had run it, you know, holding the reins throughout the campaign as we had held "Stop AIDS Love Life," the impact might have been different. Unfortunately, it didn't work out properly. [There were] so many issues. Commitment was one. Commitment definitely goes with financing. I'm sure everybody expected there was free lunch, and once they realized there wasn't free lunch and they had to put in some money, their level of commitment was not as strong as we intended. And then, of course, there was the bureaucracy

within the various religious institutions and then also within the public sector itself. But they were excited about it.[21]

Religious leaders were "excited" about the campaign, they received national attention in the TV advertisements, and it seemed to designers at JHU and GSMF that they had secured commitment for the long term. Much to the chagrin of JHU/GSMF staff, religious leadership worked with these AIDS organizations up until the point they realized there was no money in it for them or they faced bureaucratic hurdles in their religious institutions. Despite all the efforts to secure buy-in, and the appearance of support from religious leaders, it did not take much for these leaders to abandon the campaign.

Fast-forward a few years later to when GSCP took over USAID funding for coordinating its AIDS communication in Ghana. GSCP's central task was to put together a new national antistigma campaign. Much to the dismay of GSCP staff, JHU and GSMF did not pass along any data or documentation from the "Stop AIDS Love Life" or "Show Compassion" campaigns. Like the "Show Compassion" campaign, GSCP determined that it had to address a major source of stigma, the religious community, to reduce stigma nation-wide. I asked a GSCP staff member whether they tried to link to JHU/GSMF's earlier campaigns:

> Yeah, if possible. One is with the stigma campaign we're working on right now. Johns Hopkins had the only comprehensive stigma campaign in Ghana so far. A campaign called the "Compassion" campaign, where they worked with faith-based leaders. And we're doing a stigma campaign, as well, that focuses on adults and kind of gets at different issues. But, we're also focusing on faith-based leaders with specific material targeted to them. And, we're going to go back and find all the religious leaders they had worked with and getting them on board. We're even going to use the same people in photo shoots for the faith-based stuff so that there's a link.
>
> You know, you have five years to change the world. And then, you don't change the world. So, then, somebody else comes in and starts from ground zero and tries to change the world in five years, instead of trying to change the world in fifty years. So, we're trying to make links where possible. Part of the problem is—and it's not like Johns Hopkins, it's just what happens all the time—we can't find anything that they did. Like, there's no record, and USAID doesn't have it. Like, there are no records of what they did, evaluations of it, what worked, what didn't. When a project packs up, they pack up and go.[22]

With the lack of a smooth transition between JHU/GSMF and GSCP, GSCP designers didn't know about the failed commitment around stigma campaigns that JHU/GSMF faced with religious leaders. In the absence of this history, GSCP staff members decided they should reach out to *those same religious leaders* from the "Show Compassion" campaign to create continuity. For the religiously oriented "He didn't judge; why should you?" campaign, GSCP created posters that included photographs of some of these original religious leaders and also developed brochures and a set of training manuals for antistigma workshops to be distributed to local congregations (see figure 14).

I spoke with GSCP staff again in 2008, a year after the January 2007 launch of the campaign, to get a sense of how the campaign was going. Although these staff members didn't have evidence that stigma had decreased, since they were waiting for follow-up results from the 2008 Demographic Health Survey, they had evidence that the "comparison" campaign reached 50 to 60 percent

FIGURE 14. Ghana Sustainable Change Project's national antistigma campaign "The Holy Prophet Didn't Judge" religious print advertisement

of Ghanaians nationwide. Designers also reported that the religious-oriented posters seemed to resonate. GSCP staffers remarked that people were "clamoring" for the Jesus poster and they ran out of the "religious" posters much faster than the "comparison" campaign posters, even though they had invested more into the "comparison" campaign.[23] When I asked about the training manuals that were to be the core interpersonal dimension of the campaign, GSCP staff reported that the materials weren't being used at the level of local churches and mosques. I had a moment of déjà vu. History had repeated itself. When it came to following through, these religious leaders failed to shepherd these materials among their congregations or encourage their flocks to use the materials and attend antistigma workshops. Additionally, whereas the religious posters seemed popular, it may have had nothing to do with the stigma message. Rather, Ghanaians may have wanted free posters of revered religious leaders to display in their homes.

Cultural ombudsmen for *both* the JHU/GSMF and GSCP campaigns failed to live up to their commitments. Although religious leaders appeared engaged and dedicated throughout the design phase, the appearance of commitment did not translate to actual commitment. Between following the best practice of securing buy-in and getting verbal commitments from these leaders to champion these materials, something went wrong. Unanswered questions linger for these staffers: Did religious leaders stop caring once they got their publicity, or once they realized there was no money to be had? Did they meet resistance from their congregations? Did they get busy with other tasks and never follow through despite their good intentions? Designers have various explanations about what happened, but they will probably never get a definitive answer to why these leaders let the project languish. Designers often blame religious leaders for failing to follow through. As I see it, the problem isn't with religious leaders but with the prescriptions of these best-practice documents.

Designers' commitment to securing buy-in leads AIDS organizations to heavily invest in recruiting and retaining cultural ombudsmen. However, designers fail to recognize how fragile ombudsmen's participation is and how difficult it will be to incentivize their commitment after the launch. This is the failure of what has been called the "sustainability doctrine" of NGOs (Swidler and Watkins 2009). NGOs rely upon elites such as cultural ombudsmen to ensure the sustainability of their projects after they pack up and leave, yet the incentives for participation change after the project changes hands or when new actors such as congregations or church bureaucracies alter the arrangement. Designers had confidence that ombudsmen, as gatekeepers to these communities, would translate their participation in the design process into interventions into their communities. Both JHU/GSMF and GSCP found that gatekeepers are not the same as interventionists. Because religious leaders can keep AIDS campaigns out, AIDS organizations need their support to ensure access for their campaign into targeted communities. The problem arises when AIDS organizations assume this involvement will translate into *intervening* on behalf of the campaign rather than just *permitting* the campaign.

The work of intervention is much more costly for religious leaders. It involves uncompensated time and effort. It involves persuading other religious leaders to stop preaching about AIDS as a justification for abstinence and faithfulness. It means navigating church politics and working to change the practices of the laity, without any direct personal benefits. Coming to a meeting once a month to give their opinion is very different from asking religious leaders to change practices (e.g., stop linking HIV with immorality) and risk their reputation to make difficult changes that might meet political resistance. After AIDS organizations have created the materials and passed them along to their cultural ombudsmen, the incentives for encouraging their use diminish rapidly.

CULTURAL ENTROPY THROUGH SECURING BUY-IN

GSCP's dedication to involving cultural ombudsmen in the design process ultimately undercut its commitment to evidence-based design. As I've shown, these two paradigmatic best practices often conflicted with and undercut each other. As the concepts moved from the focus group to the stakeholder's meeting, cultural ombudsmen living with HIV objected to the "ridiculous" campaign that garnered the most support from the target audience. Despite designers' efforts to safeguard the "ridiculous" campaign with evidence, the ombudsmen's veto power compelled GSCP designers to go with the other two campaign concepts. Even though they lacked convincing evidence these other campaign concepts would work, GSCP staff members adhered to the best practices and compromised to ensure the ombudsmen's commitment to their cause. Then, the religious campaign never made it to the intended audience because the campaign strategy relied too heavily on buy-in from ombudsmen who lacked the incentive to follow through on their investment.

In the ideal world that global AIDS organizations envision in their best-practice reports, using techniques of evidence-based design and securing multisectoral involvement will lead to the production of resonant campaigns with influential community leaders willing to spread the word. Designers' desire to follow these practices often fails to produce the results best-practice reports intend and promote. With every new arrangement, best practices face new meanings and practices that disrupt the intended outcomes of following these practices. Cultural entropy happens at every turn, despite designers' devotion and faithful carrying out of best practices. In the next chapter I show how new arrangements of objects, audiences, and settings lead to more unanticipated cultural entropy, further diminishing the effectiveness of campaigns.

Displacement and Decay:
Materiality, Space, and Interpretation

AIDS campaign designers work for months to design a campaign that reaches their target audience with a clear, consistent, and culturally relevant message. Designers believe that after following best practices, they have mitigated the possibility that audiences will interpret their campaigns incorrectly after the launch. Given the gospel of best practices, designers express confidence that they have made the best possible campaign for their target audience. Designers have faith that their campaign objects embody their message and will change behavior as long as the objects reach their target audience. With the objects "perfected," the AIDS organization releases its campaign into the public sphere. By and large, *this is where the organization's work ends.*

I bring to light the unexpected lives of these campaign objects after their release into public space. These unexpected lives determine whether messages reach the target audience and whether those audiences interpret campaign objects as intended by campaign designers. When people interpret and use campaign objects in unexpected ways, these alternative interactions often undermine a campaign's ability to persuade people to change their behavior. If you can't see a billboard's message, or if you miss the point, that billboard is unlikely to persuade you to put on a condom. When this happens, the months and monies of development are squandered.

These disruptions in the communication process happen because of a tendency toward cultural entropy. From the moment organizations begin to circulate their AIDS campaign, the objects become increasingly open to disruption and deterioration. The cause of these unexpected disruptions is often material in nature, and the disruptions lead to communication failures, unintended misreadings, and misappropriations. When campaign designers fixate on choosing the right symbol and message, they fail to account for how the material qualities of their campaign objects will interact with the setting in which they are displayed. In particular, designers do not attend to such specific dimensions of the setting as the physical environment and the cultural practices people enact in the vicinity. I argue that the cultural entropy caused by the interactions between an object's materiality, its physical setting, and local cultural practice is patterned and systematic. In the cases I present, I identify three ways communication is disrupted: (1) certain settings prevent the intended message from being communicated, (2) campaign objects may decay or be obscured when exposed to the elements and local cultural practices, and (3) some campaign objects are more vulnerable to displacement, and moving the object to unintended sites may hinder intended interpretations.

By failing to adequately attend to how objects, settings, and audiences interact, practitioners of public-health communication have trouble explaining when and how communication breaks down. By focusing on material dimensions of these interactions, my data reveal three kinds of communication disruption. First, audiences may never see a campaign object, as when a tree or building obstructs the message from view. This kind of disruption is fundamentally about whether the campaign object is *perceptible*. Second, audiences may not interpret the campaign's message as the producers intended but often assume they have. On these occasions, the objects are not *legible*. Third, as in the case of the female condoms described in the introduction, audiences may find creative alternative meanings and uses for objects that they prefer over the intended use.

In Accra, as in any city, the arrangement of place and how citizens engage the city through their local cultural practices work in tandem to constrain people's "practices of looking" (Sturken and Cartwright 2001). Urban scholars have made similar observations through ethnographic attention to space and materiality (Jacobs 1961; Zukin 1995). By observing the conditions of interpretative interactions—how the physical and cultural constraints on people meet the material conditions of objects and the city—this chapter articulates how the materiality of AIDS campaigns shapes their meaning (Griswold 1987b).

AIDS Media Campaigns and Materiality

Within any setting, the interpretation of AIDS media depends on the interaction between the materiality of the object and the surrounding environmental conditions. Certain combinations of AIDS campaign objects and urban settings are *discordant*, rendering campaign objects less perceptible and legible. My specific focus is on *material discordance*—a mismatch between the

FIGURE 15. Ghana Social Marketing Foundation's Champion Condoms bus shelter advertisement, Accra Central neighborhood in downtown Accra

material qualities of an object and the physical setting where it appears. Public places rarely provide ideal conditions for reception, and more often than not, these conditions are outside of the control of AIDS media producers.

For instance, figure 15 features a bus shelter advertisement for Champion condoms in the Accra Central neighborhood of downtown Accra. In Accra, as in many developing cities, sales are not confined to semipublic settings such as stores. Rather, hawkers use every inch of public space to sell goods. This photograph shows how the market has overtaken the advertising space. In it, a hawker displays clothes for sale using the side of the bus shelter, blocking the poster from view.[1] This display of clothing reduces the visibility of the poster. The material qualities of the bus shelter make possible the obstruction of the poster. The bus shelter's height and capacity to bear weight allow hawkers to hang goods over the advertisement. In this sense, the activities of the hawkers compete with the qualities of the bus shelter that advertisers emphasize (i.e., the shelter as surface for advertising) to obscure the image.

In addition to the imposition of the market onto this image, bus shelters are innately bad sites for media. Because shelters shade passengers from the sun and protect them from rain—persistent weather conditions in tropical climates of places such as Ghana—people stand or sit in front of the media.[2] For pedestrians or cars traveling past the advertisement, these people seeking shelter obstruct the message from view. Those Ghanaians who are inside the shelter waiting for transportation direct their attention out to the road rather than inward toward the shelter and its advertisements. The placement of the shelter's bench ensures that those seated will also face away from the ad. Placed directly against the advertisements, people must sit with their bodies facing out. This unique combination of clothing sales, advertisement orientation, material qualities of the shelter, and social convention hinders the producers' attempts to maximize visibility of their campaign.

The billboard at the University of Ghana, Legon (fig. 16) presents a similar example of a disruptive setting. This billboard depicts a man with his arm around a woman, with the associated text "Don't Rush into Pre-Marital Sex. You . . ." But the rest is obscured. At the bottom of the billboard, people have pasted pictures of political candidates, three announcements for the "Legon Beach Bash," six flyers for the Baptist Student Union's "Jehova Praiz '07" concert, and more. These various announcements cover the remaining text of the original billboard: "Risk Getting Infected By HIV/AIDS!"[3] Due to the limited space for advertising events on campus, just like limited market space for hawkers, students co-opt the built structure around them. In an act of creativity, local students use this billboard as free advertising space, effectively undermining the intended meaning of the billboard as a message about AIDS. This creative use is enabled by the eye-level height of the billboard: it is just short enough to paste a flyer along the bottom that will be readable by an adult passerby. Had producers built the billboard higher—just out of

FIGURE 16. "Don't Rush into Pre-marital Sex" billboard on the University of Ghana, Legon, campus

reach for potential flyer posters—the billboard would not have afforded this use, and the perceptibility of the AIDS prevention message would not have decreased.

Based on interviews with twenty-five students passing by the billboard, it became clear that the message is less perceptible and legible than on the day it was erected. Of the twenty-five people I interviewed about this billboard, only four recognized this advertisement as an HIV/AIDS message. About half the people said that no one pays the message any attention because of the condition of the billboard. A few of these people used the language of "messy"— that its messy condition distracts from the message and makes people not want to look at it. Most students felt strongly that the billboard should be taken down or replaced because its condition symbolized a disrespect of the university. Those students who took the time to look at the message walked away frustrated by the condition of the billboard, instead of being thoughtful about the HIV transmission risks of premarital sex.

Throughout Ghana, billboards serve as a central medium of communication about AIDS. As other advertisers do, many AIDS producers like billboards because the medium tends to yield high "impression rates" (Luke, Esmundo, and Bloom 2000). Billboards offer AIDS campaigns a routinized means of communication, increasing "effectiveness" through repeated viewing. Billboards also impose their messages on public audiences more than do television or radio, on which people can flip to another station (Hackbarth, Silvestri, and Cosper 1995). Because most AIDS campaign designers in Ghana discuss billboards as a core component of their communications strategy, and because billboards are often the sole media channel for many campaigns, most campaign objects I discuss are billboards. With multichannel campaigns that include radio and TV, one might claim that the low perceptibility of a single billboard does not preclude audiences from access to another billboard or a radio advertisement. However, because most residents move through the city in habitualized travel patterns, low perceptibility of even one billboard reduces access to knowledge for all the residents who pass it.

Through efforts made by the Ghana AIDS Commission, many media-barren rural villages have a billboard that marks village boundaries with a generic message like, "Welcome to [insert village name here]. Prevent AIDS. Use a Condom." For these villages, the AIDS prevention billboard is often the *only* billboard nearby and therefore a highly visible reminder to protect oneself against AIDS. In urban Accra, campaigns not only compete against one another but also with other media. While AIDS prevention and condom billboards pepper the streetscape, media of all sorts compete for people's attention, and urban activities encroach on the space of campaigns. AIDS media producers want to maximize the visibility of their campaign but are constrained by their limited budgets. Since their funding cannot compete with corporate media budgets, they often place their campaigns in less saturated media environments (i.e., less commercially desired).

Consider the media environment of the Osu neighborhood. Osu is a hip neighborhood in Accra, with a vibrant commercial district of restaurants, shops, and nightclubs. AIDS organizations, along with corporate advertisers, target Osu because of its high traffic and the presence of commercial sex workers nearby. Osu has the highest density of AIDS images of any neighborhood in Accra. Figure 17 captures Oxford Street, the main thoroughfare in Osu, as it floods the senses with some of Accra's densest pedestrian traffic and visual culture. Areas with pedestrian traffic are well suited for media interactions because people walking by have more time with an image than people driving past in cars. None of the billboards along this street address HIV/AIDS. Multinational corporations including Western Union, Samsung, Unilever, Guinness, and Barclay's Bank dominate billboard space along Oxford Street's commercial sector, effectively pricing out AIDS nongovernmental organizations (NGOs).

As such, the AIDS imagery in Osu tends to appear on the outskirts of the neighborhood and off the beaten path, along areas with high automobile traffic but low pedestrian traffic. Most AIDS images in Osu can be found at

FIGURE 17. View down Oxford Street, the main thoroughfare in the Osu neighborhood of Accra, Ghana

the northeastern boundary of the neighborhood, within a block of Danquah Circle, one of Accra's main traffic roundabouts. As of 2008, this area had seven HIV/AIDS billboards. This dense concentration remained essentially unchanged since observation began in 2003: one billboard was removed and two new billboards added.[4] There are more AIDS images around Danquah than all other major commercial advertising combined.

In an effort to maximize the visibility of their campaigns, AIDS campaign producers strategically place AIDS advertising along the heavily trafficked Danquah Circle.[5] The billboards around Danquah are positioned along the three arteries with light pedestrian traffic—the fourth artery is Osu's busy Oxford Street. Ring Road's high density, high-speed vehicular traffic and the lack of sidewalk or shoulder dramatically diminish the presence of pedestrians. But with the busy vehicular traffic, most AIDS campaign producers presume people in vehicles passing this intersection get an eyeful of AIDS information. Only one advertiser I spoke with recognized that this might not be the case:

ORIGIN8 STAFFER: Say you are looking at people who do not drive, people who sit in commercial vehicles, in buses or tro-tros, those people are less likely to see billboards because, I don't know if you've sat in one before, except the person beside the driver, the people inside the car cannot really see the billboard because they are high up.

TERENCE E. MCDONNELL: And because the windows are so low?

ORIGIN8 STAFFER: Yeah, the windows are low. They need to push their heads out the windows to be able to see anything at all along the road. So for people like that, when people like that are your target, billboards may not be the way to go. But if you are looking at the driver, the driver will see those things on the roads as they pass.

TEM: So people who own their own cars, people who can afford to hire a taxi, who can sit in the front seat . . .

ORIGIN8 STAFFER: Yeah. Those are the people who may see billboards.[6]

Consider the "Use a Condom" billboard just one hundred feet from Danquah Circle in figure 6 (see chapter 4). In this image you can see the billboard photographed from the median across the road. Alternatively, in figure 18 the same billboard is captured from a moving tro-tro (private minibus shared taxi)—looking at the image, behind and to the right of the vertical black-and-white pole that runs down the middle of the photograph, only the gray background of the very bottom of the billboard is visible.[7] The physical characteristics of tro-tros (i.e., low windows, high seats, and crowded interior),

FIGURE 18. Ghana Social Marketing Foundation's "Use a Condom" billboard, from figure 6, obscured as seen from the inside of a tro-tro (private minibus shared taxi)

and the conventional placement of billboards (i.e., elevated off the ground) decrease the perceptibility of this billboard for those who rely on tro-tros for transportation.[8]

This example opens for consideration how the corporeal nature of movement and vision, as obscured by a tro-tro, further disadvantages those people who lack access to health information. Typically, Ghanaians who cannot afford taxis or personal automobiles rely on tro-tros for transport. These are the same people who interact with a limited number of media sources (e.g., TV, radio, newspapers). Billboards are one of the few channels of mass communication that AIDS campaigns have used to address this population, but most campaigns have not realized that traveling by tro-tro impedes the reception of their messages.

Members of the middle class, who can afford the occasional taxi but do not own their own vehicles, also tend to miss these billboards, but for different reasons. Whereas tro-tro drivers are restricted to taking the same routes along the busiest streets, taxi drivers avoid the main traffic routes unless they lack an alternative path. Since organizations place their billboards on the thoroughfares with the most traffic, and most taxis avoid these routes, taxi drivers and their middle-income passengers miss the majority of the AIDS billboards.

Organizations that place billboards in areas with high vehicle traffic reach

more wealthy Ghanaians, often not the target audience. By failing to consider the material character of the interpretive interaction, billboards placed
in areas of high vehicle traffic but low pedestrian traffic, such as the area
around Danquah Circle, have decreased visibility for the low and middle-
income passengers traveling in tro-tros and taxis. The placement of billboards
too high for tro-tro passengers to see, and along high traffic routes that taxi
drivers avoid, reduces the perceptibility of AIDS campaigns. Those middle-
class people with the resources to avoid high traffic do so, and the poor, who
have little choice in how they travel, are relegated to vehicles that inhibit their
sight line.

How did AIDS organizations miss this important observation? One explanation might stem from designers' upper-class backgrounds. As such, they
rarely travel in tro-tros and may never have noticed how the placement and
orientation of billboards, in conjunction with patterns of movement through
space, dramatically reduces the perceptibility of their AIDS media. Another
explanation stems from campaign producers' practice of discussing campaigns in generalities, not in the specific language of place. Using market research data, AIDS campaign producers worked to determine which channels
of media (e.g., print versus radio) and which sites maximize reach for their
target audience. However, rarely did they discuss how different channels of
media might function differently in situ. After campaign designers decide to
place a billboard in Osu, other location-specific material considerations could
arise: What billboard height maximizes visibility? What billboard orientation
increases audience reach: facing westbound or eastbound traffic? What colors
"pop" against this particular streetscape? These kinds of considerations never
arose in my conversations with campaign producers. By thinking of place as
a proxy for audience, rather than as a unique context with material qualities
and attendant cultural practices, AIDS organizations failed to prevent discordant settings from disrupting communication.

DECAY OF CULTURAL OBJECTS

In Accra, AIDS materials often age to the point where the intended message
is obscured. This material decay of campaign objects is made possible by the
interaction of campaign materials and the environment. Less durable materials or materials placed in harsher environments decay more rapidly. This
aging yields crucial material changes in the object that may alter interpretations. Ghanaian advertisements, and in particular AIDS media, remain in
urban space for long periods. The vast majority of AIDS billboards in Accra
documented in 2003 remained in public space through the end of 2006. By

2008, at least half of those billboards still remained. Whereas billboards in the United States tend to turn over every few months, the average life span for Ghanaian advertisements is calculable in years. Many of the AIDS media objects in Accra have visible wear and tear.

Interviews with AIDS media producers revealed two explanations for the conditions of decay. First, AIDS organizations in Ghana lack the resources to produce AIDS campaigns using high-quality materials, and most cannot afford short-term rented billboard space. Therefore, organizations construct their own permanent billboards using inadequate materials. If one of their billboards starts to deteriorate, they lack the monies necessary to replace the billboard. AIDS organizations cannot afford to replace decrepit billboards or develop new campaigns to replace old ads before they age, so producers try to maximize the value of each poster and billboard. Consequently, AIDS media remain in public space for years at a time.

Second, while some AIDS organizations are concerned with durability, the advertising firms they hire are not. When I asked producers about which aspects of design are most important when designing AIDS media, not one designer mentioned durability. Instead, these advertisers focus on maximizing campaign visibility for target audiences, using attractive images, and developing clear and catchy messages. These cosmopolitan Ghanaian advertisers mimic the design practices established in Western Europe and the United States.[9] Durability remains a low priority since most of the campaigns Ghanaian advertisers design are for corporate clients, such as Coca-Cola or Nestlé, that possess the resources to regularly produce new ads. Advertisers do not change these practices when designing materials for AIDS prevention organizations and so, often, produce campaign objects with a short life span.

The decay of the billboard adjacent to the Nima market in Accra (see fig. 1 in chapter 1) speaks to this lack of attention to durability. Nima is one of the poorest neighborhoods in Accra and has a high concentration of Muslim residents (Weeks et al. 2007). The AIDS billboard at the Nima market is the sole billboard aimed exclusively at a Muslim audience in the city.[10] The Nima billboard has some of the greatest disrepair in Accra: the photographic image is bent out of shape and covered in dirt, and the letters are peeling off the backing. Despite this considerable deterioration, the intended message is just as legible today as it was the day Family Health International (FHI) and the United States Agency for International Development (USAID) put up the billboard. Local Muslims can still read that being "faithful to your partner(s)" helps prevent AIDS.

The material decay of the billboard introduces a new set of possible interpretations that local audiences may generate. As a marker of *time*, the billboard's aged appearance may remind local Muslims how long it had been since health organizations had engaged in AIDS prevention activities in Nima. As a sign of *inattention*, locals may see the billboard as evidence of their position as a low priority for public-health officials. One man I interviewed said of the billboard: "If these organizations care about it, they will maintain it. They will clean it. They will straighten it out and then repaint it. But they don't care."[11] The decrepit condition of the billboard may inspire any number of alternative interpretations. The point here is not about *which* new meanings audiences fabricate. Rather, the point is that decay opens this object to increasing and varied alternative interpretations. Decay has uniformly negative effects for these producers who invest so heavily in communicating one intended message.

Another common form of material decay in Accra is the fading of red ink from billboards, stickers, and other media. The tropical sun fades the color red from advertising at a much faster rate than other colors. Ghanaian and international campaigns alike liberally use the color red in the design of their media. Evoking international design conventions, AIDS campaign designers in Ghana draw on the symbolic power of red, often printing the most important text and symbols in red. Considering the prevalence of red, the fading of red-colored symbolic content has a dramatic effect on the communication of prevention information.

For example, look at the billboard at the entrance to the University of Ghana, Legon campus (fig. 19). The billboard depicts a young man and woman leaning against a car holding hands and in a half-embrace. When this billboard first appeared, the text clearly read "Avoiding AIDS as easy as . . . Abstain, Be Faithful, Condomise." The word "AIDS" and all but the *ABC* of the words "Abstain, Be Faithful, Condomise," were printed in red. Over time the red text faded into a color similar to the background color. Now the image reads "Avoiding . . . as easy as . . . ABC." This "new" message, when taken with the image of the young couple, reads as gibberish, or it might display a warning to avoid romantic relationships that detract from their university studies. This image no longer permits a legible interpretation because the most *important* text on the billboard was printed in red. Students often line up in front of this billboard while waiting for the bus. When I asked these students to recall the message of the billboard behind them (without turning around), they felt compelled to turn to look at it. Only after squinting their eyes and scanning the billboard did they recognize it as being about AIDS.

The billboard outside of the Accra Girls School provides another instance of an AIDS prevention ad falling into disrepair. When originally produced, the billboard stated, "Don't Rush into Premarital Sex You Risk Getting

FIGURE 19. "Avoiding AIDS as Easy as ABC" billboard at the entrance to the University of Ghana, Legon, in which wording printed in red has faded to near illegibility

Infected with HIV/AIDS," exactly like the billboard discussed earlier. In this case, the red text of "HIV/AIDS" and the associated red ribbon have faded beyond perception for cars passing along the highway (figs. 20 and 21). With the decline in visibility of the red HIV-specific text, the more resilient text of "Don't Rush" takes visual precedence. This change in the image suggests an alternative interpretation for those audiences speeding down the adjacent highway. Their reduced capacity to interpret the billboard emphasizes their "rushing" down the road past innocent and vulnerable schoolchildren, as opposed to the "rushing" of school kids into sex. In this case, the billboard's unique pattern of decay interacts with the local environmental context of a major highway to potentially alter interpretations of the billboard.[12] Through these material conditions, the intended message of the Accra Girls School billboard undergoes a process of cultural entropy.[13]

The cultural memory of local audiences mediates the significance of decay, and therefore entropy. In a focus group interview with recent graduates of the University of Ghana, Legon, I asked if they recognized the phrase "Avoiding AIDS as easy as ABC." They all replied yes and identified it as the message at the entrance to the university. When these responses are placed in conversation with my interviews with current students in the physical presence of the billboard, the billboard's declining effectiveness is clear. But for these recent graduates, if they return to campus and interact with the faded

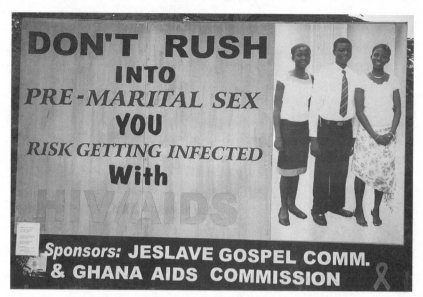

FIGURE 20. Close-up of "Don't Rush into Pre-marital Sex" billboard outside the entrance of the Accra Girls School

FIGURE 21. Accra Girls School "Don't Rush into Pre-marital Sex" billboard from figure 20, viewed from a distance of 30 feet

billboard through the lens of their memory, they will likely still see the message as about AIDS—although they may also make new meanings regarding what an unkempt billboard says about their alma mater. Similarly, those students who attended Accra Girls School when the billboard was first erected may still remember it as an AIDS message, regardless of the red text fading into the background. When looking at the billboard, they may not even "see" the disappearance of the text. But for sites such as Accra Girls School and the University of Ghana, Legon, every year brings new audiences into interaction with the images. With every passing year, the opportunities for "misreading" the text increase. In fact, when senior students of Accra Girls School were asked about the content of the billboard while away from campus, they could not recall the sign's message or the image it depicted. When in good condition, routine interactions with these billboards seem to have imprinted a strong memory. As I have shown here, these billboards' capacity to impress memorable content on an audience declines rapidly as their red content fades.

DISPLACEMENT ACROSS SETTINGS

Whereas the interactions of objects and environments cause variation in decay, the materiality of objects in interaction with cultural practices facilitates the movement of campaign materials from intended sites of reception. For instance, such organizations as the Ghana Social Marketing Foundation (GSMF) have employed "nontraditional media" to market condoms. GSMF distributed Champion Condoms–branded umbrellas to sellers of produce and aprons to pharmacists who also sold Champion condoms. GSMF staff used these umbrellas and aprons to identify sites of condom distribution for the public. By this thinking, if a Ghanaian sees a pharmacist wearing a yellow Champion apron, he or she will know that the pharmacy sells condoms and, more specifically, that it sells the Champion brand of condom. As I will show, what GSMF failed to recognize was how these objects could be displaced, leaving Ghanaians with the dilemma of deciding between risking unsafe sex and losing a potential sex partner amid the search for a condom.

The move to nontraditional media is in keeping with GSMF's attempts to extend condom distribution beyond such typical settings as pharmacies and clinics into markets and busy streets where people in need of a condom can find one quickly and conveniently. For instance, one GSMF staff member discussed attaching Champion Condoms stickers to the wood and glass display cases of informal "rock" cake sellers. Decorating display cases is a common practice among rock hawkers, so this medium suited the designers' purposes. According to GSMF staff, these hawkers hang around nightclubs and bars selling rock cakes to hungry late-night patrons. These patrons may urgently need condoms for their anticipated sexual activity, and distributing condoms through the hawkers brings the sale of condoms closer in proximity to sexual activity.

GSMF also wished to bring its condoms to the market, but it needed a way to identify the point of sale. Umbrellas are valued commodities for traders who spend hours in the sun daily. By providing market traders with free Champion Condoms umbrellas (fig. 22), GSMF both shades these traders from the sun and recruits condom saleswomen. The material qualities of the umbrella enable dual functionality: its design elements mark it as a site of condom sales while its physical structure shades the seller.

The alternative uses afforded by these nontraditional media also enable their removal from intended sites of reception. Often, when I found someone wearing a GSMF Champion apron or sitting under the shade of a Champion Condoms umbrella, they did not also sell condoms. The woman pictured in figure 23 is a seamstress who finds the pockets of the apron quite valuable, as they allow her to keep scissors and other tools at her disposal. She claims she received the apron from a friend who no longer needed it. Similarly, the avocado trader under the umbrella in figure 22 had never sold condoms, nor did she have an explanation for why she had an umbrella advertising Champion

FIGURE 22. Ghana Social Marketing Foundation's Champion Condoms umbrella shading an avocado seller on Oxford Street in the Osu neighborhood of Accra, Ghana

FIGURE 23. Seamstress wearing Ghana Social Marketing Foundation's Champion Condoms apron in the Osu neighborhood of Accra, Ghana

Condoms. The same bundle of material qualities that made these objects so good for marking unexpected sites of condom sales also enabled their creative co-optation by friends or family who valued the material properties of aprons or umbrellas.

When I asked GSMF staff members about how these campaign objects move beyond producers' intended settings, they seemed untroubled by it. Producers contended that as long as people interact with images of the Champion brand, the objects still promote the product, even if they no longer mark sites for condom sale. But this nonchalance overlooks how the displacement of nontraditional campaign objects makes Ghanaians vulnerable to the temptation of unsafe sex. With the sale of condoms at accessible sites, people could now wait to purchase condoms until a sexual encounter presented itself, instead of needing to plan for safe sex by stopping for condoms in advance at a clinic (a stigmatized source for condoms). In unfamiliar environments such as a crosstown bar or a different city, these nontraditional media facilitate this practice. Despite the lack of concern by campaign producers, the movement of stickers, umbrellas, and aprons may result in a lack of access to condoms for those who rely on nontraditional media to indicate the availability of condoms.

As these objects are displaced, the odds increase that customers who count on the opportunity to spontaneously pick up condoms will meet a market trader or rock seller who does not sell actually condoms. In that situation, the customer must weigh the risk of unsafe sex against the hassle of searching for condoms. The farther that campaign objects such as umbrellas, aprons, and stickers move from actual sites of condom distribution, the more often consumers confront situations in which they must balance their health risks against inconvenience. As they move, these objects undermine spontaneous condom purchases, and consequently sexual health, by diluting the power of these media to mark points of sale. The marketing logic of GSMF— that as long as the image is visible in public space, the advertisement is still "working"—diverts the organization's attention away from this unintended consequence.

In another example, a set of posters placed by FHI in hair salons seemed to disappear. FHI designed this campaign as a conversation starter in "third places" such as hair salons and seamstress shops where Ghanaian women chat about personal matters and local gossip (Oldenburg 1999). Ghanaian women have less access to media than men do. Also, women spend less time in public space than men do. In Accra, more women work in the market than any other occupation, so women split time between the market and the home.[14] Ghanaian AIDS organizations have found that homes are too private and markets are too public for such interventions as posters and peer education, and thus AIDS organizations preferred salons and seamstress shops for these AIDS interventions. FHI hoped that putting up an AIDS poster in a salon would cause patrons to inquire about its presence. Then the hairdressers, trained as peer educators, could converse about AIDS and sexual health in the context of the clients' personal experiences. The poster served as an icebreaker, enabling a conversation about AIDS between two people who had already developed a trusting relationship.

A staff member from FHI described what happened when staff returned to these targeted hair salons to evaluate the campaign:

> I wanted to find out what was happening to our posters, because we provided them with a lot of posters, but moving around and going to our project communities, I wasn't seeing our posters. I wanted to find out why. And there were interesting revelations. For instance I asked some hairdressers why they removed the posters and had placed them in their room. And they were saying that oh, for them, they think that the message was clear, and that sometimes you might be having sex . . . you may not insist on condom use, but if the picture is placed in her bedroom, any time she enters then her mind goes back to the message. So if she wants to have sex, it enables her to insist on condom use. Which we think was very good.[15]

The movement of the posters into the homes of the hairdressers defied the expectations of this staffer. The campaign leaked from the semipublic spaces intended by FHI into the very private spaces of hairdressers' bedrooms. This spatial shift dramatically reduced the perceptibility of that campaign because fewer people had the opportunity to interact with that message. This leakage reduced the AIDS knowledge available to local women—an audience that already lacks access to AIDS information.

As these hairdressers reduced the perceptibility of the campaign for the target audience by moving the poster out of the salon, they increased the posters' legibility and simultaneously improved their own sexual health. The poster became a tool to negotiate condom use when they moved it into their bedrooms. Cultural objects are "more likely to influence action" when they are "better situated at a point of action" (Schudson 1989, 171). People organize salon space to encourage particular kinds of behaviors (i.e., gossiping by including extra seating, hairstyling by introducing adjustable chairs). As a place, a salon is rather distant from sexual activity, especially with all the scissors and hot irons around. A woman seeing a poster about condom use is quite unlikely to actually use a condom right then and there. Alternatively, in the privacy of a bedroom, in the presence of a bed, and with the routines of intimacy, sleep, and sex practiced there, the poster becomes more legible, increasing the likelihood that the hairdressers will adopt the AIDS prevention behavior that FHI prescribes. The bedroom is a more powerful setting than the salon. Materiality plays an important role in increasing the legibility of this poster for these hairdressers. The poster's size and weight made it mobile, enabling the shift in interpretive context from salon to bedroom. Had the image been a two-story-tall billboard outside the salon, hairdressers could not roll it up, walk it through their front door, and hang it next to their bed.

According to FHI staff, the movement of the poster into the homes of hairdressers did not always increase safe sex:

TEM: So it became less a public poster for everyone to see when they came into the shop, and more a personal thing for when she goes into her bedroom . . .

FHI STAFFER: The initial idea was to put them up as public posters . . . then we realized that the posters were not allowed to be where we wanted them to be . . . people were moving them and putting them in their rooms. . . . Some people were saying that the pictures were very nice. They were appealing to them. So some people were not even associating the messages . . . they were just looking at the pictures and thought that they were nice, without necessarily knowing what the pictures wanted to them to do.[16]

For other hairdressers, the poster went up for decorative reasons—because it looked nice. For most Ghanaians, the decorating aesthetic is the aesthetic of availability. In Ghanaian homes, walls are covered with advertisements and objects purchased from street vendors or obtained from friends. The local culture of decorating with what is available elaborates material qualities of objects beyond their prescribed uses. In this case, the bright colors and "nice" pictures of these AIDS posters serve to accent a room. This example highlights the power in the "bundling of qualities" inherent in any object (Keane 2003). Since symbols are simultaneously and necessarily material, that embodiment in materiality "inescapably binds it to some other qualities . . . which can become contingent but real factors in its social life" (Keane 2003, 414). For hairdressers who find these posters attractive, the posters are more powerful as decoration than as health messages. Ironically, by working to design a more appealing poster with attractive and catchy images, campaign producers inadvertently undermined the reach of their campaign for more public audiences.

INTERSECTIONS OF DECAY AND DISPLACEMENT

Early research on HIV in Ghana and West Africa identified professional drivers and commercial sex workers as groups at high risk for infection and in a position to spread the disease. As male drivers travel from city to city, some have sex with commercial sex workers at transportation hubs, or with partners in cities along their routes (Agyei-Mensah 2001; Pellow 1994). Their sexual practices, coupled with their mobility, encouraged the spread of HIV along major transportation routes. In response to this "vector" of transmission, GSMF mobilized its institutional resources to develop the "Drive Protected" campaign (fig. 24). Beginning in November 2000 and launched nationally in May 2002, "Drive Protected" used TV advertisements and radio dramas alongside posters and car stickers to educate audiences about the dangers of HIV and encourage the use of condoms to protect oneself against contracting the disease. The campaign trained peer educators to serve as a resource for people with HIV/AIDS–related questions at major transportation hubs and to hand out "Drive Protected" stickers.[17] These stickers—aimed at "drivers, mates, porters, traders, commercial sex workers and passengers" (Ghana Social Marketing Foundational International 2003)—became one of the most visible sources of HIV/AIDS information in the country. By handing out free "Drive Protected" stickers, GSMF guaranteed quick diffusion of the campaign.

The visibility of "Drive Protected" stickers did not arise out of the taxi and tro-tro drivers' commitment to do something about AIDS. Rather, GSMF's

FIGURE 24. Ghana Social Marketing Foundation's "Drive Protected" campaign stickers on a "4 sale" tro-tro (private minibus shared taxi) in Accra, Ghana

rapid diffusion of the campaign capitalized on the drivers' preexisting cultural practice of decorating their automobiles. Ghanaian transportation workers cover their vehicles with stickers and decals: Ghanaian flags, portraits of Jesus and Bob Marley, pictures of a white baby in a straw hat called the "Golden Child," clenched fists symbolizing black power, and team logos from the local, English Premiere League, and World Cup football teams. When I asked taxi drivers about their choice of stickers (e.g., "Why white babies?"), more often than not I would hear the reply, "Because it is nice." Only when I asked about Jesus portraits or their favorite football teams would drivers energetically proclaim their affinity for the sticker, provoking long conversations about sports or religion.

As in the example of the salon posters taken by the hairdressers, these drivers have adopted a decorating aesthetic of availability. When I asked about the "Drive Protected" stickers, rarely did a driver have a cogent reason for putting the sticker on his car. Most simply explained that they "like to put stickers on [their] car." Other drivers liked the "Drive Protected" stickers because their large size shaded the back and side windows of the tro-tro, keeping the vehicles cool. On one occasion when I asked a driver why he had a sticker about AIDS on his taxi, he denied that the sticker existed until I asked him to take a look for himself. He had forgotten about the sticker until I reminded him about it. Most drivers liked the stickers because they were free, available, and attractive rather than because the drivers had any commitment to preventing AIDS.

Despite the dominant presence of "Drive Protected" across Accra's urban streetscape early in its history, over time, the campaign experienced both displacement and decay. Passing through the streets of Accra during the summer of 2003, I found it difficult to avoid seeing the "Drive Protected" campaign. The stickers covered the back windows of taxicabs, freight trucks, and tro-tros throughout the city. I observed that about one third of the vehicles at taxi stands and transportation hubs had at least one "Drive Protected" sticker, and some drivers had plastered their cars with multiple "Drive Protected" decals. Three years later, during the summer of 2006, I returned to Accra to continue my research. Much to my surprise, the campaign had all but vanished. Whereas in 2003 I could spot a vehicle with a "Drive Protected" sticker after five minutes while standing at a busy intersection, it took three weeks of observation to find a single sticker in 2006.

What explains the disappearance of the campaign? Had the stickers become controversial? Had drivers repainted their vehicles or scraped off their windows? After speaking with a number of professional drivers, the answer became clear: high market turnover for used vehicles in Accra. The vehicles imported into Ghana typically have already had a lifetime of use in Europe or Asia, and most arrive with well over one hundred thousand miles on the odometer. Every time a "stickered" car breaks beyond repair, the "Drive Protected" campaign declines in perceptibility. A second analogous cause for the decline of the campaign in Accra is the pattern of used vehicle sales. Imported vehicles enter through the Tema port, a mere half-hour drive from Accra. The greater wealth of Accra and its proximity to Tema offer prospective taxi and tro-tro owners from Accra the first look at new vehicles coming off the boat. Professional drivers in the other major Ghanaian cities of Kumasi, Cape Coast, and Takoradi typically buy vehicles that were previously owned and operated in Accra. Therefore, after a second career in Accra, cars have a third career in a satellite Ghanaian city. The outflow of vehicles from Accra to neighboring cities, along with the short life span of cars after they enter Ghana (a material condition of the car and the unfriendly road conditions), explains, at least in part, the rapid decrease in perceptibility of the "Drive Protected" campaign in Accra and the saturation of the campaign in such other cities as Cape Coast and Kumasi.

The marriage of sticker to car made possible the movement of "Drive Protected" out of Accra. The point I would like to press here is that this marriage is an intimately *material* affair. From the moment a driver applies a "Drive

Protected" sticker to a car, the perceptibility of that campaign object depends on the material conditions of the car to which it is attached—the fate of the sticker is contingent on the fate of the car. The accelerated demise of poorly maintained cars, older cars, cars that travel over unpaved or potholed roads, and cars involved in accidents corresponds to an increase in the decline of the campaign. The movement of the campaign to locales outside of transportation hubs depends on the physical constraints placed on the cars carrying the stickers. Cars travel only on roads, so the physical arrangement of streets and highways determines the spaces where the campaign stickers are visible. The mobility of the cars enables the campaign to circulate through the urban streetscape. But this mobility also enables the campaign to concentrate in one city at the expense of another.

Exposure to the elements has also adversely affected the perceptibility of "Drive Protected." During the summer of 2003, only one year after the campaign went national, I found a number of vehicles with faded "Drive Protected" stickers in their windows. Much as had happened to the red of the billboards at the University of Ghana and the Accra Girls School, the tropical sunlight had bleached the sticker and rendered it unintelligible. Figure 25 highlights the stark difference in color between a faded sticker and new stickers. Granted, the driver of this vehicle added two fresh stickers to supplement

FIGURE 25. Ghana Social Marketing Foundation's faded "Drive Protected" sticker one year after debut of the campaign—in contrast to the new stickers below it and to the left—on a tro-tro (private minibus shared taxi) near Takoradi, Ghana

the faded one, but this was the exception, not the rule. Most faded stickers I found were not supplemented. Only one year after the "Drive Protected" campaign went national, many stickers had already faded.

The combination of effects from the vehicles' pattern of movement and their exposure to the sun disadvantages access to the campaign by rural communities. The "Drive Protected" campaign tended to distribute stickers in urban transportation hubs, which makes sense when trying to maximize the distribution of the campaign. From these hubs, "Drive Protected" stickers eventually migrate out toward more rural areas, despite an initial concentration in urban sites. But for the rural communities that inherit vehicles after their use in Accra and Ghana's other major cities, the stickers have often faded to the point of illegibility. It's possible that urban audiences may retain cultural memories of the sticker and the campaign and may still be reminded to use condoms when they perceive the pink oval that remains. But rural audiences who did not have access to the campaign in its prime state of perceptibility and legibility may see only a washed-out pink oval, which means nothing to them.

Reconsidering Materiality in AIDS Campaigns

AIDS campaign designers labor to maximize the reach and clarity of their media objects. This chapter has shown how material interactions between objects, settings, and cultural practices create variation in the perceptibility and legibility of campaign messages and lead to cultural entropy. The systematic inequalities in access to AIDS knowledge made possible by these material disruptions rarely capture the attention of AIDS organizations in Ghana—or, for that matter, around the globe. This blind spot stems from conventions of campaign design that focus on symbolic aspects of media production at the expense of materiality. Organizations do not consider the consequences of the material choices they make and how those choices might enable cultural entropy.

This is changing, though, as some designers have begun to consider issues of materiality. Strengthening HIV/AIDS Response Partnerships (SHARP), working with the Ghana Sustainable Change Project (GSCP) design team, saw the need to intervene into the community of Ghanaian men who have sex with men. Because homosexuality is illegal in Ghana, most AIDS organizations have not considered designing interventions for this community. In designing a campaign for men who have sex with men, SHARP believed that public media such as billboards or TV ads would meet public resistance. To better serve this community, it developed a campaign that *discreetly* promoted safe sex. SHARP designed tiny pamphlets that could fit into the palm of one's hand, so that volunteers integrated into the community of men who have sex with men could pass on important health and HIV/AIDS information in public places without attracting attention to individuals' sexual practices. SHARP's campaign producers realized that they needed a pamphlet much smaller than the average health pamphlet because they kept the future context and interactions between the target audience and media object in mind while designing the campaign. Rather than rely on a conventional trifold health brochure format, SHARP broke with convention and made pivotal changes to the materiality of the media object. Regrettably, innovations like this are the exception and not the rule.

While I've addressed the material effects of objects and contexts on interpretation, it is crucial to note how these material conditions result from the choices of organizational actors under particular structural constraints and with particular worldviews. Economic factors partly determine the kinds and quality of media AIDS organizations use, as well as where those media are placed or distributed. Better resources would enable AIDS campaign producers to replace decaying billboards, flood the streetscape with fade-resistant bumper stickers, and bid for the best advertising locations.

However, money cannot fix everything. As I have shown, social factors also enable the displacement of campaign objects and the establishment of discordant object–setting interactions. Increasing the budgets for AIDS campaigns cannot change the pattern of the used car market, or of traffic flows through the city, or of how people use urban space to sell goods. Nor can it change the conventions of public-health campaign design universally adopted by AIDS campaigns in Ghana. These conventions privilege the design and testing of symbolic content over considerations of how the materiality of the media and the physical characteristics of place may enhance or discourage accurate interpretations.

The creative interpretation and use of AIDS campaign objects by local Ghanaians often frustrate AIDS organizations because of the substantial institutional energy mobilized around creating campaign materials that "work." Instead, organizations should rethink these unexpected moments. They are windows through which organizations may observe audiences applying local cultural schema. From there, organizations could make the proverbial "lemons" of creativity into "lemonade." Take the movement of AIDS advertisements into bedrooms as decorative safe-sex reminders as an example. The entropic behavior of these hairdressers might yield paradigm-shifting insights into AIDS campaign design: organizations could design future AIDS prevention posters specifically for sites of sexual activity such as bedrooms.

Drawing on de Certeau, people "enunciate" different meanings and uses afforded by objects through "established languages" (de Certeau 1984). These cases highlight how established languages of decoration and fashion mediate the use of AIDS prevention materials (AIDS posters and condom bracelets, respectively). No matter how much pretesting an organization does, the material effects of objects, contexts, and audiences will undoubtedly lead to cultural entropy. Next, I show how audiences continue to interpret campaigns through the established languages of AIDS that the earliest campaigns introduced, thus leaving new campaigns open to resistance and misinterpretation by Ghanaian audiences.

Scare Tactics:
Interpreting Images of Death, Illness, and Life

A TV ad for the "Stop AIDS Love Life" campaign, Ghana's first national-level campaign, opens with a long table in a dark room, covered end to end with rows of lit red stick candles. In the background plays a sorrowful trumpet solo from the sound track of *The Godfather*, lending the scene an ominous atmosphere. Then a man with a deep voice says, "There is a menace out there that affects us all. Every day, two hundred Ghanaians are infected by the HIV virus. These candles represent those two hundred people. Are you protecting yourself? The choice is in your hands." A strong gust of wind blows through the room, extinguishing all two hundred candles, as easily as AIDS extinguishes two hundred lives. The voice-over returns to conclude, dramatically, with the slogan, "Stop AIDS. Love Life." The words appear on the screen like the title of a horror movie, with "Stop AIDS" in dark red letters.

This advertisement marks a moment of transition. In the years before this advertisement, most AIDS campaigns used scare tactics to frighten Ghanaians into changing their behavior. After it, AIDS campaigns took a positive turn, universally adopting life-affirming language and imagery. The "Stop AIDS Love Life" campaign followed a parallel trajectory. This early television ad for the "Stop AIDS Love Life" campaign relied on the familiar trope of depicting the scale of AIDS deaths. Designers adopted this strategy because Ghanaians didn't think they were at risk for contracting HIV. As one staff member at the Ghana Social Marketing Foundation (GSMF) described,

> 2/3 of women and 3/4 of men did not consider themselves at risk for AIDS. Now you tell me, if you didn't consider yourself at risk for anything, why would you take precaution? We realized this is what was stymieing condom sales, but also stymieing the whole national response. . . . We looked at issues

from the sentinel data [tracking HIV infections] that the rate of people dying was 250 a day, or contracting HIV. How do you represent that? Ok, let's
represent this at the ["Stop AIDS Love Life"] launch with 200 candles. So we
decided, let's just shoot it as a commercial. So we had 200 candles that were
lighted to indicate the lives just snuffed out. It was very powerful.[1]

Although it was emotionally powerful, GSMF designers later saw this advertisement as problematic because it frightened people:

I think yes, the strategy has been to be more positive than negative . . . not to
put fear in the people. But I do remember that with "Stop AIDS Love Life,"
we made this ad we call "the candles." And people—[the ad] scared people!
People took it literally. They were like "What 200 people are dying every day?"
In the whole country that would be X number a year. People started doing the
math. They forgot that it was taken in such a way to play on your mind. But
it scared people, okay? And it became a huge talking point in various workplaces, in the home, on radio and on TV. You know, and so, we had people
asking us to come and explain what that 200 a day meant.[2]

Despite the belief that the ad reportedly got people talking about AIDS, the
organization believed that negative effects tempered this potentially positive
effect. In the years before the rise of best-practice reports, fear campaigns
based on drama rather than evidence were the norm. Evaluations of these
fear campaigns revealed that they rarely change behavior and often lead to
fatalism and increased stigmatization of people living with HIV (Sherr 1990;
Rosser 1991; Slavin, Batrouney, and Murphy 2007). These stigmatizing effects
then reduce participation in HIV testing and treatment. Best-practice reports
described these findings and prescribed a shift toward positive, life-affirming
campaigns across the globe. Scaring people into safe sex came to be seen as
inappropriate, barbaric, and ineffectual. The ad with the candles was the last
TV ad produced by GSMF and Johns Hopkins University School for Public
Health (JHU) using scare tactics.

Later GSMF and JHU campaigns included TV spots featuring testimonials by religious leaders and HIV-positive Ghanaians; these ads showed people
living with HIV and encouraged everyday Ghanaians to treat HIV-positive
people compassionately. Since 2002, campaigns across Accra's streetscape
have told people, "Your *Life* is Precious (Wo Nkwa Hia)," to "Stop AIDS
Love *Life*," to "Live and Let *Live*," and to "Reach Out, Show Compassion to
People *Living* with AIDS Today" (emphasis mine). This rapid shift from fear-
based to life-affirming campaigns shows the power of best-practice reports
to coordinate the field.[3] As AIDS organizations in Ghana reinvented their
approach and abandoned images of death and disease, they also initiated the

first coordinated national response to AIDS through the mass media. This systematic effort was led by international organizations such as Family Health International (FHI) and JHU, local nongovernmental organizations (NGOs) such as GSMF, and state initiatives such as the newly established Ghana AIDS Commission (GAC).

Most of the earliest fear-based campaigns were produced by in-house staff at underfunded divisions of the Ministry of Health or local AIDS organizations who had limited communications training. In contrast, the new life-affirming campaigns had substantial institutional and monetary support from global aid organizations such as the United States Agency for International Development (USAID) and the World Bank. These changes are significant. Before 2002, most campaign objects were pamphlets and storybooks, distributed through local health clinics and introduced to communities via health educators. These early images associating AIDS with death and signs of illness had a limited reach, passing from hand to hand via clinics rather than displayed publicly on billboards. This was before the World Bank's Ghana AIDS Relief Fund (GARFUND) flooded Ghana with money and before the establishment of GAC. With the rapid inflow of resources after 2002, campaigns became more coordinated and evidence based. Communications experts ran campaigns, outsourcing production to major local ad agencies. Gone were the skeletons and coffins. Life-affirming messages and images flooded public space via the mass media. In addition, these positive messages made their way onto the radio and TV airwaves through spots and teleplays such as JHU's "Speakeasy" and "Things We Do for Love" and the Planned Parenthood Association of Ghana's (PPAG's) "Young and Wise Choices." With the visibility that came with the institutional and financial backing of international and national-level organizations, AIDS campaign designers believed they could replace Ghanaians' associations of HIV/AIDS with death and illness with more-positive images.

Surprisingly, despite the overwhelming presence of these life-affirming AIDS messages in the public sphere, group interviews with residents of Accra revealed that Ghanaians still strongly associated HIV with the scare tactics images from early campaigns. As I will discuss further in this chapter, when I asked focus group participants to design their own AIDS poster, they usually started by drawing skeletons and people overcome with illness. Although participants often repeated life-affirming slogans like the ones mentioned from the post–2002 campaigns, it sounded as though they were parroting platitudes. Images of death and illness strongly resonated with my participants while life-affirming messages fell flat. Why have life-affirming messages failed to take hold among Ghanaian communities? I argue that life-affirming

messages were more open to cultural entropy than images of death and illness were.

Life-affirming messages are open to cultural entropy in three ways. First,
the iconography of death and illness is more emotionally resonant for Ghanaians. Compared to images of life and positive messages, the distinctive,
emotionally vivid, and symbolically coherent representations of death and
illness evoke heightened responses by participants. In large part, this is because images of death and illness made AIDS visible and legible. Second, the
color red and the red ribbon symbol have unique local meanings associated
with funerals that undermine their use in life-affirming campaigns in Ghana.
Third, people interpret later campaigns through the lens of earlier ones, often
discounting information that doesn't fit with their cognitive presuppositions.
During my group interviews, Ghanaians interpreted life-affirming messages
through death-and-illness frames. In this way, the life-affirming frames do
not replace earlier stigmatizing frames. Instead, these competing frames produce an *additive* effect.

I begin by tracing the history and use of scare tactics by health organizations. Then I account for the sweeping changes in representation in the early
years of the first decade of the twenty-first century from stigmatizing images
of death and illness to positive images and messages of life. Then, using AIDS
posters made by focus groups, I show how local audiences make meaning
around HIV and address how these later messages became open to cultural
entropy.

Scare Tactics: Ghana's Initial Response to the AIDS Epidemic

Beginning in the late 1980s and continuing through the 1990s, AIDS educational materials often symbolically associated the disease with death through
the use of skeletons or the skull and crossbones, or they linked HIV with
extreme illness by depicting "lean" bedridden patients. These early representations made AIDS more concrete, visible, and actionable for Ghanaians in
three ways. First and foremost, portraying AIDS as a "death sentence" and
associating it with particular symptoms made the disease *visible* and avoid-
able. Second, in these early campaigns AIDS was *personified* as a "killer."
Third, AIDS was embodied in particular *personae*, usually deviant or foreign
peoples. Taken together, these representations of AIDS gave Ghanaians the
tools to visually identify people with HIV and ways to think about people
with these symptoms, particularly deviant or foreign people, who might carry
the risk of infection.

AIDS AS VISIBLE AND CARRIER OF A DEATH SENTENCE

The Ghana's National Technical Committee on AIDS tethered AIDS to death by depicting a grinning skeleton with the text "Don't Catch AIDS: Know the Facts" in its pamphlet (fig. 26). Throughout the pamphlet, "AIDS" and "DEATH" are repeatedly capitalized, emphasizing a relationship between them. Inside the pamphlet introduces the disease:

> What is AIDS? AIDS is a new killer disease which is caused by a small germ (virus). It destroys the body's ability to fight diseases. Most people who have the AIDS germ may look and feel healthy and still spread the disease. Once a person catches AIDS, the result is DEATH. (National Technical Committee on AIDS n.d.)

Despite clarifying that carriers of the AIDS "germ" may look healthy, the pamphlet undercuts that claim by listing a series of symptoms associated with those who have AIDS. "How does one know that he has AIDS?" If you:

> Feel tired all the time.
> Lose weight suddenly.
> Have fever for more than one month.
> Have diarrhoea (running stomach) for more than one month.
> Have white spots in your mouth.
> Have painless swellings in the armpit or on the neck.
> Have shingles (ananse) more than once.
> Have sores in your private parts.
> Have plenty of vaginal discharge. (National Technical Committee on AIDS n.d.)

The inclusion of these symptoms makes legible for Ghanaians a shared vision of how an HIV-infected body is marked. Ghanaians drew upon a clear, stable list of symptoms whenever I asked them how they recognized someone with HIV, and foremost among these symptoms was "leanness." Being overly thin, almost *skeletal*, became tightly coupled with being HIV positive. This pamphlet, and others I discuss subsequently, made the disease *visible* for Ghanaians. By introducing symptoms commonly associated with HIV, campaigns enabled Ghanaians to identify people with these symptoms and assume they had AIDS, whether they were HIV positive or not.

The potential for death is also used as a warning in the illustrated storybook *Beware of AIDS: A Supplementary Reader for Basic Level School Children* (Dokosi 2002). The book, intended for children, is centered on a family discussion of AIDS. The Asare family is enjoying a relaxing night of television when a "Stop AIDS Love Life" message airs. This advertisement spurs Ama,

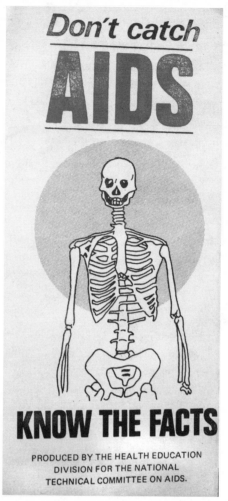

FIGURE 26. Cover image of National Technical Committee on AIDS's pamphlet *Don't Catch AIDS, Know the Facts*

the youngest of the Asare children, to ask her mother about the message. Kofi, Ama's brother, then "burst out, 'I saw a girl and boy wearing T-shirts the previous day on which were the same inscription, 'STOP AIDS LOVE LIFE'. Mama, what is all this talk about AIDS and why are there so many announcements about it?'"

This outburst initiates a frank discussion about AIDS among the Asare family. The parents discuss how HIV is transmitted, how touching someone with HIV won't lead to infection, and then Kofi asks, "Can babies also get infected with HIV?" After a brief discussion of how babies can become infected by HIV, Kofi cries about how "sad and tragic" that is, and then Mrs. Asare notes:

"Babies that suffer from AIDS look sickly. They always look pale and weak. They also have difficulty breathing and they die within a few years," she added. "AIDS has no cure at the moment, and so anyone who is infected with the AIDS virus and later develops AIDS is bound to die," Mr. Asare quickly stated. (Dokosi 2002)

Here, the book makes manifest the direct connection between AIDS and death, while also making visible how babies with AIDS look and act. The adjacent illustration depicts a cemetery populated by above-ground coffins, captioned "Beware of AIDS—It can kill you." Again, the notion that AIDS "kills" appears as a warning. Rather than with skeletons, this image represents death as a field of coffins. In context with the previous page, the book suggests that contracting HIV results in taking up residence at the local cemetery.

Next, Ama asks, "What are the signs to look out for in an AIDS patient?" In reply, Mrs. Asare says:

Some of the signs to look out for are:

When a person is always ill; HIV destroys one's ability to fight against diseases, such as diarrhoea, pneumonia, fever and tuberculosis so they easily attack an AIDS patient.
When a person loses weight rapidly.
When a person becomes very thin.
When a person becomes very weak. (Dokosi 2002)

Although *Beware of AIDS* and other campaigns of this era attempt to clarify that people should care for people living with HIV and that touching someone who is HIV positive will not put you at risk for infection, the subtext often tells a different story. These campaigns make the invisible visible for Ghanaians, giving them something to "look out for." Through the discursive and visual presentation of symptoms of HIV, AIDS organizations give Ghanaians an imagined portrait of someone living with HIV/AIDS. With this portrait in mind, Ghanaians can protect themselves by avoiding these people.

While these accounts demonstrate how campaigns make AIDS visible by listing symptoms textually, many representations of AIDS in Ghana make this point visually. One GAC-produced poster—"Don't turn your back on AIDS. STOP AIDS. Make the Promise."—depicts a thin woman so frail that she requires the support of two other women to stand and walk (fig. 27). While weight loss is strongly associated with being HIV positive in Ghana, needing the care and support of friends and family is another trope commonly depicted. These images attempt to communicate the need for the community to care for people living with HIV, but they have the unintended consequence

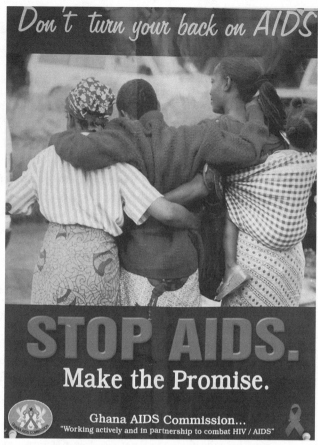

FIGURE 27. Ghana AIDS Commission's "Don't Turn Your Back on AIDS" poster

of putting a "face" on what a person infected with HIV looks like. Depicting grotesquely thin bedridden patients being cared for by hardy family members is another trope that makes visually distinct the healthy and the sick. These dramatic differences between healthy and sick emphasize the symptoms exhibited by people sick from AIDS.

Images depicting men living with AIDS from this era typically show them as shirtless, accentuating the toll of the disease through their nearly skeletal appearance. An image from a 1996 pamphlet titled "How to Protect Yourself Against HIV/AIDS and STDs," produced by PPAG and funded by the United Kingdom's Department for International Development (DFID), depicts a man who is so thin that his ribs visibly show through his skin. As if mocking him, the illustration shows a poster on his wall reminding him (and the audience for this pamphlet) that "AIDS Kills." Also present in this image is another sign of illness: visible marks across his body and face, presumably Kaposi's sarcoma lesions. At that time, Kaposi's sarcoma had yet to enter Ghanaians' popular imagination as a symptom of AIDS, and this pamphlet does not address what this symptom is. Audiences may interpret these marks in any number of ways: boils, warts, tumors, shingles, and the like. By leaving the interpretation open rather than specifying this image with a caption, the ad permits people to believe AIDS manifests in any number of ways.

Such extreme imaginings of symptoms are also made possible by sexually transmitted infection (STI) flip-books regularly used by AIDS organizations in peer education at clinics. Sexual health clinic nurses and HIV/AIDS peer educators commonly use STI flip-books to encourage people to practice such preventative behaviors as condom use and abstinence. These flip-books show grotesque close-up photographs of genitals deformed through sexually transmitted diseases. Every HIV testing and STI clinic I visited had these flip-books within arm's reach of the nurses. AIDS organization staff members I spoke with were unequivocal in their support for these flip-books. HIV/AIDS organizations that rely heavily on peer education—namely, PPAG, FHI, and Strengthening HIV/AIDS Response Partnerships (SHARP)—report using these flip-books with great success. Even when I visited Accra's Burma Camp to talk to military staff about AIDS campaigns, the official I spoke with was so proud of the camp's flip-books that he sent his assistant across the camp to retrieve one for me.

In fact, one AIDS organization staff member described an experiment the organization conducted to measure the effectiveness of the flip-books:

> I asked that [peer educators] talk about infertility, because we know that in traditional Africa, infertility is a big disaster. It is the biggest calamity that can befall a couple—barrenness. So we started talking about infertility issues [using the STI flip-books]. And it worked more like magic. People were interested because we had the STI flip charts through which we did the education and showed the pictures—people wanted to know more. And obviously you can't talk about STIs without walking the person through HIV/AIDS. So consciously or unconsciously they were taking people through things they didn't want to listen to before.
>
> To know whether the flip charts were really working, we did a small survey. We divided the peer educators into two—a control group and a non-control group. One group we showed the flip charts and gave them referral cards, and the other group we gave only the referral cards. Interestingly, those who carried the flip charts came back with all their referral cards completely

exhausted. And from that we established that using the flip chart for education was more results-oriented than doing education without these BCC [behavior change communication] support materials.[4]

This experiment convinced FHI staff that using flip-book images had a direct effect on people's *intention* to seek care. Although most of the peer educators I interviewed had only anecdotal evidence, they universally accepted that the flip-book images had powerful, direct impacts on those people who saw them.

Nurses and peer educators gave these flip-book presentations alongside condom demonstrations on model penises, the distribution of free condoms, and discussions of abstinence as part of an integrated approach to sexual health education. Health educators ostensibly use these photographs to inform communities about the symptoms of disease, so that they can identify an STI and seek treatment if they exhibit symptoms. A latent function of these flip-books, though, was to frighten people into practicing health-protective behaviors. Staff at AIDS organizations often described people's reactions to these images as "scared" or "frightened." Fear, they believed, is an effective approach to changing behavior. Clinic staff and peer educators devoutly believe that showing people these images is the *most* effective way to convince people to protect themselves from HIV/AIDS.

So how do nurses and peer educators make a connection between HIV/AIDS and these graphic images of STIs? If HIV/AIDS by itself does not produce visible symptoms on one's genitals, how do these flip-books "mark" HIV/AIDS infection? Typically, the flip-book begins by showing a series of pictures of genitals of HIV-negative patients infected with one infection: chancroid, herpes, genital warts, gonorrhea, etc. Next, the flip-book shows how HIV/AIDS enhances the manifestation of these diseases. These nightmarish images are presented with such text as, "Chancroid in a male with HIV infection often leads to severe damage to the penis." Another horrific image pictures the bloodied head of a penis that looks as though it had gone through a meat grinder. The text reports, "Part of the penis has been eaten away in this person with Chancroid. The person has AIDS."[5]

Despite ever-present claims in pamphlets produced by AIDS organizations that "some people do not develop any symptoms at all," that AIDS is a "dangerous disease" because you won't know that your partner has HIV, and that many people "feel healthy for years before becoming sick and dying from AIDS," most organizations depict visual markers of HIV/AIDS for Ghanaians.[6] By showing drawings and photographs of bone-thin, shirtless, bedridden, and diseased people, AIDS organizations are unintentionally two-faced.

They *tell* audiences that HIV is often invisible and that carriers may look healthy, but they *show* easy-to-identify visual markers of HIV/AIDS through illustrations. AIDS organizations represent a direct link between "catching AIDS" and death through images of skeletons, the skull and crossbones, coffins, and candles being extinguished. By tightly coupling meanings of HIV/AIDS with serious illness and death, these AIDS organizations sought to put fear in the hearts of the Ghanaian community. By encouraging collective fear of AIDS through these scare tactics, public-health institutions hoped to spur the public to adopt behaviors that would prevent the spread of AIDS. As I'll show next, AIDS organizations did more than associate HIV with death and visible symptoms. They personified AIDS as a "killer."

AIDS PERSONIFIED AS A KILLER

In these early representations of AIDS, the disease is often talked about as a "killer" or something that "kills." One instance of the notion that "AIDS Kills" appears on a red PPAG bumper sticker (fig. 28) in which a depiction of the skull and crossbones warns of the deadly nature of AIDS. This bumper sticker offers audiences three ways of avoiding death by AIDS: the ABCs of abstinence, being faithful, and condom use.[7] PPAG asks its audience to "stop" and "think" about how the consequence of AIDS is death, encouraging viewers to choose one of the three prescribed behaviors it suggests.

By framing AIDS as a "killer," organizations personify the disease and metaphorically make AIDS an opponent (Lakoff and Johnson 1980). As the hand-painted message at a polyclinic in Accra argues, "AIDS is a Killer: Kill AIDS before it kills U" (fig. 29). The sign also labels AIDS an "enemy" and

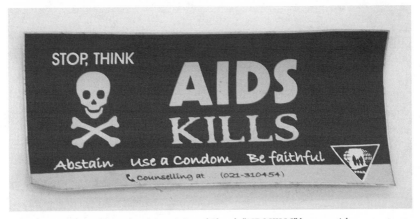

FIGURE 28. Planned Parenthood Association of Ghana's "AIDS KILLS" bumper sticker

FIGURE 29. Hand-painted "AIDS Is a Killer" message at a polyclinic in Accra, Ghana

calls on Ghanaians to "avoid it." By calling AIDS a "killer" and an "enemy," this sign orients Ghanaians' behavior toward AIDS and the people carrying the disease. When AIDS is viewed as an opponent, it becomes something the people can "defeat" by taking action. In the case of this clinic's message, good hygiene, sterile needles, and cleanliness (and avoiding "quack doctors"!) are all paths to "killing" AIDS. While this poster suggests "killing" AIDS with good medical sense, casting AIDS as an enemy opens the door to other ways to "defeat" one's opponent.

For instance, the Ghanaian military also called upon people to defeat their opponent AIDS by taking action. A poster produced for the military claimed that "AIDS is deadly," and in response soldiers should "Crush it" by using condoms.[8] While the text suggests the poster is meant to promote condoms, the image itself is more violent. It depicts a military boot stomping down on the text "AIDS" as if a soldier were subduing an enemy combatant. Such depictions of violence are typical in the personification of AIDS. Another poster, "KNOCK! HIV/AIDS Out of Ghana," produced by GAC, depicts a boxer punching toward the audience. Another ad produced in the series shows a soccer player striking the ball, with the caption "KICK! HIV/AIDS Out of Ghana." The danger is that these images direct Ghanaians' treatment of people living with HIV. When Ghanaians are encouraged to kill AIDS, crush it, punch it, and kick it, transferring this abstract idea to a person is not a huge leap.

AIDS AS PERSONAE

In addition to personifying AIDS as an opponent, making concrete for Ghanaians the need to fight it as an invading enemy, these first campaigns linked AIDS to particular personae. Within many Ghanaian communities, HIV was already associated with foreigners and outsiders. Cases of AIDS in a village were blamed on migrant workers (often from Côte d'Ivoire, where HIV prevalence is much higher) or on traveling Ghanaians from other villages (Anarfi 1993; Yankah 2004). Ghanaians adopted strategies to avoid AIDS by having sex only with known people in the community and avoiding "lean" people who looked symptomatic of AIDS:

> You were safe from the disease as long as you had sex with familiar people . . . and who else would be considered safe sex partners: men and women who looked plump and fleshy. . . . Knowing this, men sometimes avoided the stigma by simply overeating to become fleshy or drinking excess beer to acquire pot bellies. (Yankah 2004)

Beyond giving people visual categories of distinction such as "fat" and "thin," AIDS campaigns equated HIV with particular behavioral categories of people. For instance, one story titled *Had I Known* . . . makes a clear link between sexually active women and HIV.

Produced by the National AIDS Control Programme and the Ghana Ministry of Health, *Had I Known* . . . tells the stories of Yaa and Adwoa. Yaa and Adwoa were good friends until Adwoa decided to follow in the footsteps of Naomi and Mary, two women who jumped from "one man to the other." Yaa warns Adwoa against being seduced by Naomi's and Mary's lifestyle because to do so would be "courting trouble," a trouble called AIDS. After twelve years of implied sex work and the "good life," Adwoa returns to the village dressed in fancy clothes. She tells Yaa that she's changed her name to "Freekie" and tries to give money to Yaa. Adwoa/Freekie says to Yaa, "I can see that you are still moving with that miserable wretched Kwame. Well, life is sweet and I have everything I want. Here take this money and buy better dresses." Yaa replies, "Thank you but I don't need your money. Kwame may be poor but he is the man for me." Soon, Yaa learns that Adwoa/Freekie has been hospitalized. In the final panel, Yaa goes to visit Adwoa/Freekie. When Adwoa/Freekie sees Yaa, she states, "Yaa, look at me today. I should have listened to you. I went chasing the good things in life and now look at me. I have AIDS! Had I known . . ." Compared to Adwoa's effervescence earlier in the narrative, the image of her lying sick in bed and exclaiming, "I have AIDS!" shows the audience how far she's fallen. She once celebrated the good things in *life*, but now she's condemned to illness and *death*. She is weak and thin, with bony feet and narrow forearms, and her hair isn't styled. By comparing the fates of Yaa and Adwoa, the audience learns that one can avoid AIDS through faithfulness and shunning greed; but desiring wealth and following an immoral path such as sex work will likely lead to contracting HIV.

Other storybooks link HIV to rapists and introduce parties as a serious threat to the moral and physical purity of young women. *Mavis, a Pearl of Great Price*, a book sponsored by GAC and written and illustrated by a young secondary school student, tells the story of Mavis, a beautiful and obedient fifteen-year-old girl who is cloistered by her father. Her friend Lucy invites Mavis to her sixteenth birthday party, and Mavis asks for her father's permission. Reluctantly, her father permits Mavis's attendance, even though Lucy arrives dressed provocatively and talks to him as if her were a "sugar daddy." At Lucy's party, the other guests include two young men named Abdul and Addae, both of whom take an interest in Mavis. Mavis tastes something funny in her soft drink and gets woozy. She passes out and awakes the next morning, naked, in Lucy's bed. Mavis is confused about what has happened and when she asks, "Where's my dress?" a complicit Lucy hides what happened by saying that "the room was hot." Mavis goes home, still ignorant that she was raped. Some time later, "dark spots darkened [Lucy's] light skin" and "that plump body steadily grew lean." Mavis learns that Lucy and Abdul have died. When Mavis reports this news to her father, he insists that Mavis tell him about what happened at Lucy's party. Mavis insists that all she knows is that she woke up in Lucy's bed.

Mavis is admitted to the University of Ghana, Legon, with hopes of becoming a doctor, but before classes begin, she gets sick with diarrhea and grows thinner. At the hospital, the doctor reveals to Mavis's father that she has AIDS. Confused and angry, he cannot explain how his virgin daughter could have AIDS, until he remembers that night years ago when Mavis stayed overnight at Lucy's party. Her father cries, "'Now I know . . . now I understand. Oh wicked Lucy, that rotten liar!' . . . Mr. Amfo's pearl of great price was lost. Wicked AIDS robbed him of his only child." For Mavis, choosing to hang around with sexually promiscuous friends even once led to her demise. This story suggests that sexually promiscuous friends are likely HIV positive, are envious, dress provocatively, talk back to fathers, lie, and invite rapists (who also have HIV) to parties. Even though Mavis resists being morally corrupted through her associations with Lucy, she cannot help being bodily corrupted by associating with these "wicked" people.

Couching lessons about AIDS in broader morality tales was a common way in which Ghanaian AIDS organizations drew moral boundaries around the types of people who carried AIDS. Other materials, such as the STI flip-books, also do this work. By marking the types of people who have the most extreme cases of infection, the flip-books link HIV to categories of people that most Ghanaians believe act immorally. By actively categorizing some bodies as different, and even deviant, these images promote guilt by association. For instance, the flip-books label when a patient is homosexual or bisexual, effectively tying HIV/AIDS and the behaviors that lead to STIs to non-heterosexual sex. Such statements as "Anal warts in a bisexual man (Bisexual refers to a person who engages in both vaginal and anal sex)" and "Early signs of syphilis in the anus of a person who admitted to being a homosexual (a homosexual is a male who have sex with another male)" align infection with what many Ghanaians view as licentious behavior.[9] Additionally, flip-books mark some bodies as criminal. Another image depicts an anus covered in massive growths, with the caption, "This young man was a prisoner. He is infected with venereal warts. He admitted having anal sex in prison."[10] In addition to trying to frighten their audience into safe sex and abstinence, these flip-books police normality and moral boundaries. By showing how HIV/AIDS magnifies the harm done by STIs, they also actively stigmatize populations viewed as "immoral" within Ghanaian culture: homosexuals and prisoners.

These AIDS campaigns suggest a deep history of representing HIV-positive Ghanaians through vivid symbols of death and illness. Through these campaigns, Ghanaians came to fear AIDS while simultaneously learning how to identify people living with HIV/AIDS. Early HIV/AIDS campaigns gave Ghanaians categories of people to watch out for: young people who engage in premarital sex, loose women, sex workers, lecherous men, potential rapists, homosexuals, and prisoners. As Carol Heimer has argued, "Teaching about prevention almost necessarily stigmatizes those who are infected" (2007, 565).

When AIDS was personified and linked to personae, embodied in people with particular symptoms or who belong to certain social categories, Ghanaians could also stigmatize and ostracize them. These depictions played an important role in making HIV visible and legible—able to be read in the social landscape—through physical manifestations of disease.

AIDS campaigns portray people living with HIV as morally tainted and intensify stigma by linking HIV to marginal populations. When AIDS campaigns indicate that HIV is a direct consequence of sex work, homosexuality, prison life (and therefore criminal activity), or adultery, they fundamentally misrepresent people living with HIV in Ghana. These depictions distort the truth. Results from the Ghana Demographic Health Survey reveal that most people living with HIV are not from marginalized populations (Martin and Logan 2005). When organizations depict symptoms and link AIDS to these "others," they enable stigma by confirming suspicions that people with HIV deserve it because of their immorality. AIDS stigma is about recognizing the "unhealthy other" against whom people can define themselves as healthy (Crawford 1994). "The mark inflicted by AIDS, other sexually transmitted diseases, and to a certain extent, all serious affliction is an inscription of otherness. The visible component of this otherness is the *external* object of abjection" (Crawford 1994, 1335). This marking is necessary for Ghanaians to maintain the social boundary between the moral, healthy self and the immoral, unhealthy other.

Studies in Ghana and elsewhere have shown that the consequences of generating fear and promoting stigma around AIDS are vast. "Misconceptions are built on the stigma attached to the disease . . . the general opinion [in Ghana] is that sufferers of the disease must be killed or at best be confined" (Anarfi 1993, 20). People living with HIV whom I interviewed reported being isolated by their community, banished from their homes, and beaten by their family members. Linking AIDS with death caused the general population to fear contact with people infected with HIV. Individuals' fear of being "outed" as HIV positive and the stigma they would face has led to low rates of voluntary HIV testing in Ghana (Luginaah, Yiridoe, and Taabazuing 2005). Public-health organizations inadvertently undermined their own efforts at preventing HIV by making HIV legible to local communities in ways that encouraged stigma.

Shifting Strategies: Affirming Life

Around the turn of the twenty-first century, international public-health organizations ascertained that fear-based communication approaches have this unintended consequence of increasing stigma. Best-practice documents adjusted their prescriptions accordingly. For instance, in 2002 Family Health International published *Behavior Change Communication for HIV/AIDS: A Strategic Framework*. In this publication, the authors insist on using only positive campaigns:

> The theme should be positive. It is now commonly understood that fear campaigns and campaigns blaming particular groups are ineffective. Most experts agree that fear tends to focus an audience's attention on what not to do, or what to avoid. Approaches are more effective when they promote positive messages that state clearly what audiences can and should do.
>
> Themes should also avoid blaming or stigmatizing. Messages that blame a particular group can backfire, especially in AIDS programs, by diverting audiences' attention from their own needed behavior changes. Such messages can also encourage discrimination, stigma and even physical harm to PLHA [people living with HIV/AIDS] and other vulnerable groups. Stigma and denial can in turn cause people to avoid services that may benefit them. (FHI 2002, 14)

In response to this tide shift in the thinking on health communication, AIDS organizations globally developed campaigns that encouraged prevention by promoting life rather than threatening death. AIDS organizations in Ghana followed suit. Due to concerns that early Ghanaian campaigns using scare tactics led to unintended negative effects, the field of health organizations in Ghana quickly changed communication policies, vowing to promote health behavior through positive messages that wouldn't encourage stigma or fatalism.

The most prominent campaign to proactively engage in a positive, life-affirming agenda in Ghana was the USAID-funded "Stop AIDS Love Life" campaign. Designers' concerns about avoiding stigma and choosing positive messages informed even their choice of color. Despite the common use of red for AIDS campaigns previously in Ghana and throughout the world, JHU designers opposed the use of red and opted instead for yellow:

> The general rule for choosing a color for an AIDS campaign would have been to use red, the international color for HIV and AIDS. But we chose yellow because red is a very serious symbol for the main, traditional group in Ghana, the Ashanti. Red is their national color. Even if they are Ashanti, red is their color. Out of respect. Red would have created the wrong impression. People within those traditional areas might tend to think that they are being stigmatized, so we decided to use a color that would be very friendly and would be loved by everybody. The yellow signifying gold is our heritage. We chose gold; we chose yellow.[11]

JHU chose yellow because it was "friendly," "loved by everybody," and signified the nation's "heritage" as the Gold Coast, which designers felt would unite Ghanaians around their common goal of stopping AIDS. The stigmatizing effects engendered by previous campaigns haunted the design of new campaigns like a specter, making the staff at Johns Hopkins hyperaware of the ways color, symbols, and messages might stigmatize.

The principal image for the campaign was the "Stop AIDS Love Life" image, reproduced on TV ads, billboards, posters, pamphlets, T-shirts, and other objects (see figure 8 in chapter 4). The image sought to "shatter the silence" around AIDS in Ghana, and it represented this idea by depicting a hand bursting through the center of the billboard, a hand that doubled as the "popular international symbol for 'stop.'"[12] Attempting to overcome stigmatizing associations, organizations sought new ways to encourage productive conversations about AIDS through "positive behavior modeling." This strategy of positive behavior modeling continues on this billboard as it suggests that Ghanaians take proactive steps toward preventing AIDS by adopting the ABCs: "Abstain (from sex), or Be Faithful (together), or Condom Use (every time)."

"Stop AIDS Love Life" quickly became the most prominent and well-known campaign in Ghana through its nationwide circulation via mass media and peer education. My participants recognized "Stop AIDS Love Life" as the most visible AIDS campaign in Ghana. Even eight years after the campaign's launch, it remained one of the best-known slogans around HIV. "Stop AIDS Love Life" is one of the most, if not *the* most, commonly reproduced slogans among local audiences. I found the slogan painted on banners advertising non-HIV-related events, on the sign for a basket weaver, and on a trash can at the Kaneshi fabric market. Putting aside the possible entropic interpretations of what it means to have this message on a trash bin, people clearly felt passionate enough about AIDS to take it upon themselves to spread this message further.

Similarly, the Agege Traders' Association made a hand-painted reproduction of the "Stop AIDS Love Life" billboard (fig. 30). The message here is somewhat different (it encourages people to "Show Compassion to AIDS Victims"), but it retains the positive spirit and is yet another example of local, hand-painted redeployments of the campaign by local groups. The "Stop AIDS Love Life" message resonated with people committed to doing something about AIDS. These examples are evidence that the message became more than just a slogan circulating through the public sphere. These creative redeployments show how "Stop AIDS Love Life" became an important part of the shared discourse around AIDS in Ghana.

As this sign by the Agege Traders' Association shows, the idea of showing

FIGURE 30. Agege Traders' Association hand-painted sign reproducing Johns Hopkins University School for Public Health's "Stop AIDS Love Life" billboard in Accra, Ghana

compassion to people living with HIV/AIDS also took hold at the community level. The language of "show compassion" originates from the "Stop AIDS Love Life" brand and appears in the similarly visible (and yellow) "Reach Out" campaign (fig. 31). "Reach Out, Show Compassion" continued this trend of adopting positive imagery, even seeking to counteract the high levels of stigma caused, in part, by earlier campaigns. As JHU staff described to me, "Reach Out, Show Compassion" stemmed from designers' feeling that they needed to change the character of campaigns and improve the social conditions for people living with HIV:

> As the ["Stop AIDS Love Life"] campaign unfolded, we realized that people were not receiving those with HIV and AIDS very well. They were not treating them well, and the source of the problem is that until people learn how to treat those people with HIV and AIDS properly, they will not understand HIV/AIDS themselves. If you are able to create that compassion in them, to move them to understand, you can. Also that communities should start coming together to create a caring atmosphere in developing programs that meet the needs of people living with AIDS, their families, and so on. So the creation of "Show Compassion."[13]

JHU staff sought to improve people's understandings of people living with HIV, reduce stigma, and create a "caring atmosphere." Notice too, that the

FIGURE 31. Johns Hopkins University School of Public Health's "Reach Out, Show Compassion" billboard, in the Airport Residential neighborhood of Accra, Ghana

billboard uses the language of "life" by asking Ghanaians to "show compassion to people *living* with HIV/AIDS, <u>today</u>." Again, JHU distanced itself from fear campaigns and instead worked to create life-affirming campaigns that would establish a supportive environment for people living with HIV.

Incongruously, despite these efforts to depict positive images, this campaign continued to show illness (although less explicitly and dramatically than in past campaigns). For instance, when I asked JHU staff about the use of hands in this campaign, my respondent replied:

> Now the choice of that hand was to extend your hand to somebody who is sick. So you see two hands. One is weak and one is strong. The weak one is the person living with HIV/AIDS and the strong one is the unaffected person. . . . You reach out, touch him, and pull him along with you.[14]

Although this billboard avoided the link between AIDS and certain death, it still identified symptoms of AIDS by depicting a strong (read: healthy) hand holding and "pulling along" a weak, sick hand.

The theme of helping hands supporting the weak appears in another life-affirming advertisement produced by the Ghana AIDS Commission. "Wo Nkwa Hia" ("Your Life Is Precious"), is a campaign that appeared shortly after the advent of JHU's "Stop AIDS Love Life" campaign. To represent the preciousness of life, the campaign depicted a hand holding a newly hatched baby chick (fig. 32). Read one way, this representation placed even more distance between HIV/AIDS and death and disease by portraying *new* life. The image

FIGURE 32. Ghana AIDS Commission's "Wo Nkwa Hia" ("Your Life Is Precious") billboard, in the Labone Estates neighborhood of Accra, Ghana

also plays on a metaphor of fragility and weakness. This strong hand has to protect and care for that "precious life" because the threat of AIDS is ever present, as the red warning "AIDS IS REAL" forcefully declares in the lower right corner of the billboard.

These campaigns relied on the language of "love" to encourage prevention and compassion. Organizations believed that encouraging people to "love with care" and "stop AIDS" by showing a "love" of "life" through engaging in the ABCs of HIV prevention would motivate them to adopt preventative practices to protect themselves and their loved ones. Love is also strategic in its symbolic opposition to hate. AIDS organizations reframed the relationship between the community of people living with HIV and those who are HIV-negative through the language of love. These framings discouraged stigma and hate, and they exhorted the uninfected to embrace practices of love and care.

As I have shown, AIDS organizations in Ghana made a conscious effort to reframe AIDS after an era of scare tactics. Rather than continue with fear-inducing messages, they adopted best practices and designed upbeat campaigns that affirm the value of life, encourage positive changes through loving and caring for one's neighbor, and seek to unite Ghanaians around the goals of AIDS prevention. For a variety of reasons, designers in Ghana expressed confidence that this new positive approach would change how Ghanaians understand AIDS, improve the treatment of people living with HIV, promote changes in sexual behavior, and increase demand for such services as HIV testing and care. First and foremost, these new campaigns were backed by far greater resources than earlier campaigns had been. With these monies, organizations could produce evidence-based mass media campaigns that reached greater numbers of Ghanaians than had earlier interventions comprised primarily of storybooks, pamphlets, and STI flip-books circulated via clinics and peer education.

Structural shifts occurred contemporaneously with the appearance of these life-affirming campaigns and made possible the decoupling of the tight link between AIDS and death and disease. Ghanaians with high T cell counts gained access to antiretroviral therapy (ART), which made it possible to "live with AIDS." Similarly, condoms have to be available and affordable if people are to use condoms as a way to "Stop AIDS Love Life." Before the early years of the first decade of the twenty-first century, affordable condoms were available only at clinics, but the subsidization of condoms and the efforts of GSMF brought affordable condoms to a variety of locations throughout the city. The designers I interviewed felt confident that these new initiatives equipped them to turn the tide. However, despite these structural changes, my interviews with focus groups of local Ghanaians reveal how images of death and disease still resonate strongly. Next, I discuss the AIDS posters drawn by my participants and how the imagery they depict mimics and inflects the representations put forth by the earliest AIDS campaigns.

How AIDS Campaigns Shape Ghanaian Meanings of HIV

Has interacting with these institutionalized representations of HIV/AIDS in the public sphere affected Ghanaians' meaning making around AIDS? If so, how? Using evidence from focus group interviews with Ghanaians and the posters they drew in 2008, I find that interacting with AIDS campaign interventions has shaped Ghanaians' understandings of AIDS in unexpected ways. Campaigns provide a language (both verbal and visual) that constrains the ways Ghanaians think about AIDS. Despite efforts by organizations to *replace* stigmatizing imagery that associated AIDS with death and illness, I find that later campaigns had an *additive effect*. Instead of replacing their stigmatizing understandings of AIDS with life-affirming readings, Ghanaians creatively synthesized the range of meanings provided by the evolution of AIDS representations, ultimately favoring the scare tactics of early interventions.

At the beginning of my focus group interviews with residents of Accra,[15] I asked them to collaborate in designing and drawing an AIDS poster. After giving them a box of colored pencils and a large blank sheet of paper, I asked them to "come up with a message about AIDS that your community needs to see and hear." What is striking about the images created by focus group participants is how similar they are to one another and how they draw upon the "visual language" of AIDS campaigns that once circulated through the public sphere.[16] Ghanaians called on this language to make a poster: they drew pictures and chose slogans nearly identical to images and discourse from publicly available campaigns. Consider the poster drawn by schoolteachers at an elementary school in Accra (fig. 33). In their poster, the teachers make a link between AIDS and death by relying on symbols of death reminiscent of, if not identical to, Ghana's earliest representations of AIDS. By depicting a skull, a skull and crossbones, and a coffin, these teachers fixated their representation of AIDS around "death and danger" (the explanation they offered again and

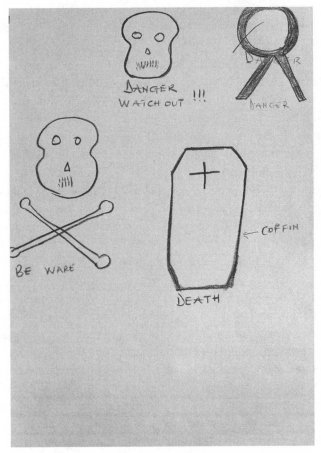

FIGURE 33. Focus group AIDS poster drawing, by primary school teachers (with ribbon colored red)

again for the symbols they chose). They said that "AIDS is going to bring death, so you should watch out."

When I asked them how their poster differed from AIDS images they see throughout Accra, they said they felt this poster was distinct:

PARTICIPANT: It is really different. Because the signs we see there tells that there is danger.

TERENCE E. MCDONNELL: So most HIV/AIDS advertisements don't do that?

PARTICIPANT: They don't do that. The advertisements use symbols and messages that people don't understand.

TEM: What symbols do other AIDS advertisements use that people don't understand?

PARTICIPANT: Like the ABCD . . . people understand the pictures but they don't read the text. They have no impact.

TEM: Are there ways in which this poster you've made is like other AIDS posters you've seen?

PARTICIPANT: It is totally different.

TEM: Then why haven't organizations made a poster like this one?

PARTICIPANT: Because they don't talk to people when they select the symbols and messages. And I also think the tone—the tone shouldn't be too harsh. Because if someone has it, they wouldn't want the person to start seeing death, they want the person to approach death gradually. So they think it has to be mild. They don't want the patient to feel bad. So they make it mild. But then that language is too mild for some people. For some it might make people living with HIV/AIDS feel bad, but for those who don't have it . . . They need to see something more stronger. Some people were saying AIDS or no AIDS life must goes on. And some men say they don't like to use a condom because it doesn't feel real. If such a person sees this, he will realize he has to be more careful.

For this group of teachers, the poster they created warns people about AIDS by using symbols and images their community understands. Unlike the life-affirming ads they see around them that are too "mild" or that use symbols people in their community do not understand, and therefore have "no impact," this poster is clear and dramatic. Surprisingly, while their poster resembles imagery and language from the earliest interventions, they did not recognize this resemblance. This finding suggests that the images of skulls and coffins that came immediately to mind had suffused into the collective unconscious even when people lacked firsthand exposure to the pamphlets or storybooks that relied heavily on images of death.

Their discussion demonstrates a nuanced understanding of the toll such dramatic images have on people living with HIV but places this understanding in tension with the need to persuade HIV-negative Ghanaians to change their behavior. They understood that their poster might make people living with AIDS "feel bad" and recognized that the campaigns out there were careful not to be too harsh and avoided confronting people living with HIV with images of death. They weighed these potential negative and stigmatizing effects for people living with HIV against their need for harsher images that would have a greater impact among HIV-negative people. These teachers viewed the campaigns currently on the streetscape with skepticism. Anecdotally, they identified many people in their community as lax about their AIDS risk, leading them to believe that current campaigns sacrificed prevention for antistigma. For those people who "don't have it" and don't like to use a condom, the teachers thought that demonstrating the consequences of this behavior—namely, that AIDS leads to death—would force people to "be more careful."

In another example, a focus group of Osu community members drew an "after and before" AIDS poster (fig. 34). After receiving my prompt, one woman immediately proposed—without hesitation, reflection, or debate—that they should draw a skeleton and skull and crossbones. The rest of the group quickly agreed, even before discussing what the idea of the poster should be. After drawing the skeleton with a skull and crossbones floating overhead as a "sign of warning," the group moved on to discussing what message they wanted to share with their community:

MALE PARTICIPANT 1: AIDS is real. Either abstain from—well, not abstain from sex. Always use a condom. That is—if you want to go behind your wife . . .

FEMALE PARTICIPANT 1: Oh, and choose life.

As they deliberated about the slogan, they suggested taglines that were commonly available in campaigns from the public sphere: "AIDS is real," "abstain from sex," "always use a condom," and "choose life." Having drawn a skeleton and skull and crossbones but seeing no clear way to connect the skeleton to the slogans they had identified, they seemed unsure of how to proceed. They would pause to think and then start an idea, only to stammer or noncommittally switch to another idea. After a lengthy silence, during which they looked at one another, seemingly hoping others in the group had a way forward, I had the sense that they were discouraged. I then pushed them forward by asking, "Why'd you choose a skeleton?"

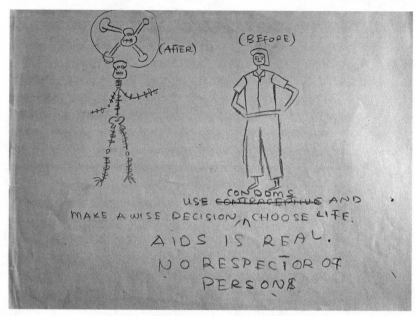

FIGURE 34. Focus group AIDS poster drawing, by residents of Osu neighborhood of Accra, Ghana

MALE PARTICIPANT 1: Because if you are talking about the disease of HIV, you may die. And—

FEMALE PARTICIPANT 1: And it depreciates to this stage. They become so weak and look like skeletons. Helpless and weak.

Here they articulated two meanings for the skeleton. One participant connected HIV to death, as represented by the skeleton, and another described the skeleton as symbolizing the symptoms of people living with AIDS: They are "helpless and weak." After the idea emerged that the skeleton could represent disease rather than death, the group circled around the idea of incorporating the skeleton into a "before and after" narrative. When they had committed to the before and after approach, they confronted a problem: by being so quick to get the skeleton down on paper, they put what should be the "after" image of the skeleton in the "before" position (i.e., to the left side of the page, an automatic position for anyone in a culture of left-to-right writing). As one participant admitted, "we should have rather drawn it so that this picture is here and this picture is here." They then drew a healthy man in the "after" position but were careful to label which image was "before" and which was "after" to clear up any confusion.

Taken together, these two posters demonstrate just how strongly Ghanaians associate AIDS with death. Choosing images such as skeletons, coffins, and the skull and crossbones felt natural to the focus group participants. Consensus came quickly, if not instantly, suggesting that this interpretation was cognitively at hand, and this connection between AIDS and death appeared automatic (DiMaggio 1997; Vaisey 2009). Though the life-affirming campaigns in the mass media never associated AIDS with skeletons, early health pamphlets had a powerful influence on how Ghanaians understand AIDS. This is surprising considering the limited circulation of these images. One explanation might stem from the fact that the majority of Ghanaians do not know someone with HIV.[17] These early images, fueled by gossip, rumor, and uncertainty about AIDS, anchored Ghanaians' understandings of AIDS to death, with skeletons as the symbol foremost in their mind. Alternatively, Ghanaians who have seen a friend or relative wasting away from AIDS might also associate this image with the disease.

Additionally, despite the efforts of the "Stop AIDS Love Life" campaign to link AIDS with yellow rather than red, AIDS and red were still tightly coupled for my focus groups. When AIDS organizations in Ghana used red in their campaigns, they reported that they were drawing on international conventions around AIDS representation. For the Ghanaians in my focus groups, the use of red was grounded in *local* meanings of red. While staff at JHU went with yellow to celebrate Ghana's history as the Gold Coast and to avoid stigmatizing the Ashanti people who were traditionally associated with the color red, the Ghanaians I interviewed understood the meaning of red differently. As I will show, red symbolized death and danger.

Returning to the first poster I discussed (fig. 33), the elementary school teachers went right for the red colored pencil after I gave them my prompt, and the first image they drew was the red ribbon, though not for the reasons one might expect. For many cultures in the industrialized West, red ribbons work denotatively as a shorthand for AIDS. One might assume the teachers followed this common practice of using a red ribbon to mean AIDS, but they understood the red ribbon as a "bow" that carried a different connotation.

FEMALE PARTICIPANT 1: What is natural to portray AIDS to the community, I believe red is danger. You see red, you see danger. And the symbol is a bow. That's what it is, danger. So, if you use the bow as a sign on the right top corner, everyone will be alarmed to watch. [*The other teachers are confused*] Bow, Bow, Bow, B-O-W, you know the bow!

MALE PARTICIPANT 2: And arrow?

FEMALE PARTICIPANT 1: No, like this [*she uses her hand to depict the loop of the red ribbon*]. As we make bow for a funeral, we tie it, like with lace. That is right [*in response to the teacher drawing the red ribbon*].

Although at first there was little consensus around what the red ribbon meant as a symbol for AIDS, or even that the drawing was a depiction of a ribbon, this group was familiar with the symbol from campaigns they had seen. Without an internalized narrative of what the bow represented, they deliberated and improvised justifications for the red ribbon on the spot. It was automatic for this group to associate red with AIDS and to connect it with the local meaning of red as representing death and danger. However, coming up with justifications for the bow symbol required serious deliberation. Local meanings of red and bows, especially when decorating funerals, structured their justification for using a bow.

Ghanaians don't use ribbons to represent causes as is done in other parts of the world. Without that shared practice, my respondents did not recognize the red ribbon as a transnational symbol representing AIDS as a "cause." This teacher assumed that AIDS organizations intended to represent "bows," thus imbuing this choice with a new set of meanings. Ghanaians commonly use bows to decorate major events such as weddings, funerals, or "outdoorings" (when Ghanaians celebrate the birth of a new baby). Seeing the symbol as a bow, and not as an awareness ribbon worn to mark support or as an abstract representation of AIDS, this focus group followed her lead in associating the red ribbon with the Ghanaian practice of decorating homes to honor the death of a loved one. A second respondent continued when I inquired, "why a bow?"

FEMALE PARTICIPANT 2: Because, normally, we use that a lot. It should be hanging as when you have a funeral. You tie it like lace, that type of bow. So when we are doing a [funeral] decoration, for people to be attracted, really, we use a bow. So if it is a red bow, it signifies something. If it is white, it is a victory sign. If it is red, it is danger. So I prefer we use red. And everybody understands, from children to adults, we understand red as death and danger.

Ghanaian funerals are extravagant events, with great effort put into decorating homes for the period of mourning. Three color schemes are typically associated with Ghanaian funerals: white on black, black on black, or red on black. People wear funeral attire and decorate their homes with ribbons in these colors. I understand from conversations with Ghanaians that when the elderly die a "good" death of old age, the family and friends festoon the funeral in black and white. However, funerals adorned with red and black are associated with tragic or unexpected deaths. The depiction of a coffin with a cross is a clear representation of mourning and funerary ritual.

Read this way, the use of red in conjunction with symbols of death worked within the practices of local sense making. Red was already associated with death and tragedy. Extending red to represent AIDS was logically and culturally consistent. As the quotation from the second female participant makes clear, in addition to using red to mark death, red served as a symbol of warning. In their poster, skulls and crossbones are also drawn in red, one skull accompanied by the text "Danger Watch Out!!!" Depicting death through the use of red came up when the focus group participants from Osu discussed their skeleton drawing in figure 34. When I asked about what colors they might use, since they completed the whole drawing in brown, they said, "We should have used red or black for the skeleton." This consistent use of red is not random, and it reveals the color's powerful symbolic connection with death and warning.

Red not only serves as a warning and a symbol of death but is also used by Ghanaians to distinguish HIV-infected people from those who are uninfected. Rather than using images of death, a group of secondary school teachers wanted to depict someone who is "sick and dying of AIDS." When I asked how that would look, the teachers discussed the variety of signs that identify someone with AIDS. They first proposed to depict a man who is "lean, or has almost depleted the flesh from the body." Another suggested that they depict "people with the sentence of AIDS, that is, some of the symptoms of AIDS that are common to the person, the boils and other things which should be also shown." Why, I asked, should they depict these signs of illness? The answer was simple: if they showed signs of illness, they could convince others that AIDS was a real danger. "People have heard of AIDS, but people don't believe in its existing. So by showing those signs, or those things, they will be able to know that, really, AIDS is real. It should say 'AIDS is a Killer' or 'AIDS is a Slow Killer' because AIDS kills slow." Here the personification of AIDS as a killer appears, much as in the earliest campaigns.

Just as consensus seemed to have been established about what to depict, one teacher added a caveat:

FEMALE PARTICIPANT 1: I just wanted to add that it is not everybody who shows sign of the sickness, if they are a carrier, if they carry the virus, but still look normal. Like two normal people, two people who are healthy, one who is an AIDS carrier, the other who is not. Even though they all look normal and don't show any signs of sickness. Let's draw a healthy person and write 'beware of those who are healthy because they could be carriers of HIV.'"

Now the group needed to reconcile two competing images of AIDS. On the one hand, AIDS was visible. By depicting someone who was sick, lean, and covered in boils, they could convince their fellow community members that AIDS was a killer. On the other hand, HIV was invisible. You can't tell who might have the disease because HIV can be carried without signs of illness, which raises one's risk of infection.

Central to this debate was the question of whether representing people as sickly would create fear and stigmatize people with HIV. In response to one person saying the group should depict a person so sick that people would "run from" him or her, another participant disagreed:

FEMALE PARTICIPANT 2: I just don't think it's right. I think education will be more appropriate than putting fear into the person. I think it's to under-stand what the disease is all about and—and, not necessarily tracing out those aspects to put fear, but to make the person more aware that these things can happen if you do this. So, don't do this, or don't get into this thing. But, don't—don't bring it up with the main problem of putting fear into the people. I don't think it's good for the human being. We should be careful about the impact, the psychological impact on the human being. Not just—I think it would be selfish to just put fear into them—we are so desperate to get people out of AIDS that we try anything? Fear? It's not appropriate.

This conflict between the impulse to instill fear in the community by depict-ing illness through the use skeletal images and the desire to protect people living with HIV from stigma posed a problem for the group to solve. The participants deliberated over these issues at length.

Just as these competing visions of AIDS appeared intractable, someone suggested drawing a person in red to depict the presence of the disease. The emotional dynamics of the group changed when red came up: participants started speaking loudly, talking over one another about how to use red, nod-ding heads and leaning forward around the table. These physical expressions of emotion and excitement signaled that the idea resonated among the group members. The use of red solved the problem created by their competing vi-sions. It allowed them to represent someone as healthy and asymptomatic, but infected, while also communicating the danger and warning that using a fear-based skeleton approach would permit. The ultimate poster (fig. 35) first shows two people who look similar, one depicted in green, the other in red with the text, "EVERYBODY IS AT RISK." Then, it portrays a person on a bed, also drawn in red, and two other people drawn in green looking over

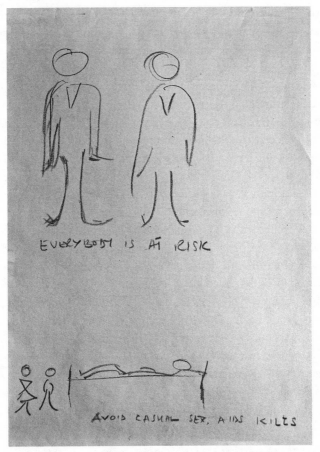

FIGURE 35. Focus group AIDS poster drawing, by secondary school teachers (with top figures colored one red and one green, bottom figure in bed red and two figures beside it green)

the AIDS patient, with the text, "AVOID CASUAL SEX, AIDS KILLS." I later probed the group about the meanings of red and green and asked why these two people were drawn in different colors. Despite wanting to depict HIV as invisible, their strategy still made HIV *visible* through the color red:

MALE PARTICIPANT 1: The green color will show that this is not a carrier. Then the red. So you see they are all normal, but this one is a carrier.

TEM: So why does green mean healthy and not a carrier and red mean they are a carrier?

MALE PARTICIPANT 2: Because red means Danger. There is danger. Green means health. When you look at vegetation when they come up healthy, they come up green.

The use of red offered a resonant solution to the competing meanings of the group. Depicting one person as red allowed the group to communicate both infection *and* danger, while circumventing their concerns about reinforcing fear and stigma. Despite the attempt to show how invisible HIV carriers can be, these teachers still felt compelled to do the representative work of showing difference: healthy (green) versus not healthy (red); not dangerous (green) versus dangerous (red); HIV negative (green) versus HIV positive (red). This use of the color red to mark illness continues in the bottom half of the poster, where there appears a red stick figure lying on a bed, looking especially thin compared to the green figures standing beside the bed. If depicting someone on his or her deathbed wasn't enough to mark the person as someone with AIDS, the use of red does the parallel symbolic work.

My focus groups with HIV-positive Ghanaians shared similar understandings of red as expressing warning. HIV-positive Ghanaians had such strong *negative* associations with red that they actively sought to avoid using the color because of its perceived stigmatizing effects. Both of my focus groups with people living with HIV/AIDS chose not to use the red pencil. When I asked one group about why they used green in their poster, they instead started talking about red with anger and frustration (fig. 36). They said, "We don't have red, because some people take HIV to be danger. You see. Even now, a mark, you see something that is red, people feel fear." They went on to tell stories about the stigmatizing effects of the public's fear of people living with HIV, and one person described how his community boarded up his

FIGURE 36. Focus group AIDS poster drawing, by HIV-positive Ghanaians (with figures colored green)

home while he was away and exiled him from their community. They chose green as the central color for their poster, not because they felt a strong commitment to green in particular but because of their preference for any "bright color." They did not select green for its resonance, as they admitted yellow or gold could work just as well. What *was* resonant was their aversion to using red. They felt strongly that the use of red in campaigns negatively affected people's perception of them. The other colors were defined by their difference, resonant simply because they were *not*-red (de Saussure 1998).

Another HIV-negative focus group linked red to the visibility of HIV when its members used the color to demarcate the transition from HIV negative to HIV positive. The poster uses four panels to create a narrative of how a fruit hawker contracts and suffers from HIV (fig. 37). In the first panel she is HIV negative, wearing a purple dress. In the second panel she wears that same purple dress while receiving a blood transfusion from tainted blood so brightly portrayed that the color jumps off the page. In the third panel she is depicted wearing a red dress and looks thinner. She grows lean and weak as she becomes increasingly ill, such that she needs the support of a man to stand up (resembling the image in figure 27 shown earlier in this chapter). For this group, the red dress served to make visible the presence of an invisible HIV infection in the absence of other characteristic signs—for example, Kaposi sarcoma lesions. In the fourth and final panel, she lies in a hospital bed, drawing on the familiar representation of people dying of AIDS from earlier storybooks, looking weak and manifesting Kaposi sarcoma lesions.

In this poster, not only is the hidden infection made visible through the color red, but other common markers of illness that AIDS organizations made available in the public sphere also appear: people living with HIV who need help walking, get thinner over time, and lie on hospital beds with their bodies covered with lesions. When I asked the focus group participants to explain what they drew, one participant explained how it was not the disease that made people lean, but the awareness that they are going to die:

PARTICIPANT 1: We've drawn someone who is lean, lying in a bed almost dying. If you don't know you have the virus, you lead your normal life. But immediately when you get tested and you learn you have the virus, you stop eating and you get lean. But so whereas you don't know, you think you are normal, you eat your normal food, you do your daily activities, your regular routine. But the moment you detect that you have the virus then you start thinking, you stop eating, you distance yourself from social activities, so the awareness makes them feel lean, but not the actual sickness. That awareness that you are going to die, it is psychological. They

FIGURE 37. Focus group AIDS poster drawing, by secondary school teachers (with woman's dress colored purple in top two panels but red in bottom two)

don't care for themselves once they learn they have HIV . . . they think, so where do I eat? So where do I take my medicine? [*Others nodded in agreement.*]

These participants continued to make a strong connection between AIDS and death, but they identified another cause for the symptom of leanness: the social and psychological effects of being HIV positive. This explanation likely comes from antistigma campaigns that raised awareness of the experiences of people living with HIV. Their discussion resembles an antistigma TV ad made by GAC. Although the ad asserted, "Life is precious," the ad's dramatic depiction of negative effects of HIV—depression and social distance—made a greater impression on Ghanaians.

This commitment to showing the "reality" of AIDS by depicting widely recognized and visible symptoms of AIDS continued with the next focus group. Much like the primary school teachers who believed most AIDS campaigns were "too mild" and thought they must warn people of the danger of death associated with contracting AIDS, this group of University of Ghana, Legon, graduates now working in the Ministries wanted to depict someone who was sick with AIDS:

PARTICIPANT 1: I think the reality of the disease is much different when you see a commercial on TV depicting someone with AIDS. It might be different when you see someone who has actually got it dying of AIDS. What I personally think is you need to see someone with actual symptoms . . . I think that is more effective.

By depicting healthy people living with HIV—often in association with these more life-affirming campaigns—AIDS organizations presented an account of the disease that seemed fictional to these Ghanaians. Rather than using actors who represented the picture of health, they wanted *real* HIV-positive people displaying *real* symptoms. "Here in Ghana there are so many people who do not understand what they are seeing. They say who is like this? We should use *real* persons. Pictures will not make the same kind of impact that real people would." As these participants drew their poster, they were frustrated by how a drawing would not have the same impact as a photograph. Later, when I showed this group a photograph of a grotesquely thin man with AIDS on his deathbed, they all responded that the photo was what they were trying to represent through drawing. In fact, this was a common response to that image among my HIV-negative focus groups. When I asked why showing someone with symptoms is more effective than showing someone healthy with HIV, one participant replied, "When I see someone who is healthy and they say it is an HIV patient, to me I think it is not true." Many Ghanaians find it hard to believe AIDS organizations when they show images of normal, "healthy" people and claim they have HIV.

The university graduates' ultimate drawing used the "before and after" structure we saw earlier. In their poster, they first drew "John" as healthy and HIV negative, and then they depicted John as thin, skeletal, bald, and living with AIDS (fig. 38). When I asked them what text should be associated with this image, one participant said, "Stop AIDS Love Life." Another followed,

FIGURE 38. Focus group AIDS poster drawing, by Ministries staff

"AIDS Is Real." This idea was quickly seconded: "We should put 'AIDS Is Real, beware.' That should be the theme . . . it should be 'AIDS Is Real.'" I asked them, "Is that the most important message? AIDS Is Real?" One participant quickly replied:

PARTICIPANT 2: People know there is something called AIDS, but they tend to believe it is for a certain kind of people. I don't know how to explain it. When I'm at home, I don't see any AIDS. So when I hear about it I think it is only for these class of people. I wouldn't think it could happen to me. Because the truth is, that is how people tend to think, even though we are all aware [of] its existence, we tend to believe we won't contract it, rather only these certain types of people.

To make AIDS more "real," they felt the need to make AIDS visible. Although their picture only makes AIDS visible by representing a skeletal image of a man with HIV, this quotation shows their desire to link AIDS to "a certain kind of people" because they, and people from their community, are not at risk. Early campaigns linked AIDS with sex workers, strangers, criminals, and immoral sexual behavior, and the Ghanaians in this focus group were still seeing AIDS as connected to particular personae. This association of HIV with "other" people from "other" places allows them to believe that their communities remain untouched by AIDS. Not seeing AIDS at home is symbolic, then, in that it allows people to maintain the illusion that their community is morally pure.

Rejecting the link between leanness, HIV, and marginalized groups, HIV-positive focus group participants sought to resist and contest the use of skeletons and depictions of lean, sick people infected with HIV to represent AIDS.

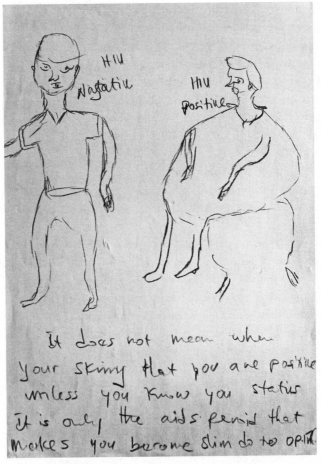

FIGURE 39. Focus group AIDS poster drawing, by HIV-positive Ghanaians

Specifically, they attempted to invert representations of the emaciated HIV-infected people by showing how obese people could also be HIV-infected (fig. 39). As they say in the poster, "It does not mean when your [*sic*] skinny that you are positive unless you know you[r] status. It is only the AIDS period that makes you become slim." In this sense, they attempt to undermine the practice of associating AIDS with people who are skinny. This could also be read as a transgressive representation that aligns "big men" with HIV. In Ghana the expression "big men" can be used to describe both large men who are wealthy enough to overindulge and men of high prestige such as traditional leaders or politicians—often the two overlap.

As I discussed earlier, images of symptomatic people living with HIV were not very visible in public; the campaigns that showed sickly AIDS patients and skeletons circulated hand-to-hand via pamphlets and storybooks rather than through mass media AIDS campaigns. The HIV-negative Ghanaians in my focus groups by and large did not personally know someone with HIV, did not "see any AIDS" in their communities, and associated HIV with "immoral" behavior and unfamiliar "others." "AIDS Is Real" slogans throughout the streetscape offer a ready-made explanation for why HIV is perpetuated: Other people don't believe AIDS is real, and so they continue to engage in "immoral" behavior. HIV-negative Ghanaians in my focus groups desperately wanted to make HIV visible to these others because visibility makes AIDS tangible. Making AIDS visible, they believed, will keep people from engaging in "immoral" behavior. This sentiment appeared in the Osu focus group, which also used the slogan "AIDS Is Real" on its poster (fig. 34).

PARTICIPANT 1: Some people still don't believe that AIDS exists. You'd be surprised that when you ask someone, they may have heard of something called AIDS, but they don't know anything about it.

TEM: But most research in Ghana says that most Ghanaians know of HIV/ AIDS, so is there a difference between knowing and believing?[18]

PARTICIPANT 1: The knowing part might be that people have heard of it before. But they haven't gotten any information . . .

PARTICIPANT 2: They don't know of anyone suffering from AIDS. For that matter some people don't believe AIDS exists. They think they are unsusceptible to AIDS.

PARTICIPANT 1: When you go to Togo you see these harlots, most of them don't believe there is AIDS. They think it is just used to scare them out of practicing their trade. And they think it only affects the poor in society because it is mostly only those kinds of people who you see dying of the virus. So they feel AIDS is so far away from them.

Ghanaians reinforce moral boundaries when they try to show that "AIDS Is Real" by depicting lean bodies, sores, and skeletons. When they claim to believe in AIDS but have no firsthand experience with it, they set themselves up as morally superior to those who refuse to believe in AIDS and engage in what they consider immoral acts, such as sex workers from Togo or poor people who sin through idleness. In addition, they believe that making AIDS visible in their posters provides a needed public service. If people don't believe AIDS is real, they must prove its existence through harsher campaigns that make plain the horrors of AIDS. Such vivid campaigns, these Ghanaians believe, will push those engaging in immoral behavior toward a more righteous path.

The issue of stigma and life also came up for this group from Osu, the only group to explicitly use the language of "life" on its poster (fig. 34). When I asked them why people should "choose life," one participant replied:

MALE PARTICIPANT 1: Well, even though it is difficult for those of us in Ghana, if all you are eating is a bowl of kenkey with shiito, with hot pepper, you still enjoy it, even though life is hard. It is better to have life and to live a poor life than having AIDS and dying a horrible death before your time. Because recently on the news, there was this lady who had AIDS and her family members could not care for her anymore, she was all weak and feeble, and couldn't do anything, and they went to drop her in the deep gutter. So mostly when you don't hear anything about AIDS it is because of the stigma. Even if I had it, I wouldn't tell people because I don't know what they are thinking about it, who they will go and tell, how they will look at me, you know?

For these participants, choosing life was not terribly life-affirming. Under the shadow of AIDS, choosing life was always placed in the context of "dying a horrible death." Choosing life reminded them of the opposite: people living with HIV being thrown out with the trash. They do not see choosing life as a choice of happiness for HIV-positive people. Rather, it is a choice of stigma and keeping oneself hidden from the world. So even when Ghanaians advocated that people "choose life," that choice was inflected with death, weakness, and stigma. If the discourse of life has taken hold for some Ghanaians, the positive imagery and valence of life-affirming campaigns have not.

The Additive Effects of Campaigns and Cultural Entropy

With the dramatic shift to life-affirming AIDS campaigns in the early years of the first decade of the twenty-first century, designers believed they could *replace* Ghanaians' negative, stigmatizing understandings of AIDS facilitated by the earliest AIDS interventions. And why wouldn't they? They had more resources allowing them to reach more people than ever before. They had adopted the best practices of campaign design that prescribed ways to make clearer, culturally sensitive, and resonant campaigns. Condoms were more widely available, ART was introduced to meet patient demand, and voluntary counseling and testing centers were publicly visible. The government publicly endorsed the work of AIDS prevention through the creation of the GAC. Designers had confidence that this new positive approach would increase prevention, testing, and treatment, while also reducing stigma.

Based on my focus group interviews with Ghanaians, I've shown that the life-affirming messages saturating the streetscape have not taken hold. Despite valiant attempts by AIDS organizations to reframe HIV in ways that affirm life, HIV-negative Ghanaians continue to represent AIDS with images of death and disease. The images they use bear a strong resemblance to early representations that made direct connections between AIDS and skeletons, coffins, the skull and crossbones, and visible markers of illness. Yet though life-affirming prevention and antistigma messages did not replace Ghanaians' strong associations with these "negative" images, they have made available discursive alternatives.

AIDS images in the public sphere provide a language, both visual and verbal, that structures meaning making about AIDS. By and large, the Ghanaians in my focus groups adhered to the institutionally available discourse and imagery of AIDS. In this sense, AIDS campaigns in Ghana are doing *something*, even if they don't work as intended. In making their posters, HIV-negative participants replicated the imagery of early campaigns and the slogans of current campaigns: skeletons, coffins, and bedridden patients paired with such taglines as "AIDS Is Real." This finding was true for HIV-positive Ghanaians as well; they acknowledged and reinforced the imagery of wasted bodies and the associations of red with danger by using their opposites to make their points. To understand the meaning of an HIV-positive "big man" or green ribbons, one must draw on the meaning of emaciated people living with HIV and red ribbons, letters, and signs that link AIDS with danger. These focus groups demonstrate how images of skeletons and sickness and the use of the color red powerfully "anchor" people's thinking on AIDS (Ghaziani and Baldassarri 2011). Clearly, the attempt to clean the slate and reframe AIDS in life-affirming, nonstigmatizing terms did not replace Ghanaians' visual associations of AIDS with death and illness.

The fact that these drawings closely resemble the scare tactics of Ghana's early response to AIDS suggests that life-affirming campaigns haven't resulted in the intended effect. Most of the focus groups raised the issue of stigma, which suggests a growing awareness of stigma and the effects on people living with HIV. However, while my HIV-positive focus groups felt the issue of stigma deeply, this topic generated debate rather than consensus in the HIV-negative focus groups. Certainly, HIV-negative Ghanaians discussing issues of stigma and the potential negative effects of the scare tactics their posters perpetuate suggests a positive step forward. The fact that they defaulted to the images of death and illness that came to mind automatically, or identified resonant ways to use red to visibly mark people living with HIV, suggests that AIDS education in Ghana has a long way to go. Although such positive slogans as "Stop AIDS Love Life" and "Life Is Precious" often emerged in focus group discussions, HIV-negative focus group participants rarely, if ever, appeared committed to such ideas. This language usually arose when the group was searching for what to say. These life-affirming ideas are institutionally supported—this is what Ghanaians are *supposed* to say about AIDS—but when the HIV-negative participants started to reflect on these catchphrases, they became uncertain about what they meant. When pressed to explain why someone should stop AIDS and love life, or even to describe what that slogan means, participants grew inarticulate and appeared to grasp at phantoms. How does "loving life" stop AIDS?

It is surprising that life-affirming campaigns have had such limited effects, considering the comparative advantages of these campaigns. Early campaigns, often produced by people untrained in communication, featured cheaply produced pamphlets and storybooks that circulated through interpersonal means such as peer education and visits to health clinics. Newer, life-affirming campaigns were designed by communications experts, used evidence-based methods, targeted specific audiences, circulated through both mass media and interpersonal means, and enjoyed far greater resources than previous campaigns. Why were these new campaign ideas unable to replace the old?

One reason is the stickiness of the scare tactics imagery. Images of skulls and crossbones grab people's attention. Photographs and drawings of wasted skeletal bodies were memorable because they were so out of the ordinary. Even though they weren't widely circulated, these concrete images of illness and locally recognizable symbols of death, danger, and warning made sense of an abstract, unfamiliar disease for Ghanaian communities. These images are more believable and grounded in everyday practice: depictions of disease symptoms are present throughout the country, and Ghanaians are used to relying on these depictions. Ghanaian herbalists, doctors outside the clinic system, and traditional healers place hand-painted signboards outside their businesses to advertise symptoms they treat and to enroll patients. In this sense, the early AIDS campaigns used representations of AIDS that were materially closer to the disease and were already embedded in local visual culture and practice.

When the game changed, moving campaigns away from scare tactics, AIDS campaign designers needed to divine ways to visually represent AIDS optimistically so as to avoid undermining their efforts. This proved to be quite a challenge due to the material constraints of representing AIDS. Positive, literal representations were few and far between. How do you make a symbol for AIDS that is grounded in the reality of the disease without showing symptoms or death? It is the invisibility of HIV to the naked eye that creates this problem. Designers could depict a virus, a rather neutral presentation, but that probably would not have resonated with the Ghanaian public. One could label a healthy-looking person as HIV positive, but many in my focus groups suggested that this strategy leads people to question whether AIDS is real.

Instead, organizations chose to represent life, often with abstract symbols such as a baby chick, with generic images of Ghanaian people in romantic relationships, or with pictures of people in their daily lives that resembled images on most ads around town.[19] In this sense, the life-affirming campaigns either seemed too different from AIDS or made AIDS seem too normal, leading my participants to complain that they were not harsh enough. Out-of-the-ordinary images such as skeletons and emaciated bodies stuck with them, while generic images did not. The hands of "Stop AIDS Love Life," "Show Compassion," and "Life Is Precious" were absent. The repeated use of hands as a symbol, though useful for conveying "stop," "compassion," and the need to "protect" life, appears disconnected from AIDS. Symbols that are decoupled from the disease and only meaningful in the world crafted by the campaign were less resonant with Ghanaians, even though many of these campaigns were supported with pretesting. One of the reasons for this incongruence is that the pretesting was biased. During pretesting, designers pitted these campaigns against other concepts that used similarly generic life-affirming imagery that was decoupled from the disease, without more-grounded alternatives. When, say, one of the three abstract, life-affirming concepts tests better, it gives designers confidence that such campaigns will work. Had more vivid images of death and illness been included in the testing, my evidence suggests that this more vivid imagery would have tested better.

In this way, the early campaigns that were based on gut instinct rather than evidence employed vivid imagery that made AIDS visible and legible for the Ghanaian public. This imagery aligned with Ghanaians' imaginings of disease, quickly becoming a shared reality for most Ghanaians in the absence of other representations. These images provoked discussion, spreading from the ground up, and became more entrenched as they spread. These first campaigns had a primacy effect, in that it appears Ghanaians remember these images better and more quickly than the more optimistic visuals that appeared later. These cultural understandings of AIDS established a stable visual language that Ghanaians used to make sense of the disease, thus anchoring their future meaning making. Ghanaians believe the "harsher" images represent the disease more effectively than the recent "mild" campaigns. The stability and cognitive centrality of early campaign images led to the cultural entropy of these later campaigns. When participants discussed the importance of living and celebrating life in the age of AIDS, they couched it in imagery and narratives of death and illness. Rather than replacing the old understandings and representations of AIDS, the new campaigns were interpreted through the lens of these old representations, destabilizing designers' intended meaning and undermining their ability to persuade.

New objects and ideas, then, add more than they replace. Designers work from an old model of culture that sees culture as coherent and cultures as mutually exclusive—to have one idea about the world is to not have another idea. This model of culture lacks empirical support. When people learn something new, they do not forget the old. Old understandings of AIDS that associate the disease with notions of death, danger, and illness seem to be working for Ghanaians. HIV-negative individuals in my focus groups appeared confident that their understandings of AIDS helped keep them safe and avoid contracting the disease. So when new, hopeful ways of making sense of the disease began to appear, people added these ideas to their cultural toolkits but lacked occasions to use the new ideas (Swidler 1986). Ghanaians have little reason to routinely deploy more-optimistic views when the old frightening imagery still works to organize their understandings of AIDS. My focus groups make clear that Ghanaians are familiar with life-affirming discourse but lack practice in using it. Such ideas are secondary to the more routinized, primary "cultured capacity" to interpret AIDS through scare tactics (Swidler 2001).

This tendency changes for people living with HIV when they get tested and realize they are infected. They seek out new ways to understand their condition, improve their self-esteem, and stabilize their identity. In so doing, they find themselves more aligned with the life-affirming antistigma messages. Whereas the HIV-negative participants embraced negative meanings first and unconvincingly drew upon life-affirming language later, my HIV-positive focus groups sought to actively counteract the lingering images of people living with HIV as sickly with images of health and the language of life. Still, these attempts to change how people think of AIDS ultimately reinforce associations of AIDS with death, danger, and illness by drawing on their opposites. In this way, they too share both negative and positive cultures of AIDS, cognitively drawing from negative images first but using more deliberate cognitive processes to bring these more positive views to the fore (DiMaggio 1997; Lizardo and Strand 2010; Vaisey 2009).

Are AIDS media campaigns effective interventions? These data suggest they are not. Until campaign designers recognize the additive nature of culture, campaigns around the world will continue to face entropy due to the discursive/emotive power of early campaigns. While Ghanaians are aware of AIDS campaign messages, the ideas promoted by health organizations seem to float on the surface, appearing in deliberation but not driving participants' drawings or their actions. Even though the ideas promoted by AIDS campaigns are backed by resource-rich institutions and circulated throughout the public sphere, Ghanaians have not moved these new ideas from their discursive to their practical consciousness (Giddens 1984; Lizardo and Strand 2010). Ghanaians' internalized understandings of AIDS view people living with HIV as skeletons, less than human, and harbingers of death. These understandings are stable meaning systems that motivate action and resist the new symbols and messages proffered by AIDS campaigns. There is a feedback effect too: if Ghanaians are to adopt this less fatalistic view of AIDS, they need opportunities to discuss such ideas and put them into practice. When a commitment to scare tactics suppresses talk of AIDS among Ghanaians and marginalizes people living with AIDS such that they are invisible, the opportunities to put new ideas into action are few and far between.

Conclusion

Throughout the book, I've emphasized examples of entropy that undermine the cultural power of campaigns. To be clear, some campaigns in Ghana certainly had cultural power. The Aganzi campaign of the Ghana Social Marketing Foundation (GSMF) changed the how Ghanaians thought about condoms. Historically, GSMF promoted a variety of subsidized condoms, under the brands of Champion, Panther, Protector, and Bazooka. All were basic yellow latex, sold cheaply, and widely available. After years of work on HIV and some success increasing condom sales, the organization's sales stagnated. GSMF relied on increasing condom sales to demonstrate success to funding agencies and therefore needed to increase market share and spread condoms to new markets.

GSMF realized that its suite of brands had reached middle- and lower-class Ghanaians but not wealthy Ghanaians. Expensive international brands aimed at wealthier Ghanaians (e.g., Durex) had been available in the Ghanaian market for some time. To "combat the influx of foreign condoms," as one advertising agency staffer suggested, GSMF researched an upmarket condom that could compete for the market share that Durex controlled. Background market research suggested that sexual performance was a primary concern of these men:

> Men wanted to have, um, sex for longer periods. [This finding] was astonishing cause the research available, the notion on the ground that men wanted to get in and out of bed as quickly as possible was wrong. Ghanaian men wanted to please their partners, and some of them couldn't.[1]

GSMF decided to invest in a condom that fulfilled men's desire for enhanced performance: Aganzi.

The Aganzi condom was unlike the other basic subsidized condoms GSMF branded. It had a chemical retardant that improved men's staying power. It used black latex to match Ghanaians' skin color, and it was also lubricated, ribbed, and mint flavored. Though Durex had begun to sell upmarket ribbed condoms in Ghana, none used black latex. GSMF believed that positioning itself as second best to Durex, with a slightly cheaper price point and vastly improved material qualities, would give GSMF a market advantage.

The development of Aganzi coincided with GSMF's serious budget woes due to shifts in foreign aid for subsidizing condoms. GSMF dismissed the idea of raising the unit cost of Champion, Panther, and Bazooka to fill the budget gap. Doing so would undercut the organization's mission by pricing middle- and low-income users out of the market. Aganzi became the solution. GSMF could use the profits from Aganzi to shore up its budget while continuing to sell its other brands at the subsidized price.

Rather than being promoted as protection against HIV or pregnancy, Aganzi was marketed through the lens of passion, pleasure, and romance. On Valentine's Day GSMF passed out gift packages of Aganzi condoms and chocolates at elite hotels in Accra. The campaign used images of orgasmic women (see figure 11 in chapter 4) and depictions of postcoital tousled bedrooms (figure 10 in chapter 4) with such taglines as "Go Wild" and "Unleash the Burning Passion within You." In light of Aganzi's novel material qualities and sexy marketing campaign, other condom brands *paled* in comparison. As one staff member at Origin8 told me, "Those who've experienced Aganzi hardly use any other cause it's more of a one-of-a-kind condom. There's no other condom that operates the same, with the same feel and everything."[2]

Despite the limited marketing budget, the Aganzi marketing worked: "It sold like hot cake. I'm not sure about the figures but it was astounding. People kept buying and buying and buying and stocking it because it's a symbol of a good night ahead."[3] Sales of Aganzi exceeded expectations, meeting GSMF's goal of condom promotion. Rather than following the typical health communication strategies of attempting to increase people's perceived risk, Aganzi resonated with people's preexisting desire for exciting sex and fear of sexual inadequacy. Aganzi was successfully understood by users to symbolize sexual pleasure and performance, resisting entropy at the object level. The trouble is, it may have worked too well.

Aganzi increased entropy in the larger cultural system, shifting the meaning of other condoms relative to Aganzi's performance-enhancing qualities. Now, to pull out a basic yellow latex condom, when a sleek black condom with ribbing, lubrication, and flavor exists on the market, indicates to your partner that you *do not* care about her pleasure.[4] The choice between condom brands was no longer between functional equivalents. Aganzi created a hier-archical status system in the market between condoms that enhanced sexual performance and condoms that did not. It is important to note that Aganzi's capacity to shift the field of meanings also extended to less-wealthy Ghanaians who were the target audience for the old subsidized brands. In 2008 when I asked middle-class Ghanaian men which condoms they preferred, those who used condoms preferred Aganzi, whereas Champion had been the most com-mon response five years prior. When asked what their second-choice condom would be, many said there was no equal. Rather than settle for Champion or Panther, some men reported that they would try forgoing condoms altogether if they were short on cash or found Aganzi was sold out at the pharmacy. The appearance of Aganzi also facilitated rumors that some condoms couldn't be trusted. Some people now said that Champion wasn't reliable. Condoms such as Champion that once got the job done were no longer considered up to the task.

Initially intended to be profitable so as to subsidize sales of budget-friendly condoms, Aganzi's success ironically came at the expense of consistent con-dom use among the Champion set, thereby undermining the organization's primary mission. Campaigns, condom brands, and cultural objects are not independent. The case of Aganzi demonstrates how crucial it is to consider how microlevel interpretive arrangements and field-level ecosystems are co-constitutive (Bourdieu 1993). As meanings stabilize around one object, new practices and ways of thinking enter into the system and ultimately destabi-lize other objects. Firsthand experience with a new object—a condom unlike any other—extended the range of condoms' meanings for Ghanaians beyond symbolizing risk and mistrust to signifying confidence and pleasure. As men reoriented themselves around Aganzi, the broader meaning system around condoms destabilized. This new preference for expensive performance en-hancement in turn creates new challenges for AIDS organizations that need to reach a population of Ghanaians who cannot afford Aganzi. Attention to cultural entropy, then, orients us to think ecologically across objects within the field, highlighting how moments of stability are simultaneously moments of instability.

Whereas most of the cases of cultural entropy I have presented suggest that entropy reduces the potential power of a cultural object, I have also come across occasions when entropy enhances objects' power. In some cases, en-tropy increases the capacity of an object to have the *desired* effect, just not via the path designers intended. The primary case of this is when hairdressers and seamstresses who had been trained as peer educators took condom pro-motion posters into their own bedrooms. In other cases, such as the female condom bangle bracelets, an object becomes energized by unintended uses, is established as a cultural practice and spreads, and stabilizes in ways that undermine institutional efforts. This is power, just not power aligned with an organization's intentions.

When discussing entropy, sculptor Robert Smithson once remarked, "All predictions tend to be wrong . . . planning and chance almost seem to be the same thing" (1996, 304). The same could be said for AIDS media campaigns: more planning, more rigorous standards, more community involvement in the design process, more money, all without predictable results. Throughout this book I have demonstrated the myriad ways AIDS campaigns undergo a process of cultural entropy at every stage of their life course. When best practices and campaign objects travel from one arrangement to another, opportunities for entropy multiply as stability established in one arrangement is vulnerable to misinterpretation, misuse, or creative appropriation in another. More than just the shifting between arrangements, arrangements themselves can never be perfectly stable. More likely than not, entropy will emerge in any arrangement.

At the end of a lengthy design process, campaign designers feel confident that the intended meanings of their campaign will be clear, resonant, and culturally relevant for the target audience. They believe that by following best practices they have stripped away the possibility that audiences will interpret the message in alternative ways. Designers' faith in these practices leads them to miss how their own practices undermine their communication goals. Best practices give designers a static view of culture that camouflages dynamic, complex cultural patterns out there in the world: stakeholders change their minds after they back a campaign, audiences get distracted, campaign objects decay, cultural practices displace campaigns and audiences from the intended sites of reception, alternative meanings of the color red overshadow life-affirming messages, claims of a local cure for AIDS cast doubt on "official" messages, and on and on. Truly, planning and chance "almost seem to be the same thing." Stability is a temporary state (and often a fiction) that demands a good deal of cultural work—like routines and rituals—to shore up meaning among a small group of committed designers and stakeholders. As soon as campaigns leave these seemingly stable arrangements, enter into the messiness of urban life, and meet the fractured, multiple cultural capacities of Ghanaian audiences, intended meanings and uses fall victim to entropy.

All of this entropy adds up. Complex and contradictory understandings of AIDS, bolstered by the cultural landscape, create ambiguity for the public. Design practices that purport to make resonant AIDS campaigns do not. These diluted campaigns meet the material reality of urban life, which pushes campaigns out of the intended sites of reception or decays them to the point of misinterpretation or disregard, further weakening their impact. Finally, when audiences interact with these campaigns, they interpret new messages through the lens of the old messages the campaigns were designed to replace. That Ghanaians are very familiar with these new campaigns— scoring highly on indicators of reach and recall—conceals the cultural entropy under the surface. Dig a little deeper and it becomes clear that these campaigns minimally influence how Ghanaians understand AIDS or act in response to the crisis.

Cultural Entropy and the Limited Effects of Persuasion Projects

Theorizing cultural entropy is crucially important as these instrumental attempts to control meaning are on the rise. We've seen a dramatic growth in systematic attempts to shape and control how people understand the world and act in it, for both good and ill: advertising to sell products, propaganda to dehumanize enemies, political campaigns to influence how people should think about an issue, or health campaigns that hope to reduce the spread of deadly diseases. These efforts are increasingly sophisticated, rigorous, and evidence-based. Early sociologists had a great concern for the antidemocratic effects of these media, believing they had the power to align the masses and facilitate the exploitation of people (Lasswell 1938; Adorno 2001). As institutions become more rational in their approach to controlling meaning, one might expect the worst. Hegemonic power combined with scientific approaches to communication should lead to institutions' increasing capacity to control populations through the media.

Yet, as these persuasion industries attempt to control us, their media are increasingly *mediated* and open to disruption—there is more entropy in the system. While the incidence of instrumental communication is on the rise, the *effects* of instrumental communication appear to be in decline: as time goes on, it takes more and more money to have the same effects (Sethuraman, Telles, and Briesch 2011). The exponential expansion of media industries and platforms creates more clutter and diminishes the possibility of having a "monopoly" over a message (Lazarsfeld and Merton 1948). Audiences have more control over how media circulate than ever before, making sites of reception harder to manage and making it difficult to channel the energy invested in campaign objects along intended paths.

Globalization has led to increased opportunities for innovation because the mediascape has never been so diverse with cultural goods and ideas (Appadurai 1996). Changes in available media alter the material infrastructure of cities, shaping the "physical ambiance" of urban locales and establishing new networks of circulation and spaces for creativity (Larkin 2008). Populations grow increasingly heterogeneous, meaning that campaigns reach beyond the target audience, and other cultural groups increasingly influence target audiences, making it difficult to treat audiences as coherent. Increasing mediation, alongside the growing cultural complexity of the global urban metropolis, leaves campaigns open to entropy (Hannerz 1992). Cultural entropy at the field level, then, helps extend explanations for limited media effects.[5]

Instrumental attempts to use culture and media to shape behavior face increasing challenges, and not just in the developing world. A recent evaluation of provaccination messages in the United States found that images of sick children actually *increased* parents' expressed belief in a link between vaccination and autism (Nyhan et al. 2014). A recent "#IAmARepublican" campaign designed to diversify the Republican Party and make it more relatable was hijacked on Twitter and turned to mockery (Castillo 2014). A 1998 antidrug campaign distributed pencils emblazoned from tip to eraser with "TOO COOL TO DO DRUGS." When the pencil was sharpened, the message became the prodrug slogan "COOL TO DO DRUGS," then "DO DRUGS," and finally just "DRUGS" (Hepburn 2014). Cultural entropy helps us understand why effective campaigns are rare and why the project of using culture instrumentally may be doomed from the start. Extending cultural entropy to recent scholarship on instrumental communication suggests the concept has broad relevance to diverse persuasion projects.

Countries attempt to use culture instrumentally to increase tourism, entice foreign businesses, or encourage patriotism through marketing techniques. In the enviable *Branding the Nation*, communications scholar Melissa Aronczyk interviewed brand consultants who expressed confidence in their ability to reshape the meaning of place through the science of marketing. After put into action, however, these branding efforts proved less effective than expected. As Aronczyk observes, "when brands are seen *not* to work . . . this is deemed a fault of application rather than a fault of logic . . . in this view nothing is wrong with the principles or practice of nation branding" (2013, 167). Cultural entropy is exactly what brand marketers miss, having "misrecognized the visionary and potent ability of brands." When consultants branded Ireland around its economic viability and then the economy crashed, one consultant suggested Irish people no longer believed in the new identity. Brand managers viewed this as a problem with investing too strongly in an economic rather than a cultural frame: "the Irish have found that what they are telling themselves about themselves is not true, or is no longer true" (Aronczyk 2013, 168). Rather than viewing this disruption as a consequence of cultural entropy, in which shifting external conditions destabilize a once stable message, brand managers view it as a problem of choosing the wrong frame—a problem which could have been foreseen with more or better advance planning. Similarly, sociologist Lauren Rivera (2008) shows how attempts by Croatia to market itself as a tourist destination were actively rejected by the majority of her Croatian interviewees, undermining the ability for the state to have "narrative control." Cultural entropy suggests the problem isn't the choice of frame—most frames will face disruption. Instead, the problem is in the belief that they could stabilize the meaning of *nation* in the first place.

Political activists also frequently attempt to harness culture to achieve their goals. Sociologist Sarah Sobieraj's excellent book *Soundbitten* (2011), on activist groups' attempts to secure media coverage, similarly implies the importance of cultural entropy. Social movements use protest as a means to garner media attention and get their message out. Movement organizations have become increasingly rational in their attempts to control their message by investing in preprotest training for activists. Organizations teach their activists how to stay "on message" through short, rehearsed sound bites that work within TV news formats and how to appear reasonable so as to make their message seem legitimate. Trained participants carried posters and wore costumes that were designed to attract attention. Sobieraj finds that the energy invested in these efforts is wasted. When activists implemented these strategies in new interpretive arrangements with reporters, communication broke down. Attempts to appear legitimate and professional undercut reporters' interest in covering authentic events. Journalists didn't want to write about an event that was "designed." Sobieraj observed, "Failure was so common that activists proceeded to define even the most meager coverage as an accomplishment" (105). Some few activists realized journalists wanted something more authentic, and to adapt to changing conditions, they began "rehearsing spontaneity" with their protest participants (93)! In response, journalists become more skeptical of these performances, going out of their way to seek out authenticity. To ensure that they reported on authentic events and people, journalists interviewed informants who were marginal to the organization. Sampling from the fringe led to news reports, quotes, and images that misrepresented the organization and its issues, undermining activists' goal of using the media to communicate their intended message to a broader audience. Sobieraj suggests the problem wasn't that "they didn't conform to the implicit rules of newsmaking, but because they were following the wrong rules" (83). I posit an alternative explanation based on cultural entropy. Instead of following the wrong rules—a view that treats the rules as static—the rules may be constantly shifting. As activists adopt more instrumental strategies, reporters become increasingly skeptical, requiring new strategies to meet the new rules. A processual account that takes a longer view may reveal additional field-level mechanisms that explain these failures.

Taken at the object level, the instability of arrangements offers new material mechanisms that help explain limited effects. The relative independence of material and symbolic qualities of objects enable them to take on a life of their own, encouraging unintended meanings and uses that divert campaign energy away from intended goals. When these alternatives spread, they sometimes stabilize in ways that directly undermine a campaign's capacity to work. This finding suggests new avenues of research that move beyond coding the content of messages for frames or engaging in semiotic deconstruction, instead considering the role of materiality in meaning making.

It is easy to assume that materiality matters more in the developing world, where harsher conditions and fewer resources lead to poorly made objects. Yet media campaigns made in the United States and Europe are no less material than campaigns in developing countries. Campaigns in wealthy industrial countries may be shiny and slick, but these are material qualities too. If anything, intense competition over the symbolic content of advertising and branding in wealthy nations, coupled with the taken-for-granted nature of infrastructure there, may make those campaigns more vulnerable to unintended material disruptions.

In another example of activists attempting to spread their message through the media, my research on AIDS campaigns by the AIDS Coalition to Unleash Power (ACT UP) in the United States suggests that it faced cultural entropy through material mechanisms. ACT UP used vibrant protest art that both attracted the attention of reporters and could communicate the organization's message when reprinted in newspapers. ACT UP graphic artists realized that effective visual techniques for drawing attention in public might not work when reprinted. One ACT UP New York graphic designer noted that the organization's dramatic posters with red ink on a black background turned all black when reprinted in black-and-white, obscuring ACT UP's message and subverting its goals.[6] The material *translation* of the image from poster to newspaper photograph rendered it illegible. Cultural entropy due to material mechanisms happens all the time. A recent J. C. Penney company billboard advertised a teakettle that *resembled* Hitler when you squinted at it (though, troublingly, that led the teakettle to sell out overnight; Thompson 2013). A lighted Elmhurst Emergency and Trauma Center sign had the bulbs in the *E* and *S* of the word *Elmhurst* burn out, making "Elmhurst" ironically read "lmhur t"—or "I'm hurt" (Lee 2009). Some of these cases of entropy are more devastating than others. Future research on cultural entropy should evaluate how widespread and damaging cultural entropy is to organizational efforts by assessing the degree, rate, and scale of entropy.

Organizations, Isomorphism, and Failure

Attention to cultural entropy reveals how organizational practices undermine their own goals. Because the curtain is so rarely pulled back to reveal how institutional practices operate on the ground, public-health practitioners and scholars give these practices too much credence. AIDS organizations' convergence around best practices follows the now familiar institutionalist account of isomorphic convergence. According to this account, organizations go about a process of adopting the same procedures and standards as other organizations. This convergence was meant to reduce public confusion about AIDS by making clearer, more persuasive campaigns, but ultimately it had the opposite effect. Rather than aligning the public's understanding of HIV with AIDS organizations' intentions, systematizing the design process led to ineffectual campaigns that cost more and were easily ignored. Organizations fetishized the design process, focusing on the means rather than the ends and forgoing evaluations, which decreased their capacity to adapt after the campaign's launch.

Additionally, convergence around best practices led to opportunities for divergence in implementation.[7] After best practices became the currency of accountability, organizations competed over the kinds and quality of data they collected to differentiate themselves from others in the field. This competition led organizations to enact best practices differently, creating different styles of campaigns. Overinvestment in securing multisectoral support then put best practices in conflict, resulting in weaker campaigns that ultimately lacked the support designers thought they secured. Paradoxically, then, routinized design that appeared to permit the navigation of complex cultural terrain instead created opportunities for entropy. These insights call attention to the limited capacity of institutions to create standard systems that produce messages with stable interpretations.[8] The ability to control culture, then, is more an appearance to keep up than an actual organizational capacity.

The concept of cultural entropy also engages recent work on accidents and organizational failure. Like the cases of cultural entropy I presented, catastrophic failures are difficult to predict. A growing literature offers social mechanisms for technological accidents, from the *Challenger* space shuttle to the Three Mile Island nuclear power plant. Such technological failures are surprising because society has so much confidence in the abilities of engineers to know complex systems and control them. Sociologist Diane Vaughan's classic study of the 1986 *Challenger* disaster identifies organizational culture as a mechanism. NASA established a culture of acceptable risk and false confidence that led to the *Challenger*'s O-ring failure (Vaughan 1996). In this sense, the failure was knowable and the organizational standards and routines led personnel to miss it. This is similar to the overconfidence and blind spots created by best-practice documents in the organizational culture of AIDS organizations. Through entropy, organizational practices orient both NASA workers and campaign designers away from evaluations that might reveal misinterpretations and misuses.

More recent approaches identify mechanisms for failure outside the organization. Some unpredictable accidents are epistemic (Downer 2011). Like Merton's unintended consequences, these accidents are problems of knowledge, errors emerging from "unknown unknowns" rather than from organizational culture. According to Downer, aircraft engineers cannot test materials under every condition (e.g., the salty sea air of Hawaii) for the expected length of use, and so their understanding of materials is necessarily simplified. Given this simplified knowledge, planes can tear apart despite good maintenance routines. Although AIDS organizations collect a great deal of information about audiences, that information is necessarily incomplete. Additionally, AIDS organizations do not consider or cannot manage other sources of entropy, such as the materiality of objects or the complexity of settings. However, organizations can learn from epistemic accidents, gathering more information and establishing new routines to reduce the likelihood of failure or miscommunication.

By comparison, Charles Perrow's "normal accidents" occur due to unexpected irregularities that emerge in dynamic, complex systems.[9] Whereas myopic organizational cultures and problems of limited knowledge certainly encourage cultural entropy, the cases of failure I observed more often resembled normal accidents. Such catastrophes are inevitable, though rare, and often emerge from small, seemingly insignificant failures that compound and cascade into bigger problems. Normal accidents are unlikely to recur and are therefore difficult to prevent with new routines or knowledge. If technical systems are complex, cultural systems are that much more so because they lack the systemic controls that reduce the likelihood of accidents to rarities. The behavior of aluminum or uranium is more patterned and predictable than that of people with their inherent erraticism and creativity. Add to that the endogenous instability of interpretive arrangements, in which objects, people, and settings interact. Whereas normal accidents are always possible but rare, the misinterpretation and misuse of objects due to cultural entropy are likely, and—in the long run—likely unavoidable. A rare normal accident can easily spread as a cultural practice: who could have foreseen condom bracelets, let alone expected the diffusion of the practice?

If these scholars develop a "sociology of mistakes," this book starts work on a sociology of misinterpretation (Vaughan 1996). Theorizing misinterpretation and cultural entropy has direct relevance to organizational theory. Sociologists argue that certain motivations—for example, profit, efficiency, legitimacy—shape organizational behavior. Research on disaster has added avoidance of catastrophic error. I'd like to add cultural entropy to this list. Even if organizations have yet to recognize the full extent of cultural entropy, the routines and standards they impose on the design process attempt to limit it. The rise of public relations and marketing departments suggests just how invested organizations are in clear communication. Organizations of every stripe need to communicate to the public, and communication failures have serious consequences for the survival of the organization.

Implications for Health Communication

Best practices of campaign design are built on the assumption that designers can create media objects with stable meanings by refining their message through iterations of evidence-based design and obtaining the support of cultural stakeholders. The cases of cultural entropy I presented call this assumption into question. The institutional constraints placed on campaign designers through best-practice reports and the pressure to demonstrate accountability undermine organizations' capacity to spot entropy and to react and respond to it. Campaigns' perceived stability is a temporary facade, a brief moment at the end of a long design process when, in a controlled environment, an object's meaning appears coherent with great potential to inspire change.

A key implication of the argument laid out in this book is that health communication science will never eliminate entropy and create consistently effective campaigns by following best practices. The dynamism of interpretive arrangements suggests that campaigns will always be subject to cultural entropy. Cultural practice and context powerfully shape meaning *after* designers launch their campaigns, regardless of the techniques used to refine and control the meaning of their message before the launch. By shifting the focus away from developing best practices to the realities of cultural entropy, I suggest that the premise (and promise) of controlling populations' sexuality through methodically designed media campaigns is largely unfounded.

The consequences of this commitment to best practices are not limited to restrained creativity and the diverting of resources from evaluation toward design processes and pretesting. At their core, these best practices orient organizations toward eliminating the possibility of communication breakdown. Message consistency and clarity are paramount. The more that organizations invest in, and fetishize, the design process, the more the returns on those investments diminish and the less they are able to manage entropy at later stages of the campaign's life course. Every additional dollar spent on the best practices of pretesting or securing support goes less far because the visible sources of entropy are effectively controlled for while hidden, unanticipated, and largely unpredictable sources of entropy go unrevealed.

It is difficult to predict which campaigns will persuade and which will not, which will succumb to entropy and which can resist. Best practices serve a legitimating function, improving the likelihood for success only to a limited degree. As I've shown, best practices encourage designers to spend months developing a single campaign that aligns stakeholders around a single message. This strategy places organization's eggs (resources) in a single basket, making the effects of entropy more devastating—a minor but widespread disruption of their message may cripple months of effort.

I make a radical proposal. Rather than resist entropy by crafting increasingly rigorous and demanding best practices, organizations might instead *accept the likelihood* of cultural entropy. This proposal challenges designers' conventional wisdom that a single, carefully crafted and tested campaign with multisectoral support is preferable. Instead, organizations could launch multiple, distinct campaign ideas at once, spending less money and time on any one design in advance. This approach allows organizations to invest resources in following these minicampaigns, observing how people respond and directing additional resources to the campaigns that have cultural power, or harnessing patterns of entropy that appear productive. If organizations observed how campaign objects work in everyday life, tracing how campaigns travel down dark alleyways or take a shortcut to their destination, they would gain better insight into local culture than a Knowledge, Attitude, and Practice (KAP) survey or focus group sequestered from the real world could ever provide.

Making multiple campaigns would also free designers from the demands of coordinating stakeholders and securing buy-in around a single message. Getting all parties to agree on a campaign message eliminates dynamic and original campaigns from consideration, leading organizations to settle on mundane campaigns that satisfy the lowest common denominator, perhaps at the expense of persuasiveness. This alternative approach allows designers to try out contradictory messages, controversial imagery, or unconventional tactics that might have more cultural power.[10] In this sense, organizations should minimize (though not eliminate) best practices of design in favor of more freedom to test more innovative campaigns in the public sphere. Given the likelihood of cultural entropy, a fleet-footed, experimental design phase that seeks out entropy is preferable to ill-informed attempts to predict in advance what will stabilize and efforts to align stakeholders that weaken the persuasive potential of a campaign.

When planning and chance are the same thing, it is better to spend less effort planning and instead observe what works in practice. Future conditions are too time-consuming or expensive to predict, so being *reactive* is more effective and efficient than being *proactive*. I don't mean to suggest that this approach will make campaigns immune to entropy. Even if an organization finds one campaign strategy that resists entropy more than others, that campaign is still susceptible to entropy. In fact, its success will likely increase its circulation, which will likely increase its openness to entropy. Nonetheless, embracing entropy is a more efficient approach that may lead to greater rates of success. Rather than waste time debating which lure might be perfect for catching fish, drop multiple lines into the water and then use more of whichever lure actually gets the fish to bite.

Rethinking Culture and Communication

Cultural entropy offers a lens through which to understand the dynamic ebb and flow of meaning and objects. The concept of cultural entropy makes visible moments of contingency and novelty that are usually hidden or taken for granted as interpretive interactions unfold over time and space. Cultural entropy is often patterned and widespread, even as the paths of entropy are difficult to predict. This perspective contrasts with views that treat culture as coherent and static, with objects as central to this stabilization. Such views overemphasize situations in which culture works, giving the false impression that culture works more often than not. Static views of culture offer a model of culture's relationship to action that does not map onto the unpredictable ways people interpret and use AIDS campaigns.

People and organizations send objects into the world, determined to shape belief and behavior in ways that suit their interests. In so doing, they distribute their agency, their *will* (Gell 1998). People, like health communicators, believe they can stabilize meaning in objects, giving their message durability and the capacity to spread beyond their own limited reach, powerfully changing belief and behavior accordingly. In so doing, they assume that their intended meanings are knowable and that others will try to understand those intentions.[11] They believe that, first, culture is widely shared, relatively coherent, and controllable; second, aligning messages with culture will shape belief and behavior; and third, objects are neutral media through which to spread these messages.

These assumptions are misplaced, especially when it comes to objects. To say that culture is shared is not to say culture is stable. Whereas the sharing of meaning can happen only through objects, where ideas are externalized into material form, objects communicate ideas imperfectly and only partially stabilize meaning. Instead, objects communicate meaning in interpretive arrangements of people and settings, each with symbolic and material qualities. The qualities and connections within particular arrangements lead objects to afford a number of meanings and uses, from which people select one or more. In this way, the dynamism inherent in arrangements puts intended meanings at risk. Alternatives always exist, which people can call forth at any time. This openness is limited, though, bound by the character of the arrangement and further constrained when objects are incorporated into routine or ritual. In this way, cultural entropy is unlike deconstructionist and postmodern approaches that look to elaborate the possible meaning of texts; elaboration that sometimes implies an unlimited openness. A key point here is that my theory of cultural entropy also breaks from postmodern approaches that promote the semiotic or linguistic notion of culture as primarily composed of arbitrary symbols. I take an empirically—and *materially*—grounded approach that reveals what meanings and uses actually emerge in interpretive arrangements, identifying the mechanisms of their emergence.

Surprisingly, cultural entropy happens even when the audience *wants* to understand the intended meaning, and not only on those occasions when people take "negotiated" or "oppositional" stances and intentionally co-opt or resist messages through "poaching," "*détournement*," and "culture jamming."[12] Unlike these situations of tactical resistance, I find misinterpretations and misuses of campaign objects even though Ghanaians want to do something about AIDS. For the people using objects to communicate, then, these accidental disruptions corrupt the intended meanings embedded in objects and divert those objects from their paths of travel, leaving them open to alternative meanings and uses in new contexts. The energy invested in these campaigns dissipates and diverges.

Sociologists, too, envision too much cultural stability. As I've already argued, this is especially true for sociologists taking an audience-based approach, who often attribute too much stability to cultural groups and social position. For these scholars, the meaning of an object is relatively stable within cultural groups but destabilizes when moving across groups. Even fields that acknowledge instability, such as science and technology studies (STS) and actor-network theory (ANT), focus their efforts on explaining stability, theorizing objects as central to the accomplishment of stability.[13] Although objects certainly play an important role in stabilization, these literatures overstate objects' capacity as a stabilizing force and undertheorize how objects just as easily facilitate the destabilization of meaning and practice. The study of cultural entropy tackles this question of instability head on.

These theories tend to treat objects and people as unidirectional, as if their presence in a network of associations is all that is necessary to produce consistent action. In this formulation, instability comes from new actors entering the network and introducing new problems to be solved. Their central mechanism for the generation of instability postulated by these analysts consists of shifts within and across arrangements. Cultural entropy contributes to this literature by suggesting ways to analyze instabilities in consistent arrangements. The different "actors" in any arrangement are dynamic and multifarious, rather than static and coherent.[14] Thus instability is inherent in arrangements, such that objects are both symbolic and material, people are embodied and analytic, and settings provide meaningful context as well as physical constraints. As a result, even if the assembled actants in an arrangement have not changed, the arrangement is still open to instability and cultural entropy.

I have argued that mechanisms of entropy emerge in the openness of arrangements, with particular attention to how much "room to maneuver" there is in any arrangement (de Certeau 1984, xvii). When each object as treated as essentially *the same*, rather than viewed in actual arrangements, a cultural object appears more stable: if it worked in one arrangement, it should work in others. Following the same object across multiple arrangements—best-practice reports and campaign objects, in my case—makes visible the varieties of meanings and uses people can attribute to it. The same billboard can mean different things over time even if the arrangement doesn't change: it can decay, or audiences may interpret it through a new lens.

The cases I presented show the value of distinguishing between identical campaign objects as they circulate through the public sphere. By analyzing objects in situ, I am able to identify the dynamism of every arrangement and then trace the trajectories of objects as they "unfold" and "disperse" through new arrangements (Knorr Cetina 2001). Even if the object does not change, every setting and every audience is dynamic. Nonetheless, as I have shown, objects do change due to their materiality: red ribbons turn pink, and then white, under the sun. In this way, every arrangement has enough wiggle room to permit new and unpredictable interpretations and uses.

Pushing beyond the well-established field of research on the diffusion of innovations that treats every object or practice as the same, a cultural entropy approach considers how people *innovate what is diffused* (Rogers 2003). It attends to the varieties of "enunciation" and the unintended appropriation of objects with attention to how those alternatives circulate and either stabilize or face further entropy. Seen this way, culture is dynamic and tends toward instability; instrumental attempts to channel culture face real challenges in crafting meanings, embedding those meanings into objects and then directing their flow.

Most studies of meaning from cultural sociology assume that people interpret and use cultural objects under ideal conditions. In this book I've taken a different approach by attending to the act of meaning making in the imperfect, real-life, material conditions of specific interactions. We've now come full "diamond," demonstrating how campaign objects respond to conditions in the social world and then change that world through processes of production, circulation, and reception, which in turn reconfigure the social world (Griswold 1986). In writing this "biography" of AIDS campaigns in Accra, I have shown how each life stage of campaigns exacerbates cultural entropy in unique ways (Kopytoff 1986). Zeroing in on the social world, the production and design, circulation, and reception of campaign objects revealed various mechanisms of cultural entropy that subverted AIDS organizations' goals of ordering meaning and behavior around HIV.

I produced a cultural topography of the social world of Accra that suggests that the urban setting's rather unstable, often contradictory, and always *ambiguous landscape* creates the demand for AIDS campaigns while it also opens those campaigns up to cultural entropy. Ghanaians concurrently believe in scientific understandings of AIDS and faith healing and the role of witchcraft in spreading the disease. *Convergence* in the commitment to best practices but *divergence* in their enactment led to a process of production that stifled creativity while also undermining designers' commitment to potentially resonant campaign concepts. Campaigns created in a relatively stable arrangement of designers, focus groups, survey data, and cultural stakeholders then met the instability of everyday life. These campaigns faced unpredictable interactions with cultural practices and spatial arrangements as they circulated, highlighting how communication through objects is often contingent on *materiality*.[15] The meanings and uses of objects change as objects (billboards) decay and people move objects (posters) to unintended locations.

As I have argued, reception studies tend to overemphasize audience-based explanations for polyvocality, suggesting that people interpret the world through membership in particular social groups (e.g., nations, genders, ethnicities). The *field of competing objects* introduces an additional source of entropy. The stabilized symbolic associations made available by earlier campaigns cognitively structure how audiences make sense of the disease, above and beyond group membership. Although HIV-positive Ghanaians may represent AIDS differently than HIV-negative participants do in focus groups, their understandings of HIV are still anchored in the shared symbols and discourse of earlier campaigns. For Ghanaians, these stabilized understandings of AIDS made it difficult to switch from scare tactics to buoyant life-affirming campaigns. AIDS campaigns, then, created "established languages" for Ghanaians by giving people images and a discourse through which to make sense of HIV (de Certeau 1984). The earliest campaigns had a long "referential afterlife," leading Ghanaians to interpret new life-affirming campaigns through images of death and illness, corrupting the intended meanings of these later campaigns (Fine and McDonnell 2007; Goffman 1981).

Cultural entropy makes another major contribution to reception theory by demonstrating just what is at stake in polyvocality. The cost of alternative interpretations is too often unaccounted for in reception studies. This omission may be a function of the choice of cases, usually art objects in which artistic intention was largely unknowable and where multiple contradictory interpretations were valued. In these studies, what mattered was interpretation, not intention. Cultural entropy brings intention back in. It matters whether an object effectively communicates its intended message because people and organizations rely on objects as tools of power (Mukerji 2010). Tracing whether a campaign produced by an AIDS organization, political candidate, activist group, ad agency, or government successfully communicates its message, persuades its audience, and ultimately changes that audience's beliefs and behavior is crucial in understanding the relationship between culture and power.

Finally, the reality of cultural entropy raises questions the about the means-ends, purposive models of action that inform these communication efforts. If AIDS organizations can capture people's "culture," or "attitudes," or "behavior," they can know why people behave the way they do and harness culture to achieve their goals. If culture or attitudes influence meaning making and action, aligning their campaign messages with an audience's culture or attitudes should result in changes in behavior. These abstractions—that "culture" or attitudes cause people to behave in patterned ways—paper over what people actually do, how they experience the world and choose paths of action within in it. It misses the flow of intention and result, the way objects push back and change course. A focus on cultural entropy considers exactly these questions, offering a more pragmatist account that grounds explanation in what people actually do with objects, how they make meaning, and how objects establish and reify paths of action.[16] By drawing on metaphors of energy, tracing flows of intention and action, and keeping my eyes open to contingency, surprise, failure, and innovation, culture appears exceptionally dynamic.

This power and unpredictability of the everyday to induce entropy certainly frustrates those attempting to impose order on everyday life. Even as entropy undermines modern interventions, one should not be too quick to dig in and resist its influence. Many of the moments of cultural entropy I witnessed offered new and positive possibilities for accomplishing AIDS organizations' goals. Female condoms could be promoted as both protective and then fashionable as bracelets. Designers could produce "bedroom posters" intended to facilitate condom negotiations. By recognizing people's association of red ribbons with funerals, AIDS organizations could harness this connection to help make AIDS deaths more visible and accepted. The solutions to social problems can appear just as easily through happy accidents as through careful research. New possibilities open up when one attends to these tiny innovations, rather than getting stuck in ineffectual practices and generic campaigns. Trusting in the creativity of the everyday may point a way forward, a way emerging from the mētis of local cultural knowledge and practice. Seeing, now, the potential energy of misinterpretation and the inventiveness of mistaken uses, I hope we can embrace the entropy.

Methodological Appendix:
Social Iconography

To measure cultural entropy, I developed what I call a *social iconography* of AIDS media campaigns. A social iconography is a study of the social practices, interactions, and contexts around visual symbols. Typical iconographic studies analyze only the content and form of visual culture, with some historical considerations; in contrast, this project seeks to understand how people interact with images in practice, attending to how people use and interpret those images in context. This focus on how images work in situ, for the people who interact with them, differentiates this study from more traditional iconographic studies of AIDS imagery that focus on the semiotics of AIDS representations (Crimp and Rolston 1990; Patton 1990; Gilman 1988; Sturken 1997; Treichler 1999). Such studies deconstruct the symbolic content of AIDS prevention advertisements and protest art without treating them as objects that audiences use and interpret in everyday life. My interest is in how people interpret and use AIDS images, above and beyond a semiotic analysis of their symbolic content.[1] To understand entropy, we need to treat objects as instances of "agency, intention, causation, result, and transformation," not just semiotic codes to be decoded.[2] Treating cultural objects as objects enabled me to demonstrate how meanings made in context mediate the effectiveness of AIDS campaigns.

In creating a social iconography, I addressed how meaning is made at every step of the communication process: from the production of campaigns by international AIDS nongovernmental organizations (NGOs) and Ghanaian state-run organizations, to the circulation of these media through public space, to the interpretation of campaigns by local audiences.[3] By taking a "biographical approach" that follows interactions with an object across its life course, I can better capture producers' intentions and subsequent divergences

(Kopytoff 1986). Thus far, I've been careful to define moments of entropy *in relation to the intentions* of AIDS campaign designers.[4] Cultural entropy is most visible when comparing the effects an object engenders during the audience's interaction with it to the meanings and uses creators intended for that object. Entropy is most easily measured when—as in public-health campaigns or advertising—people employ cultural objects to achieve recognizable ends.[5] In such cases, scholars can nail down the intentions of the organizations producing cultural objects.[6]

By following this communication process from start to finish, I identified sources of cultural entropy at both the production and reception stages. First, I show the ways that organizations' attempts to control and contain understandings of AIDS by following a rational, evidence-based approach to campaign design actually undermine their goals. Second, I demonstrate how the designers' systematic alignment of campaigns with local audiences' cultural knowledge and practices ultimately fractures when interacting with everyday context and cultural practice.

Throughout this research I adopted a mixed-method approach that enabled me to assess how the production, circulation, and reception of AIDS campaigns shaped cultural power and entropy. These methods are also unusual, though not unheard of, for research on cultural objects. Most work on meaning making and cultural objects typically studies only one dimension (e.g., the production of culture) and often relies on a single data source such as critical reviews or focus groups.

Assessing Campaign Production and Producers' Intentions

To assess the practices that AIDS campaign producers used to enhance the cultural power of their campaigns and to identify these producers' intentions, I interviewed the campaign design staff of AIDS organizations and the advertising firms with which they often worked. I also engaged in ethnographic observation of the production of Ghana's recent national antistigma campaign to understand how organizations managed the competing interests of a number of stakeholders and the creative process of image making. I was fortunate to be able to interview staff from the universe of AIDS organizations producing media campaigns in Accra. In addition, I spoke with their contracted advertising agencies and, when possible, their funding agencies. I also interviewed staff at stakeholder organizations (e.g., state ministries, religious organizations, organizations of HIV-positive Ghanaians, international agencies such as the Joint United Nations Programme on HIV/AIDS [UNAIDS] and the World Health Organization [WHO]) about their participation in campaign design. These interviews were one-on-one, semistructured interviews that typically lasted about two hours but often ran as long as three hours. Most of the campaign staff members I interviewed were Ghanaian. Most of the foreign-born respondents were Americans, and a few were Europeans. I asked my respondents questions about media design, image strategy, intended meanings, audience targeting, site selection, and campaign evaluation. These data capture the logics and priorities that inform AIDS campaign design. Additionally, campaign design staff members often revealed important data on campaign reception with narratives of their field experiences.

In 2006, the Ghana Sustainable Change Project (GSCP) organized the design of a national-level antistigma campaign. I observed the stakeholder meetings where campaign concepts were presented, people debated the pros and cons of each campaign strategy, and producers narrowed down ideas, discussed issues of representation, and ultimately finalized the campaign for public consumption. This observation permitted me to witness competing meanings and agendas at work and to assess how AIDS campaign producers managed the needs and expectations of these stakeholders.

Measuring AIDS Knowledge Distribution and Observing Object–Setting Interactions

To understand how patterns of circulation and urban space shape meaning making, I observed how billboards and posters worked in their unique settings, photographed AIDS campaigns throughout urban space, and mapped the density of images across Accra's streetscape. In addition, I spoke with key disseminators of AIDS information: clinic workers and peer educators.

To identify AIDS campaign objects throughout the city, I systematically traveled the high-traffic routes through Accra—the same routes that AIDS campaign producers targeted—in every mode of transportation (i.e., private cars, taxis, shared cars, and tro-tros [private minibus shared taxis]). I walked methodically through the Osu neighborhood visiting local bars, restaurants, pharmacies, and shops, which helped me discover campaigns in unexpected places. I also visited most of Accra's polyclinics and hospitals, a number of schools, and some churches and mosques. To analyze the distribution of AIDS media, I mapped their appearance throughout Accra, which enabled me to assess image density across space. I documented the presence of AIDS materials and the conditions of interaction through photographs and field notes for every instance of a campaign. I treat each instance of AIDS media as a unique case. For each case, I account for three factors: (1) its different audiences and their local cultural practices, (2) the physical context of interpretation, and

(3) the placement, orientation, and condition of the object. I also investigated the activities in which people engaged while in the presence of these media.

I privilege the analysis of an individual poster or billboard in its distinctive context rather than assessing the aggregate effect of the set of posters throughout a city. Nonetheless, my approach differs from particularist trends in ethnographic methods that spend a great deal of time with one group (e.g., Fine's ethnographies of idioculture; Fine 1987) or at one place (e.g., Duneier's *Slim's Table* or Liebow's *Tally's Corner*; Duneier 1994; Liebow 2003). I found that observing the *conditions* of interaction around specific advertisements and sites and then comparing across them helped me identify patterns in how interpretation was structured. Following Gibson, attention to the material conditions of interpretation permitted me to identify the potential interpretations a billboard might afford (Gibson 1979).

As in any city, Accra's physical qualities structure people's "ways of seeing" AIDS media (J. Berger 1972), and local culture constrains people's "practices of looking" (Sturken and Cartwright 2001). Urban scholars have made similar kinds of observations through ethnographic attention to space and materiality.[7] By observing the conditions of interpretative interactions—the physical constraints of people and the material conditions of the city—I articulate how the materiality of the object–setting interactions encourages some interpretations while discouraging others (Griswold 1987b).

Key actors also influence the conditions of interpretive interactions with AIDS media. I was interested in how clinic nurses, peer educators, and pharmacists mediate the power of AIDS materials and how these staff use pamphlets, penis models for condom demonstrations, and sexually transmitted infection (STI) flip charts. I informally interviewed nurses at a youth clinic, polyclinic, and STI clinic, along with peer educators working with AIDS organizations. I asked these respondents about the materials they considered effective, how they "knew" what worked, and how they might make changes to AIDS materials.

Meaning Making and the Reception of AIDS Knowledge

I collected a variety of reception data to assess meaning making and resonance when audiences interpret AIDS media. I did so through informal interviews at the sites of AIDS media, focus group interviews with residents of Accra, and interviews with community leaders. In 2008 I conducted informal interviews with Ghanaians as they passed AIDS billboards on foot. I spent an hour at each billboard and introduced myself to passersby as a researcher with an "interest in advertising" (I did not mention my interest in AIDS). The number of respondents at each billboard ranged from five to thirty. In addition to data on local interpretations of these media, I was able to assess foot traffic for each location. At each billboard I would ask respondents to first describe the billboard and then articulate their understanding of its meaning and its purpose by narrating what was happening in the photographic or artistic depictions. I then asked whether the billboard was appropriate for the location and whether they believed it was having a positive or negative effect. I was particularly attentive to respondents' remarks about the physical condition of the billboard.

I also conducted seven focus group interviews with Ghanaians living in Accra to assess their response to AIDS media campaigns specifically and AIDS knowledge generally. Community members from one neighborhood comprised two of the focus groups; schoolteachers (one group from a primary school, two from secondary schools) comprised the membership of three focus groups; and HIV-positive Ghanaians with ties to a local AIDS organization populated the final two focus groups. Each group contained men and women. The groups included individuals from a range of class backgrounds. Group size varied from four to eight people. Interviews typically lasted one and a half to two hours. Participants were not paid for their participation, but they did receive light refreshments. HIV-negative focus groups were recruited by my Ghanaian research assistants and conducted near their residences or workplaces. HIV-positive groups' interviews were arranged by ActionAid Ghana and conducted at its offices.

I began my focus group interviews by asking participants to collaborate in designing and drawing an AIDS poster. After giving them a box of colored pencils and a large blank sheet of paper, I asked them to "come up with a message about AIDS that your community needs to see and hear." I recorded their conversations and kept notes on their physical and emotional reactions. When they were satisfied with their poster, I probed for more information about how they chose the images and messages. This task revealed more than the meaning of a single billboard. It made visible the meanings associated with AIDS that circulated through rumor, myth, and local understandings of disease, above and beyond the meanings supplied by official sources such as health organizations. Respondents' discourse around how AIDS campaigns *should* look as they drew their posters was much richer than their paraphrasing of the billboard slogans. The discourse, choices, and drawings elicited by this exercise unearthed a number of cultural phenomena. This method brought to the surface the symbols and meanings that resonate with the community when thinking about AIDS. It revealed that respondents made some meanings automatically, while other meanings were contested and deliberated, a distinction I will elaborate further. This process sparked debates over which

messages their neighbors most needed to hear and revealed which representations of those ideas were most resonant. Most important, this technique
revealed these patterns without overdetermining participants' responses.

After the group participants finished drawing and discussing their poster,
I showed respondents preselected images and asked them to reflect on their
meaning in relation to AIDS, much like a traditional focus group. The images
I showed my respondents were representative of images that appeared on
AIDS advertisements throughout Ghana. To be clear, these were not specific
AIDS campaign images but images and symbols that were common in campaigns. In so doing, my respondents had an opportunity to reflect on the
publicly available symbols associated with AIDS without AIDS campaign
text constraining their responses and priming specific meanings. In total, I
selected twelve images, including symbols commonly linked to AIDS (red
ribbon, condoms), images representing religion (Islamic crescent, Christian crucifix), Ghanaian national and cultural symbols (Ghana's flag, kente
cloth, chief), medicine and science (hypodermic needle, nurse/pills), along
with images of people (a skeletal AIDS patient, happy professional men, a
weak woman being supported by friends, commercial sex workers at a testing
clinic). I randomized the order of these images before the first focus group to
avoid introducing bias through the order of presentation, and then I kept that
order consistent across the focus groups. Comparing participants' responses
to each of these images yielded a measure of coherence around the meanings
of these symbols for residents of Accra.

Finally, after discussing the images individually, I mirrored the first exercise of drawing a poster by showing the group the entire set of twelve images
and asking them to create another poster for me, using three of the twelve
symbols. The posters drawn at the beginning gave me a good measure of the
symbols and meanings that came easily to mind without biasing participants
with prompts. One problem with relying solely on the drawn posters is that
"retrievability" and "resonance" might be confounded; without prompts,
images that seem resonant may only be selected because people *remember*
them (Schudson 1989). By asking my focus groups to make a second poster
using the images I gave them, I created a check on their drawing: How consistent were the messages and images across the two posters? If they chose
similar images and messages for both posters, even after seeing a set of competing images associated with AIDS, then that suggests that their selection
of images was motivated by internalized culture, not prompted by external
cues.[8] In addition, choosing three images of twelve allowed me to do more
systematic intergroup comparison; relying only on the drawn posters might
have produced a wide range of representations without clear patterns.

Whereas this last exercise fruitfully supplemented and functioned as a check on the productive activity, it would have been insufficient by itself. If I had used only the set of twelve symbols—or, for that matter, photos of actual billboards as I had initially planned—I would have missed an important cluster of cultural associations. Stigmatizing images of skeletons, illness, and death resonate and persist in the public imagination of citizens, even though public-health campaigns have avoided or actively scrubbed these images from their visuals and language. Ultimately, the drawing exercise gave me access to different and more valid information than what I would have found if I had asked participants to analyze the set of images produced and distributed by AIDS organizations.

I also wanted to measure which AIDS campaigns my participants and interacted with. As such, I presented the focus group with a series of the campaign slogans that have appeared most frequently in public space. This activity aimed to measure both the "reach and recall" of AIDS campaigns, and also how they rated comparatively. Like the images in my initial set of twelve, I first randomized these slogans and then kept their order to maintain consistency across focus groups:

Stop AIDS Love Life
Don't be Shy, Use a Condom
Who Are You to Judge?
Don't Turn Your Back on AIDS
If It's Not On, It's Not In
Wo Nkwa Hia, Your Life Is Precious
Like Fire, AIDS Is Preventable
AIDS Is Real
Keep to Your Partner, Help Stop AIDS
Don't Go Mungo Park, Always Wear a Condom
Love with Care
AIDS Gaskia Ne [AIDS Is Real]
Reach Out, Show Compassion
Wo Ye Metcho [They Are Macho]
Be Young and Wise, Abstain from Casual Sex
Reach Out to People Living with AIDS
If Your Gift Is for Sex, Keep It
Don't Rush into Premarital Sex, You Risk Getting Infected with HIV/AIDS
Always Be Prepared
Abstain, Be Faithful, Condom Use

After asking which of these slogans participants had seen or heard, I asked them to identify which campaign they most commonly saw or heard. Then I wanted to know whether these campaigns had infiltrated the consciousness of everyday Ghanaians. So I asked the following two questions: (1) Of these campaigns, which have you heard people discuss the most? and (2) Do people use any of these campaign slogans in everyday speech?

I also wanted to know whether they thought these campaigns affect people's behavior. I asked the following two questions: (1) Do you think any of these campaigns have changed people's behavior around AIDS? Which ones? and (2) Which campaign best changes people's behavior in response to AIDS? Finally, I wanted to know if any of these campaigns had created local controversies, so I asked them to identify campaigns that were controversial.

In the final portion of the focus group, my participants filled out a short individual survey on media practices and AIDS knowledge. Many of the questions were pulled directly from the 2003 Ghana Demographic Health Survey (DHS). Using identical questions enabled me to compare how my respondents were similar or different from the random sample of Ghanaians who had taken the survey. Although the sample was small, their answers were comparable to DHS results.

I opened the survey with a series of demographic questions: gender, age, occupation, education, language spoken in home, marital status, religion. Then I inquired about media practices by asking how regularly they watched TV, listened to the radio, and read the newspaper. From there, I wanted to learn about their sources of AIDS knowledge. I asked about their most common source of AIDS knowledge, which source they trust the most, and what form of media they rely on most for their AIDS information (when they rely on media). Then I asked a series of questions about their AIDS knowledge. I asked about how to avoid HIV transmission, which groups were most at risk for contracting HIV, whether they personally knew someone who was HIV positive, whether there was a cure for AIDS, and whether they would purchase vegetables from someone who was HIV positive.

Finally, in addition to these focus group interviews, I interviewed community leaders (such as school principals and religious leaders) along with everyday residents of Accra (taxi drivers, store owners) about the presence of AIDS campaigns in their communities. I wanted to get a sense of their familiarity with various organizations, whether they had experienced any peer education, and what changes they thought needed to be made in response to AIDS. When people personally displayed AIDS images (i.e., bumper stickers, or "Condoms Sold Here" posters), I asked where they got the image, why they put it up, and what their experiences have been with people's response to the image.

A Note on the Novelty of These Methods for Public Health

In this study, I compare campaigns from multiple organizations and across time and space. These methods innovate on typical AIDS campaign evaluations that study only a single campaign. If campaigns are evaluated at all, public-health organizations correlate the reach of the campaign with changes in AIDS knowledge and behavior through small-n pretest/intervention/posttest studies. In these studies, the act of interacting with an AIDS campaign and the ultimate data collected in survey are so distant as to render that data suspect. My detailed attention to meaning at the microlevel improves on these evaluations by laying out the process by which these interventions resonate or fail. Although I cannot know whether seeing an AIDS billboard affected people such that they used a condom the next time they had sex (since researchers can't do ethnographies of people's bedroom behavior), my approach provides a higher-resolution picture of the relationship between communication and action. By moving beyond evaluations that simply ask if people have "seen" a campaign, my work attends to the ways people make meaning around these objects in context, and it identifies "aberrant decodings" of these media (Eco 2003). The insight that cultural entropy leads people to interpret AIDS media in ways contrary to the intended message provides a more nuanced understanding of why AIDS campaigns have suppressed effects on behavior.

Acknowledgments

This research was generously funded by the National Science Foundation (0503367), multiple fellowships from Northwestern University, and the Martin P. Levine Memorial Fellowship Award of the Sexualities Section of the American Sociological Association. Book indexing was made possible by the Institute for Scholarship in the Liberal Arts, College of Arts and Letters, University of Notre Dame.

Portions of this manuscript have been published elsewhere.

With kind permission from Springer Science+Business Media: *Theory and Society*, "Drawing Out Culture: Productive Methods to Measure Cognition and Resonance," 43, 2014, 247–74, Terence E. McDonnell. Copyright 2014 Springer Science+Business Media Dordrecht.

McDonnell, Terence E. 2010. "Cultural Objects as Objects: Materiality, Urban Space, and the Interpretation of AIDS Campaigns in Accra, Ghana." *American Journal of Sociology* 115:1800–52. Copyright 2010 University of Chicago Press.

McDonnell, Terence E. 2008. "The (re)Presentation of an Epidemic in Everyday Life." *Social Psychology Quarterly* 71:321–23. Copyright 2008 American Sociological Association.

Despite the vision of the cloistered scholar, hunkered down in a library and feverishly writing in solitude, writing a book is a collective process. I am deeply indebted to the mentors and colleagues who have helped give the book its shape. First and foremost, Wendy Griswold has been there every step of the way. For her constant support and consistently good advice I am grateful. Wendy knew exactly how to push my thinking and when to let me chase an idea down the rabbit hole. Thanks for being confident that I'd emerge (mostly unscathed) with something worth writing. I am also thankful to my other mentors at Northwestern University for challenging me and always pointing me in the right direction: Nicola Beisel, Carol Heimer, Jeffrey Sconce, Aldon Morris, Gary Alan Fine, Art Stinchcombe, Ann Orloff, Celeste Watkins-Hayes, Wendy Espeland, Charles Camic, Marika Lindholm, Bruce Carruthers, Bernie Beck, Richard Joseph, and Paula England. While at Northwestern, my writing group, comprised of Corey Fields, Berit Vannebo, and Kerry Dobransky, was a constant source of support. When frustrated with HIV/AIDS research, which was often, I could always commiserate with J. Lynn Gazley and a cup of coffee in her living room. I traded many chapters with my coconspirator Japonica Brown-Saracino, who encouraged my writing and made writing a book seem possible. The Culture and Society Workshop at Northwestern was my intellectual home for years, and many of the seeds of the good ideas in this book were planted in that community. I'm also grateful to all those people at Northwestern who made it a magical place to spend my twenties, especially Steve Hoffman, Ellen Berrey, Wenona Rymond-Richmond, Eric Poehler, Coleman Hutchison, Kieran Bezila, Gabrielle and Chris Ferrales, Nathan Wright, Michaela DeSoucey, James Taylor, Harvey Young, Heather Schoenfeld, Alan Czaplicki, Michael Sauder, Tim Hallett, Victor Espinosa, Theo Greene, Liz Onasch, Amin Ghaziani, Geoff Harkness, Amit Nigam, Nehal Patel, Neeraja Aravamuden, Lori Delale-O'Connor, Christine Wood, Christie Gardner, Faiza Mushtaq, and Sarah Mesle.

Thanks also to my colleagues at Notre Dame and Vanderbilt for all the encouragement along the way, especially Rory McVeigh, Ann Mische, Christian Smith, David Gibson, Erika Summers-Effler, Amy Langenkamp, Mary Ellen Konieczny, Elizabeth McClintock, Megan Andrew, Bill Ivey, Elizabeth Long-Lingo, Bruce Barry, Richard Lloyd, Tony Brown, Laura Carpenter, Dan Cornfield, Katharine Donato, Larry Isaac, Holly McCammon, Richard Pitt, JuLeigh Petty, and Bonnie Dow.

Thanks to Doug Mitchell for your wisdom, good cheer, and enthusiasm for my work. Thanks also to Kyle Wagner and everyone at the University of Chicago Press for making the process go so smoothly. I also raise a glass to Lori Meek Schuldt for her meticulous copyediting.

Conducting research in Ghana can be a trying task. Having friends makes it much more enjoyable. Thanks especially to our Ghanaian friends and family: Victor Bannerman-Chedid, Hannah Quartey and the Quartey family, Evelyn and Fred, Dan. Thanks to our expat community Marta and Rob Taylor, Rebecca and Phil Napier-Moore, Lothar Smith, Julie Dorn, Jeremy Pool, Corinne Singleton, Marina Andina, Thomas Switala, Lindsey Craig, Adele Poskitt, Jacqui Pilch, Naureen Karachiwalla, and Will Pritchard. I'll never forget those many nights of candlelit card games and drinking *akpeteshie*.

I was fortunate to meet a number of excellent scholars of Ghana early on in my research, John Anarfi, Akosua Darkwa, and Francis DoDoo—I appreciate your advice. Thanks also to my informants for sharing their knowledge and time with me. I may at times be critical of the project of health communication, but I was always bowled over by your passion, commitment, and professionalism.

I've had a number of research assistants over the years who worked on the book. Thanks to Kari Christoffersen, Amy Jonason, Erin Bergner, Erin Rehel, Katherine Everhart, Brad Vermurlen, Emmie Mediate, Julia Mulligan, Helena Dagadu, and Anne-Marie Blackmore. My superlative research assistant Kelcie Vercel deserves a special shout-out for going above and beyond the call of duty. She's read this book almost as many times as I have.

I enjoyed the benefit of excellent feedback when chapters from this book were presented at the Harvard University Culture and Social Analysis Workshop (thanks to Maggie Frye, Bart Bonikowski, Orlando Patterson, and Michele Lamont), Stanford University Graduate School of Business Organizational Behavior Workshop (gratitude goes to Amir Goldberg, Jesper Sørensen, J. P. Ferguson, and Sarah Soule), Yale University's Workshop in Cultural Sociology (much appreciation to Philip Smith and Anne-Marie Champagne), the University of Chicago's Spring Institute, the New School's Politics of Materiality meeting, and at numerous conferences.

A number of sociologists have been supportive of my work over the years and helped me think through ideas over informal chats and coffee. I owe much respect and admiration to Sarah Corse, Chandra Mukerji, Ann Swidler, John Mohr, Susan Watkins, Tia DeNora, Jeff Alexander, Robin Wagner-Pacifici, and Geneviève Zubrzycki.

I've been blessed to have colleagues who were willing to read chapters and occasionally have a drink with me. Thanks to Dustin Kidd, Iddo Tavory, Chris Bail, Fred Wherry, Kraig Beyerlein, Steve Vaisey, Ashley Mears, Shaul Kelner, Gemma Mangione, Fiona Rose-Greenland, and Fernando Domínguez Rubio.

Lynette Spillman read the entire manuscript at an especially important moment of my revisions and offered indispensable advice that helped strengthen the book. She's an incredibly generous and friendly colleague and I'm lucky to work with her.

Omar Lizardo and Jessica Collett are the best neighbors/colleagues a guy could ask for. They are always ready with a glass of wine and words of wisdom when things get especially tough. In particular, I owe Omar a debt for his shrewd evaluation of my work, his always constructive advice, his encyclopedic knowledge, and his ability to comment on chapters at lightning speed.

Talking to Steven Tepper is more fun than a [fill in the blank]. He's brimming with ideas and our conversations generated a number of insights about cultural entropy that found their way into this book. I miss having him down the hall.

I couldn't have written this book without the constant advice and support of Jennifer Lena. We were writing partners at Vanderbilt, but that friendship has continued long since. Jenn's pragmatic counsel, willingness to read my work, and unceasing encouragement kept me going. Thanks for your wit and for never letting me take myself too seriously.

I'm grateful to those close friends and family who always had faith that I would finish but never stopped ribbing me about it: Keith Karem, Dustin Burke, Jason Baker, Ryan Whittier, Brian Horne, Ian Carswell, Justin Bell, Garron Hansen, Rachel Scherrer, Kelly Dempski, Natasha Makarenko, David Davick, Meghan Sullivan, Kaity Fuja, Paul and Abi Ocobock, Jessi and Jeff Goodwin, J. J. and Alexandra Wright, Bill Jackson, and Vicki and Dan Schultz.

Special thanks to my parents, Patrick and Denyse McDonnell, and my sister and her husband, Brianne and Jesse Langille, for their constant encouragement. Thanks, Mom and Dad, for making the sacrifices you made so that I could be writing this sentence. Though this book can in no way makes up for everything you've done for me, I hope you see this accomplishment as one small way to honor you both. I love you all.

Finally, Erin. You are my heart, and my partner. Your insights made this a better book, and your sacrifices made it possible. *You have always spoken the truth to me, with love.* Thanks for introducing me to Ghana and for always being the shoulder I could lean on. With Liam and Mara you've given me two amazing kids and a perfect life. This book is for you. I love you.

Notes

Introduction

1. "The most obvious limitation to a correct anticipation of consequences of action is provided by the existing state of knowledge" (Merton 1936).

2. Models such as the "health belief model" (Rosenstock 1974), "theory of reasoned action" (Fishbein and Ajzen 1975), "social cognitive theory" (Bandura 2001), and others are widely discussed and debated within the field of public health. More cultural approaches have criticized these models for failing to attend to meaning and context (Dutta 2008).

3. See Mannheim 1955 on how "functional rationality" drives out "substantive rationality."

4. As Bielby and Bielby (1994) argue, in situations of ambiguity, organizations adopt more routines and rules to improve the likelihood of success (and legitimate their existence). Although such routines may improve campaigns, such improvements are limited and do not guarantee success.

5. "Formal schemes of order are untenable without some elements of the practical knowledge that they tend to dismiss" (Scott 1998:,7). See also Scott 1990.

6. The field established its footing in this time period, with the publication of *Health Communication* in 1989 and the *Journal of Health Communication* in 1996. Major books on campaign design also made an appearance in this period; namely, Backer, Rogers, and Sopory 1992, Edgar, Fitzpatrick, and Freimuth 1992, and Maibach and Parrott 1995.

7. Eisenstein (1979) shows how the printing press and the circulation of biblical texts encouraged religious disjunctions and change. Benjamin (1968) suggests how mass reproduction of art allowed for it to be repurposed and reinterpreted outside its intended ritual context.

8. Cell phones have also become widely available. As I was leaving the field in 2008, organizations had invested in texting as a new frontier in AIDS organizations' communication strategy. They found that text communication worked well for reaching hidden populations such as men who have sex with men. Though Internet access expanded while I was in Ghana, it had not yet become a site for AIDS communication. Over the course of this study, Internet use was primarily confined to pay-by-the-hour Internet cafés such as Busy Internet. For more on Internet in Ghana at this time, see Burrell 2012; Griswold, McDonnell, and McDonnell 2007.

9. Compared with clinics or hospitals, peer education, news and entertainment, church or mosque, schools, workplace, government, or traditional healer. More than twice as many people

reported AIDS media campaigns as a source of information than the next most commonly reported source of peer education. Peer education and media campaigns were reported as the most trusted source almost as often, with media campaigns having a very slight edge.

10. Akwara et al. 2005. The World Health Organization defines a *generalized epidemic* as a prevalence of 1 percent or more of the population.

11. Anarfi 1993; Côté et al. 2004.

12. To this last point, Oster's (2012a) study of sexual behavior and HIV prevalence in Africa (including Ghana) suggests that prevention intervention uptake, changes in sexual behavior, and declines in HIV prevalence have more to do with external factors such as economic improvements and improved life expectancy. Oster also suggests that HIV knowledge does not impact behavioral response.

13. *Comprehensive knowledge* means knowing that consistent use of condom during sexual intercourse and having just one HIV-negative and faithful partner can reduce the chances of getting the AIDS virus, knowing that a healthy-looking person can have the AIDS virus, and rejecting the two most common local misconceptions about HIV/AIDS transmission or prevention: that AIDS can be transmitted via mosquito bites and that AIDS can be transmitted by supernatural means (Ghana Statistical Service [GSS], Noguchi Memorial Institute for Medical Research [NMIMR], and ORC Macro 2004; GSS and ICF Macro 2009).

14. This is a percentage of people who express acceptance attitudes across four indicators: (1) are willing to care for a family member with the AIDS virus in the respondent's home, (2) would buy fresh vegetables from a shopkeeper who has the AIDS virus, (3) say that a female teacher with the AIDS virus who is not sick should be allowed to continue teaching, and (4) would not want to keep secret that a family member has the AIDS virus (GSS, NMIMR, and ORC Macro 2004; GSS and ICF Macro 2009).

15. Knowledge of condoms as a prevention method moved between 2003 and 2008 from 73.4 percent to 75.8 percent among women and from 84.5 percent to 85.0 percent among men (GSS, NMIMR, and ORC Macro 2004; GSS and ICF Macro 2009).

16. For instance, Radway (1991), Griswold (2000), Miller, Kitzinger, and Beharrell (1998), and du Gay et al. (2013) trace the production, circulation, and reception of objects. Appadurai (1986) and Kopytoff (1986) encourage the study of the "social life" or "biography" of things. Pinch and Bijker (2012) follow the development of technologies over time.

17. Griswold's (2000) own study of the production, circulation, and reception of Nigerian fiction offers an exemplary illustration of the cultural diamond approach.

18. In total I spent a year and a quarter in country: three months in the summer of 2003, six months (July through December) in 2006, and seven months (September through March) across 2007–2008.

19. I conducted interviews at the following campaign-producing organizations: Johns Hopkins University Bloomberg School of Public Health Center for Communication Programs Ghana (JHU), Ghana Social Marketing Foundation (GSMF), Ghana Sustainable Change Project (GSCP), Family Health International (FHI), Strengthening HIV/AIDS Response Partnerships (SHARP), the Ghana Ministry of Health's Health Promotion Unit (HPU), Planned Parenthood Association of Ghana (PPAG), and Ghana AIDS Commission (GAC).

20. Crimp and Rolston 1990; Patton 1990; Crimp 2002; Gilman 1996; Sturken 1997; Treichler 1999. An exception is Miller, Kitzinger, and Beharrell 1998.

21. The production of culture approach draws on theories of organizations and institutions to understand how systems of production powerfully shape cultural products (Peterson

and Anand 2004). In particular, Howard Becker's (1982) work on art world "conventions," Paul DiMaggio's (1982) work on how organizational models diffuse through fields of production.

Chapter One

1. Research has identified "concurrent" sexual relations as central to the rapid spread of HIV through sub-Saharan African countries, as opposed to serial monogamy, and Ghanaian AIDS organizations expressed concern about polygamy (Morris and Kretzschmar 1997; Epstein 2007). Formal and informal polygamous arrangements are common among Muslim and Christian Ghanaians. Christian leaders publicly frown upon the practice but tacitly accept it. Among the predominantly Christian AIDS campaign producers I interviewed, polygamy is more often associated with Islam than with Christianity. Despite the relatively low HIV prevalence among Ghanaian Muslims (when compared to Christians), FHI felt it necessary to address the most likely *potential* vector of transmission for Muslim Ghanaians: infidelity and polygamy.

2. For more on Nima, see Weeks et al. 2007.

3. FHI (alongside other organizations such as UNAIDS, WHO, and Population Services International) is one of the most influential producers of these standards through its publication of best-practice reports that advise organizations how best to design HIV/AIDS interventions.

4. FHI Ghana staff member, interview by author, December 5, 2006. All interviews with unnamed people in this book were conducted in confidentiality, and the names of interviewees are withheld by mutual agreement.

5. Quoted from author's field notes, March 26, 2008.

6. PPAG staff member, interview by author, October 9, 2006.

7. Names have been changed to ensure confidentiality.

8. Adapted from field notes, September 12, 2006.

9. See Tavory and Swidler 2009 and Smith 2004 for discussions of the complicated meanings of condoms that people navigate in Africa.

10. See Ankomah 1999; Fiscian et al. 2009; Meekers and Calvès 1997. The staff I interviewed at AIDS organizations regularly brought up the problem of exchange relationships (as distinct from commercial sex work) between young women and "sugar daddies"—married men who cared for material needs or school fees. AIDS organizations feared how power imbalances between young women and older men would lead to unprotected sex and higher HIV risk. As such, they actively crafted messages for young women to either discourage such relationships or promote the use of condoms.

11. Nonspecialist readers may want to skip this section (or even the rest of the chapter) as it is aimed at a specialist audience.

12. The hermeneutical insight that objects are not complete until they are interpreted (Gadamer 2004; Barthes 1977; Fish 1980) set a generation of scholars to understand the role of audiences in meaning. These approaches argued that readers bear as much, if not more, responsibility for meaning making as authors and texts do. Reception theorists view audiences as active "readers" of texts, not passively decoding inherent meaning (Fiske 1996). Moving away from close readings of texts for their intended meaning, studies grounded in reception theory focus almost exclusively on explaining polysemy of objects through variations in audience (Hall 1993; Griswold 1987a; Shively 1992; Liebes and Katz 1993; Lutz and Collins 1993; Harrington and Bielby 1995; Bryson 1996; Press and Cole 1999). In theory many of these authors make room for the importance of objects (Griswold 1987a; Shively 1992), but in practice most focus attention solely

on audience. This view has been critiqued for treating cultural groups as too static, suggesting that meaning making emerges dynamically in groups and interaction (Long 2003; Eliasoph and Lichterman 2003), but these approaches similarly focus on audiences as the central mechanism of meaning making. For a paper that both reviews these various approaches to reception and tests theories in combination, see Childress and Friedkin 2012.

13. "Alignment" refers to "the linkage of individual and [organization] interpretive orientations, such that some set of individual interests, values, and beliefs and [organization] activities, goals, and ideology are congruent or complementary" (Snow et al. 1986).

14. This notion of alignment or symmetry appears across distinct fields, from the "encoding/decoding" approach in media and communication studies (Hall 1993) to the literature on framing from social movements research (Snow et al. 1986). Hall states, "The degree of symmetry—that is, the degrees of 'understanding' and 'misunderstanding' in the communicative exchange—depend [sic] on the degrees of symmetry/asymmetry (relations of equivalence) established between the positions of the 'personifications', encoder-producer and decoder-receiver" (1993, 510). Snow et al. define frame alignment as "the linkage of individual and social movement organization orientations, such that some set of individual interests, values, and beliefs and social movement organization activities, goals, and ideology are congruent and complementary" (1986, 464). A parallel literature focuses on subcultural meaning making and the ways unaligned subcultures appropriate and challenge dominant culture (Willis 1977; Hebdige 1979). This theme also emerges in Bourdieu's (1984) arguments about the structural homologies of production and consumption.

15. Steinberg (1999) offers an important corrective to this trend in the framing literature by drawing on Bakhtin (1981) and taking a dialogic approach.

16. Certainly there are exceptions to this approach. Especially in media studies, audiences are thought to be creative and agentic, rather than static (Fiske 1996; Jenkins 1992; Radway 1991). Media studies also tend to focus on context to a greater degree (Fiske 1992), though their theories of meaning tend to be dominated by audience-based approaches.

17. Exceptions include Fiske 1992; Hall 1993; Senie 2002; Babon 2006; Tepper 2011.

18. A distinction Gibson (1979) makes between "attached" and "detached" objects.

19. Gibson's (1979) theory of affordances is a theory of perception, one that considers the qualities of objects and the perceptual and bodily capacities of people. Affordances are the latent set of possible actions that environments and objects enable *for particular people* with their own unique capacities. Affordance theory, then, is inherently relational. Affordance theory was later taken up in sociology by DeNora (2000) in her work analyzing the use and meaning of music in everyday life as a challenge to semiotic approaches in musicology. She adopts a more reflexive view of affordances, one that I prefer, "whereby users configure themselves as agents in and through the ways they—as agents—behave toward those objects" (DeNora 2000, 40).

20. Here I draw on work from actor-network theory (ANT) (Latour 1992; Latour 2005). ANT treats humans and nonhumans as agentic actants and values the importance of materiality. In particular, Pickering's (1995) adaptation of ANT is particularly useful for explaining such cases as the condom bracelet. He focuses attention on the dialectics of material resistance to human intention and the human accommodations made in response to that resistance. These approaches bring important insights into the power of materiality, including new conceptual tools and methods, but in my reading these theories rarely offer generalizable mechanisms that generate explanations. In this way I agree with Benson's (2014) critique of actor network theory as the "new descriptivism," something that is also true of work of much work on materiality—it

lacks a focus on sociological explanation. Rather than conceptual tools and description, I believe we can push these methodological insights toward a framework that makes visible generalizable mechanisms that explain patterns in disruption, interpretation, and use.

21. See also Callon 2007 on "agencements" and Latour 2005 on "assemblages."

22. I use Griswold's definition of *cultural object* as "shared significance embodied in form" (Griswold 1986, 5).

23. As Pinch and Bijker (2012) have demonstrated with the evolution of the bicycle, the stabilization of an object is a nonlinear process of contestation and consensus that emerges through interactions between objects and people. This process usually happens by narrowing collective understandings of objects to only certain qualities, which is exactly what AIDS organizations attempt to do when designing a campaign—they filter out alternative meanings and uses through a process of refinement. This stabilization is different from the stability made possible by "boundary objects" (Star and Griesemer 1989) wherein the interpretive flexibility of objects enables the cooperation of heterogeneous institutional actors.

24. Here I borrow Geertz's definition of a cultural system: "an historically transmitted pattern of meanings embodied in symbols, a system of inherited conceptions expressed in symbolic forms by means of which men [and women] communicate, perpetuate, and develop their knowledge about and attitudes toward life" (1973, 89). For my purposes, I'd supplant "symbols" with "objects." In this sense Geertz's "systems or complexes of symbols" (92) might be better defined as "complexes of objects" that carry symbolic content.

25. Admittedly, as used in the social sciences, energy is an inexact concept difficult to operationalize.

26. Elsewhere I've defined *resonance* as the heightened emotions people feel when an object organizes information in ways that make sense and facilitates action (McDonnell 2014).

27. As "secondary agents" for people and organizations, objects extend their intention, agency, and will to other people, communicating meaning and use through the symbolic and material qualities of those objects (Gell 1998).

28. I follow Gell's "emphasis on agency, intention, causation, result, and transformation" by tracing how objects operate in a "system of action" (1998, 6)

29. While I write about intensive organizational efforts, people imbue objects with intentions all the time, and much of what I write here extends to these examples as well. Objects vary by how crafted they are and also how clearly defined the goals are. While AIDS organizations typically intend to communicate a very specific message, an artist may intend to communicate multiple competing meanings or value ambiguity. In such a case, an artist's work may face cultural entropy if its meaning is reduced to a single interpretation or if it doesn't provoke debate about its meaning.

30. Bourdieu 1977, 83. See also Sewell 1992.

31. This definition of *culture work* is different from others; namely, Penny Edgell Becker's definition of *culture work* as "the processes by which individuals and groups interpret and deploy parts of their cultural repertoires in changing environments (1998, 467). For Edgell Becker, the work is in adapting to change; for me, the work is whether objects successfully transfer intention.

32. Elsewhere I've described cultural power as the "capacity for a cultural object to affect belief and behavior" (McDonnell 2010). The cultural power concept has appeared variously in the literature, usually linked to whether and how cultural objects have influence (Griswold 1987a; Schudson 1989; Swidler 1995). Here I directly link cultural power with intention and whether objects elicit the intended interpretation, which (depending on your interpretation) may con-

trast with Griswold's formulation. Griswold argues that novels have power: they elicit varying interpretations that allow people to debate the meaning of the book. This debate keeps it in the public sphere and makes such novels more likely to enter the literary canon. This persistence through time is certainly in line with my definition. Griswold's thinking seems independent of intention, but one could intuit that novelists may intentionally want to evoke multiple readings, making our thinking on cultural power more similar than different. This definition of cultural power excludes scenarios in which people are moved to act in unintended ways, as when a candidate's political ad so offends undecided voters that they are energized to vote for the opposition. This may be negatively resonant and may efficiently inspire action, but since that action was unintended (even antithetical), it can't be said to be powerful *from the perspective* of the politician's campaign.

33. Merely imagining alternative meanings and uses for an object does not necessarily undermine its capacity to work. A person can interpret a female condom as a bracelet, but as long as she or he uses the female condom as a condom, entropy is low. An object's capacity is undermined only when those unintended alternatives take hold.

34. I note "poachers" (de Certeau 2002; Jenkins 1992) here, to suggest that the original producers of an object are not the only ones who imbue objects with energy. Poachers, by co-opting an object to do different work, similarly energize objects and can face entropy.

35. To make cultural entropy (or cultural work) visible, one needs to compare a "brief" that accounts for the intentions of the agents to the objects' reception, influence, and impact on audiences (Griswold 1987b).

36. Importantly, when the same object is mobilized to do different work, when people intend for different outcomes with the same object, for the purpose of analysis the researcher should treat that same object as different, even though it might ostensibly be "the same thing."

37. Knorr Cetina 2001. See also Woodward 2011 on unfolding materiality of social life.

38. In this sense, I consider how interpretive flexibility continues downstream, beyond the design processes that Pinch and Bijker (2012) describe.

39. I draw on the growing use of Gibson's (1979) theory of affordances in sociology: DeNora 2000; McDonnell 2010; McClain and Mears 2012; Griswold, Mangione, and McDonnell 2013. For DeNora (2003), affordances structure action and meaning. She argues, "Questions concerning the social implications of artifacts (whether these are technologies, utterances or aesthetic materials such as music) focus on the interactional level where articulations—links—between humans, scenes, and environments are actually produced, and where the frames of order come to be stabilized and destabilized in real time . . . understood as a place or 'space' for work or meaning and lifeworld making" (DeNora 2000, 40). This structure of affordances, therefore, makes possible both stabilization and destabilization.

40. See Bakhtin 1981 on "dialogism" and "heteroglossia," Kristeva 1980 on "intertextuality," Eliasoph and Lichterman 2003 and Goffman 1959 on interaction.

41. Keane argues for how an object's bundle of qualities encourages contingency: "Redness in an apple comes along with spherical shape, light weight, and so forth. . . . This points to one of the obvious, but important effects of materiality: redness cannot be manifest without some embodiment that inescapably binds it to some other qualities as well, which can become contingent but real factors in its social life" (2003, 414).

42. Gibson (1979) argues that one could objectively measure the set of actions objects make available to an actor, regardless of whether that actor ever engaged in said activities.

43. In this sense arrangements always leave open the possibility of what Downer (2011) calls

an "epistemic accident." Entropy is unpredictable and unavoidable, is likely to reoccur, and challenges design paradigms, but organizations can still learn from cases of entropy.

44. Cultural entropy, then, grounds more postmodern approaches to interpretation that suggest objects are just "'empty vessels' awaiting audiences to pour meaning into them" (Lutz and Collins 1993, 219).

45. Here I point to theories of reproduction through action from P. Berger and Luckman (1966), Giddens (1984), Bourdieu (1977), Sewell (1992), and Hays (1994).

46. The notion of "frames of order" comes from DeNora: "The most interesting questions concerning the social implications of artefacts focus on the interactional level where articulations—links—between humans, scenes, and environments are actually produced, and where frames of order come to be stabilized and destabilized in real time" (2000, 40). Berezin makes a similar observation when she suggests that "meanings are relatively stable, within particular social, political, and cultural contexts and unstable when these contexts shift" (Berezin 1994, 1243).

47. Cultural entropy may appear to contrast with Patterson's (2014) view of culture as a "dynamically stable process," but I see a productive conversation. Patterson disagrees with the image that "we endlessly engage in meaning making in our interactions," instead suggesting that people work to harmonize and come to shared agreement about what things mean, giving culture stability. Change is possible through the pragmatic use of this "constituted" culture. Despite his discussion of change, Patterson's focus is on the stability of these pragmatic rules of interaction and their ability to orient people to particular meanings and uses. Examining and theorizing cultural entropy, then, makes possible analysis of how idiosyncratic interpretations (through error, deliberate resistance, or accident) diffuse, destabilize, and then stabilize into constituted cultural knowledge and practice.

48. Here I draw on de Certeau (1984), who viewed creativity as acts of "articulation" and "enunciation," given the disciplining power of structure. People's ways of operating create play in the machine (30).

49. By creativity, I'm interested in the everyday creativity described by such theorists as de Certeau and Joas. For de Certeau (1984), creativity stems from people's "ways of operating," the tactics people use to appropriate and resist the products imposed by the dominant order. In this sense I focus on how people "enunciate" alternative meanings given the "established languages" imposed on them by powerful institutions (e.g., AIDS organizations). That said, de Certeau's view is limited, suggesting that such moments of creativity are acts of resistance and subversion. Alternatively, Joas (1996) suggests that such everyday creativity is a matter of people confronting problem situations rather than actively resisting them. When habit and routine break down, when the automatic action of habit breaks down, creativity is "called forth." To translate to this discussion of entropy, when confronting novel situations or routine situations that stop working, people look for alternatives within the interpretive arrangement. Joas's approach to creativity better explains the moments of entropy I found—people rarely actively resisted campaigns. Instead, when objects don't do the work as intended, people found alternatives. Recently, Dalton (2004) makes an important contribution to this thinking by synthesizing Bourdieu and Joas, theorizing creativity as a product of habitus rather than a form of action distinct from habit. This view offers yet additional ways to understand how entropy is possible given a stable arrangement. One doesn't need an interruption to habit to encourage creativity. Dalton shows how—instead, creativity can be a product of routine and not just a break from it. In this way, recent work developing Polanyi's "tacit knowledge" suggests that skill enables creativity and change (Sennett

2008; Mukerji 2014). The embodied skill of a craftworker developed over time and experience in stable arrangements can opens up possibilities, new affordances within those arrangements. Importantly, though, creativity is just as much in the objects and settings as it is in the people.

50. As Tanggaard (2013) argues, creativity is not just located in cognitive capacities, the ability to apply divergent thinking, or genius. Instead, everyday creativity is "sociomaterial," located in the "environment, contexts, social practices, materiality" afforded by any arrangement (Tanggaard 2013, 21).

51. "There cannot be any representation that reproduces another entity, scene, or conception, but only constructions that purport to reproduce reality while simplifying, elaborating, accenting, or otherwise constructing actualities and fantasies. Because they create something different from conventional perceptions, works of art are the medium through which new meanings emerge" (Edelman 1995, 7).

52. Latour's essay on "mechanical grooms" (i.e., door closers) and the "missing masses" suggests how objects stabilize, and substitute for, human action (1992). When such do their work well, in the narrowly constrained, routine arrangements they are designed for, such objects are open to entropy only when they break down. The door closer does its work without people even consciously acknowledging its existence, unless the "groom is on strike," as Latour puts it. Scholarship in the science and technology studies and actor-network traditions explains how social action is stabilized in objects: "What has to be explained, the troubling exceptions, are any type of stability over the long term and on a larger scale. . . . If inertia, durability, range, solidity, commitment, loyalty, adhesion, etc. have to be accounted for, this cannot be done without looking for vehicles, tools, instruments, and materials able to provide such a stability" (Latour 2005, 35).

53. Durkheim 1995; see also Couldry 2003 on media ritual.

54. It is important to note that cultural power is not the same as stability. For organizations using culture instrumentally, which seek to communicate a clear and consistent message, stability is an important dimension to cultural power. If the message is not persuasive, even if it is legible and stable, it won't be powerful. Additionally, if a producer's intention is not to communicate a singular message but rather to generate multiple meanings, instability may make those objects powerful (see Griswold 1987a on novels).

55. For work on routine and habit and meaning from practice theory to cognitive sociology, see Bourdieu 1977; DiMaggio 1997; Ignatow 2007; Lizardo and Strand 2010; Swidler 2001.

56. Schudson (1989) suggests that objects that have been institutionally retained tend to be more powerful, as acting out of alignment with such objects leads to sanction.

57. Alexander (2004) is right, then, that the more symbols are detached from their ritual settings, the more the cultural and social dimensions of symbol and ritual "de-fuse," the more they seem like performance and the less power they have.

58. Hornborg (1992) discusses low-entropy borrowing when using the analogy of thermodynamics and entropy to describe value in markets. To create "order," new objects borrow from lower-entropy sources. In ecological terms, plants borrow from the lower-entropy sources such as sun, animals borrow from plants, with energy dissipating it in more disordered ways as you get farther from the sun. For Hornborg, theorizing the value of products, energy moves from raw materials and labor to products. Similarly, campaigns often borrow from what might be called "low entropy" symbols, borrowing relatively stable religious symbols to give coherence to their message. But what might appear like order at the level of the object actually creates more disorder in the system.

59. This argument shares affinities with Patterson's (2014) discussion of the contingent "cultural pragmatics" and cultural change at the microlevel, versus the more stable, shared "constituted cultural knowledge" in the aggregate.

60. This is what Bowker and Star describe as the "naturalization" of an object in a community of practice (1999, 299).

Chapter Two

1. Focus group member in Osu, Accra, interview by author, September 18, 2006.

2. Quoted from field notes, September 18, 2006.

3. Adapted from field notes, September 18, 2006.

4. Manglos and Trinitapoli make a compelling argument that faith healing establishes a "third therapeutic system" (in addition to biomedical and traditional healing systems), practiced widely in Malawi with the effect of reducing worry about AIDS. They argue, as I also suggest, that health decisions are complex, mediated by multiple knowledge regimes. As they argue, "health seeking is neither purely pragmatic nor purely culturally determined; it is the result of a complex interplay of individual experiences, social interactions, structural constraints, and cultural flows" (2011, 119). Similarly, Decoteau describes the hybridity of healing paradigms. "Living with HIV/AIDS actually *requires* the mixture of biomedical and indigenous approaches to healing. People believe that their illnesses come from multiple sources (which may be social, spiritual, or physiological); therefore they require multiple treatment methodologies" (2013, 20).

5. It has been reported that 99.4 percent of women and 100 percent of men surveyed in Accra have knowledge of HIV/AIDS (Ghana DHS 2004).

6. Excerpted and adapted from field notes, October 18, 2006.

7. Without a medical background, it was impossible for me to interpret these results.

8. Fees for services at ART centers were only recently discontinued, in 2012 (Ghana AIDS Commission 2014). Until then, patients would have to pay fees for treatment, which was a structural barrier for many.

9. Doctors track the progression of HIV in the body by monitoring the patient's CD4 count, and treatment depends on the stage of HIV based on the patient's CD4 levels. CD4 stands for Cluster of Differentiation 4, a glycoprotein.

10. For legibility, I typed this handwritten letter (including spelling errors) from a copy given to me.

11. These rumors continue to circulate through word of mouth and through the Internet, often making dramatic claims that evoke international conspiracy. For instance, the following text appeared on a nondescript web page:

> On August 26 1992, The Pioneer daily newspaper ran a headline "Nana Drobo Dies!" The story said that **Nana Kofi Drobo II**, an internationally renowned herbalist was reported to have committed suicide on the 25 August 1992. This follows a report in the same paper of July 5th telling of his narrow escape from attempted kidnapping and poisoning while on a trip to Tokyo, Japan in June 92. He was invited to Tokyo by several companies including the Dental and medical University, in order for them to test the efficacy of his drug, which many had claimed cured them of AIDS. A headline in the 8th September issue of the Ghanaian Times said "Nana Drobo died from 2 gunshot wounds" according to the pathologist Dr. **Kofi Adomako Boateng**, so he could

not have shot himself as was earlier reported. The Ghanaian Times of 3 October 1992 reported that five people including his secretary, driver, personal aide, and a linguist of the **Kwaku Firi Shrine**, where Nana Drobo was chief priest, were charged with his murder and conspiracy to murder. It is understood that three of the five were convicted. It is widely believed that **Nana Drobo** was murdered by international drug companies trying to protect their profits because his was the only <u>cure</u> and preventative medicine for AIDS whereas all the others were symptom suppressants. That may well be true but they are not the main criminals, the main murderers are those USA government agencies who were responsible for creating the AIDS-generating virus in their military laboratories and spreading it through heterosexual contacts and World Health Organisation (WHO) vaccinations in Africa. These people who have a vested interest in the elimination of the entire African nation, (*see Americas, page 13*) do not care how they do it, especially if the process can be profitable to them. Their objective is not just profit, it is Profitable Genocide (Global Africa Pocket News 1994).

12. As Rosnow and Fine (1976) have argued, ambiguous situations (such as the unease around AIDS early in the crisis) increase the spread of rumor.

13. GAC staff member, interview by author, December 12, 2006.

14. GAC staff member, interview by author, December 12, 2006.

15. For an excellent account of journalism in Ghana, see Hasty 2005.

16. AIDS organization staff member, interview by author, December 12, 2006.

17. According to Afrobarometer data for 2010, 88 percent of Ghanaians report that religion is "very important." See also Takyi 2003 and Luginaah, Yiridoe, and Taabazuing 2005.

18. Trinitapoli and Weinreb (2012) find that denominations in Malawi vary in the kinds of AIDS-related rhetoric and practices in which religious leaders engage, from faith healing to moral claims making to passing along biomedical or pragmatic advice. They find that congregations that use a combination of moral and biomedical strategies tend to have lower prevalence than those that solely use faith healing.

19. Trinitapoli and Weinreb (2012) describe that Africans explain HIV infection often through both proximate and ultimate causes. Proximate causes, such as unprotected sex, explain *how* people become infected. Ultimate causes, such as witchcraft, angry ancestors, or divine powers, account for *why*. See also Ashforth 2005.

20. On the four measures of "accepting attitudes toward those living with HIV/AIDS," only 10 percent of women and 14 percent of men express accepting attitudes across all four measures (GSS, NMIMR, and ORC Macro 2004, 213).

21. Takyi (2003). Takyi goes on to suggest that exposure to mass media may have a greater effect on changes in specific behavior than religion does.

22. GSS, NMIMR, and ORC Macro 2004, 104. Though these data are self-reported, AIDS organizations trust these numbers.

23. Nearly every school I visited asked that I come back to give a presentation on AIDS for the students and seemed desperate for informed, up-to-date AIDS information for the school.

24. More often than not, these materials are produced by the same organizations designing AIDS prevention media campaigns.

25. The STI flip chart serves a dual purpose: allowing people to self-diagnose an infection and frightening people into preventative behaviors via the spectacle of grossly disfigured genitalia. HIV/AIDS peer educators who use the flip-book universally praise its effectiveness.

26. According to the Ghana Demographic Health Survey, only 2 percent of women and 3 percent of men between the ages of fifteen and forty-nine sought VCT in the year previous to the survey (GSS, NMIMR, and ORC Macro 2004: 219).

27. Only 31.1 percent of women and 36.5 percent of men in Accra reported knowing someone with HIV (GSS, NMIMR, and ORC Macro 2004).

28. Just as Tavory and Swidler (2009) show how Malawians select and combine multiple understandings of condom use along different semiotic axes, Ghanaians seamlessly move between multiple meanings in different settings.

29. Hannerz (1992) aptly describes how the circulation of ideas is an "unfree flow."

Chapter Three

1. Funding and coordinating agency staff member, interview by author, December 14, 2006.

2. AIDS organization staff member, interview by author, February 21, 2008.

3. AIDS organization staff member, interview by author, February 21, 2008.

4. AIDS organization staff member, interview by author, October 15, 2006.

5. Funding agency staff member, interview by author, March 19, 2008.

6. Between 1997 and 2008, UNAIDS alone published 144 of these reports, with the bulk of the production appearing between 1997 and 2001 (100 of the 144).

7. A classic case of institutional isomorphism (DiMaggio and Powell 1983).

8. UNAIDS, "Best Practices Collection Archive," UNAIDS.org, accessed July 3, 2010, http://www.unaids.org/Services/publicationsArchive.aspx?displaylang=en&id=%7B8C720B29-0440 -44C2-8D1A-19B8CEDAD56D%7D.

9. PPAG staff member, interview by author, October 10, 2006.

10. AIDS organization staff member, interview by author, December 14, 2006.

11. AIDS organization staff member, interview by author, December 14, 2006.

12. AIDS organization staff member, interview by author, December 14, 2006.

13. Transcription of GSCP's "Who Are You to Judge?" National Anti-Stigma Campaign television spot, 2007. *Fufu* refers to a ball of starch made from the flour of the cassava plant or by pounding boiled cassava or yam. It is usually eaten with soup. Fufu is a regular part of Ghanaians' diet.

14. JHU staff member, interview by author, August 2003.

15. Origin8 staff member, interview by author, October 19, 2006.

16. Origin8 staff member, interview by author, October 19, 2006.

17. Interestingly, GSMF started selling for-profit condoms so as to self-finance campaigns. This effort to make itself self-sustainable might give it the freedom to take bigger risks.

18. These arguments parallel Krause's (2014) work on NGOs' commitment to "good projects." AIDS organizations are like other NGOs in that they are oriented toward producing "projects." Following best practices becomes the standard by which organizations and funding agencies define what is a "good" project, with unintended consequences such as orienting work around design rather than effectiveness.

Chapter Four

1. For instance, whereas the theory of reasoned action might assess individuals' attitudes toward behaviors under the assumption that attitudes affect intentions (Ajzen and Fishbein 1980;

Fishbein and Ajzen 1975), the health belief model might measure individuals' perceived severity of the condition and the threat by not taking action (Janz and Becker 1984). A culture-centered approach looks at different levels of analysis, such as communities, and foregrounds shared aspects of social life, such as context and values (Dutta 2008).

2. Other organizations I studied fell in between these extremes. For instance, the Planned Parenthood Association of Ghana (PPAG) used a combination of focus groups, community engagement, and market research. Comparing the cases of GSMF and GSCP makes clear the overall pattern.

3. GSMF staff member, interview by author, December 13, 2006.

4. GSCP staff member, interview by author, December 14, 2006.

5. GSMF staff member, interview by author, December 13, 2006.

6. Quoted from field notes, October 12, 2006.

7. Quoted from field notes, October 12, 2006.

8. JHU staff member, interview by author, August 2003.

9. GSMF staff member, interview by author, December 13, 2006.

10. GSMF staff member, interview by author, December 13, 2006.

11. GSCP staff member, interview by author, November 22, 2006.

12. Studies show that media campaigns that make messages "personal," when people identify with campaign characters, more effectively increase people's sense of risk (Basil and Brown 1994; Basil and Brown 1997; Snyder and Rouse 1995). The narrative campaigns produced by GSCP, which portray characters familiar to local communities, may inspire more behavioral change than those of GSMF.

13. GAC staff member, interview by author, July 31, 2003.

14. The left hand is the "wiping" hand and therefore symbolically unclean.

15. These elites are the opinion leaders who Katz and Lazarsfeld (2005) suggest are so important to media influence.

16. AIDS organizations in Ghana are often populated by a combination of experts from Europe or North America and well-educated Ghanaians.

17. GSCP staff member, interview by author, December 14, 2006.

18. GSCP staff member, interview by author, October 5, 2006.

19. Designers believed Ghanaians were sophisticated enough to understand the irony (their evidence suggested so), and they blamed the advertising agency for its inability to capture the concept. These same designers were well aware of the stigmatizing effects of earlier campaigns but were committed to the concept.

20. Quoted from field notes, October 24, 2006.

21. GSMF staff member, interview by author, October 8, 2006.

22. GSCP staff member, interview by author, October 5, 2006.

23. GSCP staff member, interview with author, February 21, 2008.

Chapter Five

1. Unlike this particular instance, most Champion condom bus shelters were not located near busy markets where people and goods interfere with communication of the message. Instead, most Champion bus shelters appear along major highways where few pedestrians (except bus/tro-tro passengers) will see the ad, rendering these ads less visible due to the lack of audience.

2. Just as the shelter protects people from the elements, it also protects the advertisement. Bus shelter ads tend to age at a slower rate than images open to the elements, the implications of which will be discussed later.

3. Although this text is not visible in the image, I know this to be the hidden text because this same message has appeared across Accra.

4. The eight billboards at Danquah Circle since 2003: "Life Is Precious," Prison System, Police Service, Fire Service, Ghana AIDS Commission/Coca-Cola, HIV testing billboard at the hospital, "Use a Condom," and Ghana AIDS Commission red ribbon signage.

5. Ring Road is the busiest highway in Accra as the main artery into Accra Central. Oxford Street is a major commercial thoroughfare.

6. Origin8 staff member, interview by author, November 1, 2006. Ironically, the advertising firm this respondent was working for continues to design billboards for AIDS campaigns without a shift in practice.

7. In this photograph, the very bottom of the billboard is barely visible from the window, along with the two posts holding up the advertisement.

8. Organizations need to consider billboard height more explicitly during the design phase. The "pasted-over" billboard at the University of Ghana (fig. 16) was too low, and here in the case of the billboards around Danquah Circle, the billboards are too high to be seen from a tro-tro.

9. Most of the ad agency staff members with whom I spoke had trained abroad, and some of the firms had affiliations with cosmopolitan advertising agencies abroad.

10. I haven't found any billboards aimed solely at a Christian audience. That said, the "Show Compassion" campaign attempted to speak across religions by depicting Christian and Muslim iconography. The "Show Compassion" campaign (the first national antistigma campaign) depicted the Islamic crescent in addition to a Christian cross. In doing so, the campaign attempted to speak to a pan-religious audience.

11. Quoted from field notes, March 26, 2008.

12. Those audiences who have time to focus attention on the ad, particularly audiences on foot rather than in cars or who pass this site regularly, may understand the billboard to be about avoiding premarital sex yet might still miss the intended connection between premarital sex and the risk of HIV infection.

13. This image appears outside of schools throughout Accra. This combination of fading and placement near highways occurs elsewhere, especially in front of the Accra Academy.

14. It has been reported that 71 percent of women in Accra are employed, and 60 percent of those women are engaged in "sales," meaning the market (GSS, NMIMR, and ORC Macro 2004).

15. FHI staff member, interview by author, November 3, 2006.

16. FHI staff member, interview by author, November 3, 2006.

17. The "Drive Protected" stickers depict a tro-tro wrapped in a condom against a red background. Around the image of the tro-tro, three campaign slogans appear: "DRIVE PROTECTED," "IF IT'S NOT ON, IT'S NOT IN!" and "Stop AIDS, Love Life."

Chapter Six

1. GSMF staff member, interview by author, December 13, 2006.

2. GSMF Staff member, interview by author, October 8, 2006.

3. Best practices advocate a positive approach (Malcolm and Dowsett 1998).

4. FHI staff member, interview by author, November 3, 2006.

5. UNICEF/Ghana Red Cross Society, *Genital Signs of Sexually Transmitted Diseases (STD's)*, n.d.

6. Quotations taken from pamphlets *The Youth without AIDS: Our Best Resource, Women Help Fight AIDS*, and National AIDS Control Programme's *AIDS: What You Need to Know*, respectively.

7. Taken literally, however, it isn't clear whether abstinence, condom use, or faithfulness are ways to prevent or cause death from AIDS. For people unfamiliar with HIV, the relation between the ABCs and AIDS is ambiguous.

8. This is one of a trend of advertisements that link condoms to boots, shoes, and socks: the GSMF/JHU Mungo Park advertisement and the GSMF ad using pop star Sydney.

9. *Genital Signs of Sexually Transmitted Diseases (STD's)*.

10. Ibid.

11. JHU staff member, interview by author, August 2003.

12. JHU staff member, interview by author, August 2003.

13. JHU staff member, interview by author, August 2003.

14. JHU staff member, interview by author, August 2003.

15. These interviews were conducted September 18, 2006; November 30, 2006; February 22, 2008; March 7, 2008; March 14, 2008 (two); and March 19, 2008. As with other interviews, names are withheld by mutual agreement to protect the privacy of the individuals who participated.

16. Bonnell (1997) argues for studying images as "visual language," mapping "out the repertoire of references available and suggest possible interpretations." I've mapped out this language, and focus group interviews and posters allow me to tease out how Ghanaians use and understand that language.

17. The Ghana Demographic Health Survey (2003) suggests that only about a third of Ghanaians know someone who is HIV positive.

18. Demographic Health Survey data show that AIDS awareness was essentially universal among Ghanaians by 2003. (GSS, NMIMR, and ORC Macro 2004).

19. More-generic imagery also lent itself to cultural entropy when parts of the messages faded, leaving normal images open to reinterpretation as, say, warnings to drive slowly next to a school (see the discussion around figures 20 and 21).

Conclusion

1. Origin8 staff [name withheld], interview by author, October 19, 2006.

2. Origin8 staff member, interview by author, October 19, 2006.

3. Origin8 staff member, interview by author, October 19, 2006.

4. Changing the "condom semiotics" Tavory and Swidler (2009) describe. Increasing entropy corresponds with additional complexity and polyvocality at a semiotic level.

5. See Katz and Lazarsfeld 2005 and Schudson 1986 on limited media effects.

6. ACT UP participant, interview by author, December 12, 2001.

7. These mechanisms converse with and contribute to Pressman and Wildavsky's (1984) work on failed policy implementation.

8. See Timmermans and Epstein 2010 on standards.

9. Perrow 1999. The other dimension of normal accidents is the tightly coupled systems that permit cascading effects. Cultural systems are dynamic and complex but not tightly coupled.

In this sense the mechanisms that spread entropy are not the same as those that spread normal accidents in technical systems.

10. Organizations' belief that securing buy-in and creating a monopoly over the message mitigates confusion in the public sphere is founded on a faulty premise. As the mediascape becomes increasingly diverse, it becomes harder to monopolize communication channels. AIDS organizations are fighting a losing battle as an increasingly complex mediascape makes it harder to stabilize a message. The risk of confusion (in an already confusing environment) is worth the potential benefits gained by this alternative.

11. This was essential to Goffman's (1959) thinking, that people would work to maintain interactions and the meanings expressed within them.

12. See Hall 1993 on negotiated and oppositional readings; de Certeau 1984 and Jenkins 1992 on poaching; Debord and Wolman 2006 on *détournement*; Klein 1999 on culture jamming.

13. ANT offers a powerful critique of how sociological explanations manufacture a stable "social" to which sociologists attribute casual power without accounting for objects (Latour 2005). Although ANT raises the importance of objects, the theoretical focus still emphasizes the question of how such stability arises, how networks of actors (both human and nonhuman) stabilize around the production of artifacts, scientific knowledge, or technologies. Similarly, Pinch and Bijker (2012) attend to the "invention" of the bicycle as the stabilization of interests over years of trial and error. "Boundary objects" stabilize heterogeneous scientific work (Star and Griesemer 1989).

14. For as much as ANT has made objects central to analysis through the "symmetry" principle, it also seems to objectify people, artificially stabilizing their interests to theorize their contribution to action (Callon 1986). Casper and Clarke (1998) have a nice critique here.

15. Contributing to recent work on materiality in cultural sociology: Acord 2010; Alexander 2008; Cerulo 2009; DeNora 2000; Domínguez Rubio 2014; Griswold, Mangione, and McDonnell 2013; Jerolmack and Tavory 2014; Klett 2014; McDonnell 2010; Mukerji 2014; Zubrzycki 2011; Zubrzycki 2013.

16. For a longer discussion of these issues, see Martin 2011 on basing explanation on subjective experience rather than objective categories imposed from above.

Methodological Appendix

1. Setel argues, "Much of the meaning of AIDS is generated at the level of action itself, unmediated by communicative speech acts or linguistic expression of any kind. In the absence of fieldwork, analysis of cultural materials by outsiders too easily becomes disconnected from the contexts in which these materials emerged" (1999, 12).

2. Quoted from Gell 1998, 6. To borrow language from actor-network theory, objects are "actants" (Latour 1992; Latour 2005; see also Cerulo 2009 for a good discussion). As actants, objects should be analyzed as equal to people in the analysis of social phenomena. Seen from this perspective, objects can have effects independent of human intention. I agree with the claim made by actor-network thinkers that objects can act upon us independent of the intentions of people (Latour 1992). That said, in most situations I find it more fruitful to take Gell's approach to the agency of objects that places intentions front and center. For Gell (1998), objects are "secondary agents" enacting the intentions of the "primary agents": people who create and mobilize objects.

3. I account for the links between AIDS campaigns and the other points of Griswold's (1986) "cultural diamond": the social world, producers, and audiences. Surprisingly few studies have

followed this practice, though a couple of exemplary works include Griswold 2000 and Wagner-Pacifici and Schwartz 1991.

4. As much as I'd like to complicate the varieties of outcomes that are possible when objects and people meet, I don't want to oversimplify by suggesting that designers' intentions are always clear, singular, or knowable. Historically, cultural sociologists have been skeptical of accounting for people's intentions (Wuthnow 1987). Sociologists of art regularly claim that art historians and literary critics put too much emphasis on the intended meanings of artists through close readings of the text. Instead, they argue, what matters is audience.

5. Although entropy is happening all the time, it often goes underrecognized. Studying cases of organizations that strategically use culture instrumentally makes entropy observable. Unlike studies of artists, with their multiple, conflicting intentions and meanings for their work that they may not verbalize, public-health campaign designers have narrow, knowable goals for their campaigns.

6. I follow Griswold's call to construct a "brief," or the set of constraints and influences that account for a producer's intentions (1987b).

7. See Jacobs 1961; Zukin 1995.

8. This raises the question of whether consistency across the "drawn" poster and the "selected" poster was an echo effect, that similarities are a product of "selecting" posters that confirm their original choices in the "drawn" poster. I cannot rule out this possibility, but I can say this: while the posters had a great deal of similarity in imagery, the slogans varied a great deal. If it were truly an echo effect, then I would see a similar echo in the messages they chose, which I did not.

References

Acord, Sophia Krzys. 2010. "Beyond the Head: The Practical Work of Curating Contemporary Art." *Qualitative Sociology* 33:447–67.

Adorno, Theodor. 2001. *The Culture Industry*. New York: Routledge.

Agyei-Mensah, Samuel. 2001. "Twelve Years of HIV/AIDS in Ghana: Puzzles of Interpretation." *Canadian Journal of African Studies* 35:441–72.

Ajzen, Icek, and Fishbein, Martin. 1980. *Understanding Attitudes and Predicting Social Behavior*. Englewood Cliffs, NJ: Prentice Hall.

Akeroyd, Anne V. 2004. "Coercion, Constraints, and 'Cultural Entrapments': A Further Look at Gendered and Occupational Factors Pertinent to the Transmission of HIV in Africa." In *HIV & AIDS in Africa: Beyond Epidemiology*, edited by Ezekiel Kalipeni, Susan Craddock, Joseph R. Oppong, and Jayati Ghosh, 89–103. Malden, MA: Blackwell.

Akwara, Priscilla A., Gabriel B. Fosu, Pav Govindasamy, Silvia Alayón, and Ani Hyslop. 2005. *An In- Depth Analysis of HIV Prevalence in Ghana: Further Analysis of Demographic and Health Surveys Data*. Calverton, MD: ORC Macro.

Alexander, Jeffrey C. 2004. "Cultural Pragmatics: Social Performance between Ritual and Strategy." *Sociological Theory* 22 (4): 527–73.

———. 2008. "Iconic Consciousness: The Material Feeling of Meaning." *Environment and Planning* 26:782–94.

Allen, Tim, and Suzette Heald. 2004. "HIV/AIDS Policy in Africa: What Has Worked in Uganda and What Has Failed in Botswana?" *Journal of International Development* 16:1141–54.

Anarfi, John K. 1993. "Sexuality, Migration, and AIDS in Ghana: A Socio-Behavioral Study." *Health Transition Review* 3 (Supplementary issue): 1–22.

Ankomah, Augustine. 1999. "Sex, Love, Money and AIDS: The Dynamics of Premarital Sexual Relationships in Ghana." *Sexualities* 2 (3): 291–308.

Appadurai, Arjun. 1986. "Introduction: Commodities and the Politics of Value." In *The Social Life of Things: Commodities in Cultural Perspective*, edited by Arjun Appadurai, 3–63. Cambridge: Cambridge University Press.

———. 1996. *Modernity at Large: Cultural Dimensions of Globalization*. Minneapolis: University of Minnesota Press.

Armstrong, Elizabeth A., and Suzanna Crage. 2006. "Movements and Memory: The Making of the Stonewall Myth." *American Sociological Review* 71:724–51.

Aronczyk, Melissa. 2013. *Branding the Nation: The Global Business of National Identity*. New York: Oxford University Press.

Ashforth, Adam. 2005. *Witchcraft, Violence, and Democracy in South Africa*. Chicago: University of Chicago Press.

Atkin, Charles K., and Vicki Freimuth. 2001. "Formative Evaluation Research in Campaign Design." In *Public Communication Campaigns*, edited by Ronald E. Rice and Charles K. Atkins, 125–45. Thousand Oaks: Sage.

Awusabo-Asare, Kofi, and John K. Anarfi. 1997. "Health Seeking Behavior of Persons with HIV/ AIDS in Ghana." *Health Transition Review* 7:243–56.

Babon, Kim M. 2006. "Composition, Coherence, and Attachment: The Critical Role of Context in Reception." *Poetics* 34:151–79.

Backer, Thomas E., Everett M. Rogers, and Pradeep Sopory. 1992. *Designing Health Communication Campaigns: What Works?* Newbury Park, CA: Sage.

Bakhtin, Mikhail M. 1981. *The Dialogic Imagination*. Edited by Michael Holquist. Austin: University of Texas Press.

Bandura, Albert. 2001. "Social Cognitive Theory: An Agentic Perspective." *Annual Review of Psychology* 52:1–26.

Barnett, E., K. de Koning, and V. Francis. 1995. "Health and HIV/AIDS Education in Primary and Secondary Schools in Africa and Asia: Policies, Practice and Potential; Case Studies from Pakistan, India, Uganda, and Ghana." *Education Research* 14.

Barthes, Roland. 1975. *S/Z*. Translated by Richard Miller. New York: Hill and Wang.

———. 1977. "The Death of the Author." In *Image, Music, Text*. Translated by Stephen Heath, 142–48. New York: Hill and Wang.

Bartmański, Dominik, and Jeffrey C. Alexander. 2012. "Materiality and Meaning in Social Life: Toward an Iconic Turn in Cultural Sociology." In *Iconic Power: Materiality and Meaning in Social Life*, edited by Jeffrey C. Alexander, Dominik Bartmański, and Bernhard Giesen,1–12. New York: Palgrave MacMillan.

Basil, Michael D., and William J. Brown. 1994. "Interpersonal Communication in News Diffusion: A Study of 'Magic' Johnson's Announcement." *Journalism Quarterly* 71:305–20.

———. 1997. "Marketing AIDS Prevention: The Differential Impact Hypothesis versus Identification Effects." *Journal of Consumer Psychology* 6:389–411.

Becker, Howard. S. 1982. *Art Worlds*. Berkeley: University of California Press.

———. 2007. *Telling about Society*. Chicago: University of Chicago Press.

Becker, Howard S., Robert R. Faulkner, and Barbara Kirshenblatt-Gimblett. 2006. *Art from Start to Finish: Jazz, Painting, Writing, and Other Improvisations*. Chicago: University of Chicago Press.

Benjamin, Walter. 1968. "The Work of Art in the Age of Mechanical Reproduction." In *Illuminations: Essays and Reflections*, 217–52. New York: Schocken Books.

Bennett, Jane. 2009. *Vibrant Matter: A Political Ecology of Things*. Durham, NC: Duke University Press.

Benson, Rodney. 2014. "Challenging the 'New Descriptivism.'" Accessed November 16, 2015. https://qualpolicomm.wordpress.com/2014/06/05/challenging-the-new-descriptivism-rod -bensons-talk-from-qualpolcomm-preconference/#comments/.

Berezin, Mabel. 1994. "Cultural Form and Political Meaning: State-subsidized Theater, Ideology, and the Language of Style in Fascist Italy." *American Journal of Sociology* 99:1237–86.

Berger, John. 1972. *Ways of Seeing*. London: Penguin Books.

Berger, Peter L., and Thomas Luckmann. 1966. *The Social Construction of Reality*. New York: Anchor Books.

Bielby, William T., and Denise D. Bielby. 1994. "All Hits are Flukes: Institutionalized Decision Making and the Rhetoric of Prime-Time Program Development." *American Journal of Sociology* 99:1287–1313.

Blumer, Herbert. 1969. *Symbolic Interactionism: Perspective and Method*. Berkeley: University of California Press.

Bonnell, Victoria E. 1997. *Iconography of Power*. Berkeley: University of California Press.

Bourdieu, Pierre. 1977. *Outline of a Theory of Practice*. Cambridge: Cambridge University Press.

———. 1984. *Distinction: A Social Critique of the Judgment of Taste*. Translated by Richard Nice. Cambridge, MA: Harvard University Press.

———. 1993. *The Field of Cultural Production*. New York: Columbia University Press.

Bowker, Geoffrey C., and Susan Leigh Star. 1999. *Sorting Things Out: Classification and Its Consequences*. Cambridge, MA: MIT Press.

Bryson, Bethany. 1996. "'Anything but Heavy Metal': Symbolic Exclusion and Musical Dislikes." *American Sociological Review* 61 (5): 884–99.

Buckley, Steve, Berifi Apenteng, Aly Bathily, and Lumko Mtimde. 2005. *Ghana Broadcasting Study: A Report for the Government of Ghana and the World Bank*. November 17. http://siteresources.worldbank.org/INTCEERD/Resources/WBIGhanaBroadcasting.pdf.

Burrell, Jenna. 2012. *Invisible Users: Youth in the Internet Cafes of Urban Ghana*. Cambridge, MA: MIT Press.

Callon, Michel. 1986. "Some Elements of a Sociology of Translation: Domestication of the Scallops and the Fisherman of St. Brieuc Bay." In *Power, Action and Belief*, edited by J. Law, 196–233. London: Routledge and Kegan Paul.

———. 2007. "What Does It Mean to Say That Economics Is Performative?" In *Do Economists Make Markets? On the Performativity of Economics*, edited by Donald MacKenzie, Fabian Muniesa, and Lucia Siu. Princeton, NJ: Princeton University Press.

Casper, Monica J., and Adele E. Clarke. 1998. "Making the Pap Smear into the 'Right Tool' for the Job: Cervical Cancer Screening in the USA, circa 1940–95." *Social Studies of Science* 28 (2): 255–90.

Castillo, Michelle. 2014. "The #IAmARepublican Campaign Isn't Exactly Going as Planned." *Adweek.com*. October 3. http://www.adweek.com/adfreak/iamarepublican-campaign-isn-t-exactly-going-planned-160554.

Catania, Joseph A., David R. Gibson, Dale D. Chitwood, and Thomas J. Coates. 1990. "Methodological Problems in AIDS Behavioral Research: Influences on Measurement Error and Participation Bias in Sexual Behavior. *Psychological Bulletin* 108 (3): 339–62.

Cerulo, Karen. 2009. "Nonhumans in Social Interaction." *Annual Review of Sociology* 35:531–52.

Childress, Clayton C., and Noah E. Friedkin. 2012. "Cultural Reception and Production: The Social Construction of Book Clubs." *American Sociological Review* 77 (1): 45–68.

Cialdini, Robert B. 2006. *Influence: The Psychology of Persuasion*. New York: Harper Business.

Cohen, Susan. 2003. "Beyond Slogans: Lessons from Uganda's Experience with ABC and HIV/AIDS." *Guttmacher Report on Public Policy* 6 (5).

Collins, Randall. 2004. *Interaction Ritual Chains*. Princeton, NJ: Princeton University Press.

Colyvas, Jeannette A., and Stefan Jonsson. 2011. "Ubiquity and Legitimacy: Disentangling Diffusion and Institutionalization." *Sociological Theory* 29 (1): 27–53.

Côté, Anne-Marie, François Sobela, Agnes Dzokoto, Khonde Nzambi, Comfort Amasoah-Adu, Annie-Claude Labbé, Benoit Massê, Joyce Mensah, Eric Frost, and Jacques Pépin. 2004. "Transactional Sex Is the Driving Force in the Dynamics of HIV in Accra, Ghana." *AIDS* 18:917–25.

Couldry, Nick. 2003. *Media Rituals.* New York: Routledge.

Crawford, Robert. 1994. "The Boundaries of the Self and the Unhealthy Other: Reflections on Health, Culture, and AIDS." *Social Science and Medicine* 38:1347–65.

Crimp, Douglas. 2002. *Melancholia and Moralism: Essays on AIDS and Queer Politics.* Cambridge, MA: MIT Press.

Crimp, Douglas, and Adam Rolston. 1990. *AIDS Demographics.* Seattle: Bay Press.

Dalton, Benjamin. 2004. "Creativity, Habit, and the Social Products of Creative Action: Revising Joas, Incorporating Bourdieu." *Sociological Theory* 22 (4): 603–22.

de Certeau, Michel. 1984. *The Practice of Everyday Life.* Translated by Steven Rendall. Berkeley: University of California Press.

Decoteau, Claire Laurier. 2013. *Ancestors and Antiretrovirals: The Biopolitics of HIV/AIDS in Post-Apartheid South Africa.* Chicago: University of Chicago Press.

Debord, Guy, and Gil Wolman. 2006. "A User's Guide to Détournement." In *Situationist International Anthology,* edited and translated by Ken Knabb, 14–21. Berkeley, CA: Bureau of Public Secrets.

DeNora, Tia. 2000. *Music in Everyday Life.* Cambridge: Cambridge University Press.

———. 2003. *After Adorno: Rethinking Music Sociology.* Cambridge: Cambridge University Press.

de Saussure, Ferdinand. 1998. *Course in General Linguistics.* Translated by Roy Harris. Chicago: Open Court.

DiMaggio, Paul. 1982. "Cultural Entrepreneurship in Nineteenth-Century Boston: The Creation of an Organizational Base for High Culture in America." *Media, Culture and Society* 4 (1): 33–50.

———. 1997. "Culture and Cognition." *Annual Review of Sociology* 23:263–87.

DiMaggio, Paul J., and Walter W. Powell. 1983. "The Iron Cage Revisited: Institutional Isomorphism and Collective Rationality in Organizational Fields." *American Sociological Review* 48:147–60.

Dokosi, Felix. 2002. *Beware of AIDS: A Supplementary Reader for Basic Level School Children.* Ghana AIDS Commission.

Domínguez Rubio, Fernando. 2014. "Preserving the Unpreservable: Docile and Unruly Objects at MOMA." *Theory and Society* 43 (6): 617–45.

Downer, John. 2011. "'737 Cabriolet': The Limits of Knowledge and the Sociology of Inevitable Failure." *American Journal of Sociology* 117:725–62.

du Gay, Paul, Stuart Hall, Linda Janes, Anders Koed Madsen, Hugh McKay, and Keith Negus. 2013. *Doing Cultural Studies: The Story of the Sony Walkman.* Thousand Oaks, CA: Sage.

Duneier, Mitchell. 1994. *Slim's Table: Race, Respectability and Masculinity.* Chicago: University of Chicago Press.

Durkheim, Émile. 1995. *The Elementary Forms of the Religious Life. 1912.* Translated by Karen E. Fields. New York: Free Press.

Dutta, Mohan J. 2008. *Communicating Health: A Culture-Centered Approach.* Malden, MA: Polity.

Eco, Umberto. 2003. "Towards a Semiotic Inquiry into the Television Message." In *Television: Critical Concepts in Media and Cultural Studies,* vol. 2, edited by Toby Miller, 3–19. New York: Routledge. Originally published in Italian in 1965, in English in 1972.

Edelman, Murray. 1995. *From Art to Politics: How Artistic Creations Shape Political Conceptions*. Chicago: University of Chicago Press.

Edgar, Timothy, Mary Anne Fitzpatrick, and Vicki S. Freimuth. 1992. *AIDS: A Communication Perspective*. Hillsdale, NJ: Lawrence Erlbaum Associates.

Edgell Becker, Penny. 1998. "Making Inclusive Communities: Congregations and the 'Problem' of Race." *Social Problems* 45:451–72.

Egger, Matthias, Josefina Pauw, Athanasios Lopatatzidis, Danilo Medrano, Fred Paccaud, and George Davey Smith. 2000. "Promotion of Condom Use in a High-Risk Setting in Nicaragua: A Randomized Controlled Trial." *Lancet* 355:2101–5.

Eisenstein, Elizabeth L. 1979. *The Printing Press as an Agent of Change: Communications and Cultural Transformation in Early-Modern Europe*. Cambridge: Cambridge University Press.

Eliasoph, Nina, and Paul Lichterman. 2003. "Culture in Interaction." *American Journal of Sociology* 108:735–94.

Emirbayer, Mustafa, and Ann Mische. 1998. "What Is Agency?" *American Journal of Sociology* 103 (4): 962–1023.

Epstein, Helen. 2007. *The Invisible Cure: Africa, the West, and the Fight against AIDS*. New York: Farrar, Straus and Giroux.

Espeland, Wendy, and Mitchell Stevens. 2008. "A Sociology of Quantification." *European Journal of Sociology* 49:401–36.

Ferguson, James. 1994. *The Anti-Politics Machine: Development, Depoliticization, and Bureaucratic Power in Lesotho*. Minneapolis: University of Minnesota Press.

FHI (Family Health International). 2002. *Behavior Change Communication (BCC) for HIV/ AIDS: A Strategic Framework*. Arlington, VA: FHI. http://www.hivpolicy.org/Library /HPP000533.pdf.

Fine, Gary Alan. 1987. *With the Boys: Little League and Preadolescent Culture*. Chicago: University of Chicago Press.

Fine, Gary Alan, and Terence McDonnell. 2007. "Erasing the Brown Scare: Referential Afterlife and the Power of Memory Templates." *Social Problems* 54:170–87.

Fiscian, Vivian S., E. Kwame Obeng, Karen Goldstein, Judy A. Shea, and Barbara J. Turner. 2009. "Adapting a Multifaceted US HIV Prevention Education Program for Girls in Ghana." *AIDS Education and Prevention* 21 (1): 67–79.

Fish, Stanley. 1980. *Is There a Text in This Class? The Authority of Interpretive Communities*. Cambridge, MA: Harvard University Press.

Fishbein, Martin, and Icek Ajzen. 1975. *Belief, Attitude, Intention, and Behavior: An Introduction to Theory and Research*. Reading, MA: Addison-Wesley.

Fiske, John. 1992. "Audiencing: A Cultural Studies Approach to Watching Television." *Poetics* 21:345–59.

———. 1996. *Media Matters: Race and Gender in US Politics*. Minneapolis: University of Minnesota Press.

Foucault, Michel. 1995. *Discipline and Punish*. Translated by Alan Sheridan. New York: Vintage Books.

Gadamer, Hans G. 2004. *Truth and Method*. London: Continuum.

Geertz, Clifford. 1973. *The Interpretation of Cultures*. New York: Basic Books.

Gell, Alfred. 1998. *Art and Agency: An Anthropological Theory*. New York: Oxford University Press.

Gerbert, Barbara, Bryan T. Maguire, Thomas Bleeker, Thomas J. Coates, and Stephen J. McPhee.

1991. "Primary Care Physicians and AIDS: Attitudinal and Structural Barriers to Care." *Journal of the American Medicine Association* 266:2837–42.

Ghana AIDS Commission. 2000. *Ghana HIV/AIDS Strategic Framework: 2001–2005.*

———. 2001. *Ghana HIV/AIDS Strategic Framework (2001–2005).*

———. 2005a. *National HIV/AIDS Strategic Framework II: 2006–2010.*

———. 2005b. *National Integrated IEC/BCC Strategic Framework (HIV and AIDS) 2006–2010.* October.

———. 2014. *Country AIDS Response Progress Report—Ghana.* March 31. http://www.unaids.org/sites/default/files/country/documents//GHA_narrative_report_2014.pdf.

Ghana News Agency. 2006. "FDB is Not against Development of Herbal Medicine." News release, September 15.

Ghana Social Marketing Foundation International. 2003. *GSMF HIV/AIDS Programme.* Pamphlet.

Ghana Statistical Service (GSS), and ICF Macro. 2009. *Ghana Demographic and Health Survey 2008.* September. Calverton, MD: GSS and ICF Macro.

Ghana Statistical Service (GSS), Noguchi Memorial Institute for Medical Research (NMIMR), and ORC Macro. 2004. *Ghana Demographic and Health Survey 2003.* Calverton, MD: GSS, NMIMR, and ORC Macro.

Ghana Sustainable Change Project. 2006. *Pre-Test Report for Stigma Concepts.* August.

Ghaziani, Amin, and Delia Baldassarri. 2011. "Cultural Anchors and the Organization of Differences: A Multi-Method Analysis of LGBT Marches on Washington." *American Sociological Review* 76:179–206.

Gibson, James Jerome. 1979. *The Ecological Approach to Visual Perception.* Hillsdale, NJ: Lawrence Erlbaum Associates.

Giddens, Anthony. 1984. *The Constitution of Society.* Berkeley: University of California Press.

Gieryn, Thomas F. 2000. "A Space for Place in Sociology." *Annual Review of Sociology* 26:463–96.

Gilman, Sander L. 1988. *Disease and Representation: Images of Illness from Madness to AIDS.* Ithaca, NY: Cornell University Press.

Global Africa Pocket News. 1994. "Ghana AIDS Cure Found—Scientist Murdered." *Global Africa Pocket News* 1 (2): 8. Accessed December 14, 2007. http://www.globalafrica.com/Africa.htm (site discontinued).

Goffman, Erving. 1959. *The Presentation of Self in Everyday Life.* New York: Anchor Books.

———. 1963. *Stigma.* Englewood Cliffs, NJ: Spectrum.

———. 1974. *Frame Analysis: An Essay on the Organization of Experience.* Cambridge, MA: Harvard University Press.

———. 1981. *Forms of Talk.* Philadelphia: University of Pennsylvania Press.

Griswold, Wendy. 1986. *Renaissance Revivals: City Comedy and Revenge Tragedy in London Theatre from 1576 to 1980.* Chicago: University of Chicago Press.

———. 1987a. "The Fabrication of Meaning: Literary Interpretation in the United States, Great Britain, and the West Indies." *American Journal of Sociology* 92:1077–1117.

———. 1987b. "A Methodological Framework for the Study of Culture." *Sociological Methodology* 17:1–35.

———. 2000. *Bearing Witness: Readers, Writers, and the Novel in Nigeria.* Princeton, NJ: Princeton University Press.

Griswold, Wendy, Gemma Mangione, and Terence E. McDonnell. 2013. "Objects, Words, and Bodies in Space: Bringing Materiality into Cultural Analysis." *Qualitative Sociology* 36:343–64.

Griswold, Wendy, Erin Metz McDonnell, and Terence E. McDonnell. 2007. "Glamour and

Honor: Going Online and Reading in West African Culture." *Information Technologies and International Development* 3 (4): 37–52.

Gross, Neil. 2009. "A Pragmatist Theory of Social Mechanisms." *American Sociological Review* 74 (3): 358–79.

Habermas, Jürgen. 1991. *The Structural Transformation of the Public Sphere*. Cambridge, MA: MIT Press.

Hackbarth, Diana P., Barbara Silvestri, and William Cosper. 1995. "Tobacco and Alcohol Billboards in 50 Chicago Neighborhoods: Market Segmentation to Sell Dangerous Products to the Poor." *Journal of Public Health Policy* 16:213–30.

Hall, Stuart. 1993. "Encoding, Decoding." In *The Cultural Studies Reader*, edited by Simon During, 507–17. New York: Routledge.

Hannerz, Ulf. 1992. *Cultural Complexity: Studies in the Social Organization of Meaning*. New York: Columbia University Press.

Harrington, C. Lee, and Denise D. Bielby. 1995. *Soap Fans: Pursuing Pleasure and Making Meaning in Everyday Life*. Philadelphia: Temple University Press.

Hasty, Jennifer. 2005. *The Press and Political Culture in Ghana*. Bloomington: Indiana University Press.

Hays, Sharon. 1994. "Structure, Agency, and the Sticky Problem of Culture." *Sociological Theory* 12:57–72.

Heald, Suzette. 2002. "It's Never as Easy as ABC: Understandings of AIDS in Botswana." *African Journal of AIDS Research* 1:1–10.

Hebdige, Dick. 1979. *Subcultures: The Meaning of Style*. New York: Routledge.

Heimer, Carol. 2007. "Old Inequalities, New Disease: HIV/AIDS in Sub-Saharan Africa." *Annual Review of Sociology* 33:551–77.

Hepburn, Ned. 2014. "The Pencil That Is Too Cool for School." *Esquire.com*. March 24. Accessed September 24, 2015. http://www.esquire.com/style/mens-accessories/a28061/too-cool-drugs-pencil-barry-bonds-2014/.

Herman, Edward S., and Noam Chomsky. 2002. *Manufacturing Consent: The Political Economy of the Mass Media*. New York: Pantheon.

Hogle, Janice A. 2002. *What Happened in Uganda? Declining HIV Prevalence, Behavior Change, and the National Response*. USAID Project Lessons Learned Case Study. Washington, DC: United States Agency for International Development.

Hornborg, Alf. 1992. "Machine Fetishism, Value, and the Image of Unlimited Good: Towards a Thermodynamics of Imperialism. *Man* 27:1–18.

Ignatow, Gabriel. 2007. "Theories of Embodied Knowledge: New Directions for Cultural and Cognitive Sociology?" *Journal for the Theory of Social Behavior* 37 (2): 115–35.

Ingold, Tim. 2007. "Materials against Materiality." *Archeological Dialogues* 14:1–16.

Jacobs, Jane. 1961. *The Death and Life of Great American Cities*. New York: Random House.

Janz, Nancy K., and Marshall H. Becker. 1984. "The Health Belief Model: A Decade Later." *Health Education Quarterly* 11:1–47.

Jauss, Hans Robert. 1982. *Toward an Aesthetic of Reception*. Translated by Timothy Bahti. Minneapolis: University of Minnesota Press.

Jenkins, Henry. 1992. *Textual Poachers: Television Fans and Participatory Culture*. New York: Routledge.

Jerolmack, Colin, and Iddo Tavory. 2014. "Molds and Totems: Nonhumans and the Constitution of the Social Self." *Sociological Theory* 32:64–77.

Joas, Hans. 1996. *The Creativity of Action*. Chicago: University of Chicago Press.

Johns Hopkins Bloomberg School of Public Health Center for Communications Programs. 2003. "Stop AIDS Love Life in Ghana 'Shatters the Silence.'" *Communication Impact* 15 (February).

Kaler, Amy. 2001. "It's Some Kind of Female Empowerment": The Ambiguity of the Female Condom as a Marker of Female Empowerment." *Social Science and Medicine* 52 (5): 783–96.

———. 2004. "The Future of Female Controlled Barrier Methods for HIV Prevention: Female Condoms and Lessons Learned." *Culture, Health & Sexuality* 6 (6): 501–16.

Katz, Elihu. 2001. "Media Effects." In *International Encyclopedia of the Social and Behavioral Sciences*, edited by Neil J. Smelser and Paul B. Baltes, 9472–79. Oxford: Elsevier Science.

Katz, Elihu, and Paul Lazarsfeld. 2005. *Personal Influence: The Part Played by People in the Flow of Mass Communications*. Piscataway, NJ: Transaction Publishers.

Keane, Webb. 2003. "Semiotics and the Social Analysis of Material Things." *Language and Communication*. 23:409–25.

Kelly, Jeffrey A., Janet S. St. Lawrence, Steve Smith Jr., Harold V. Hood, and Donna J. Cook. 1987. "Stigmatization of AIDS Patients by Physicians." *American Journal of Public Health* 77:789–91.

Klapper, Joseph T. 1960. *The Effects of Mass Communication*. Glencoe, IL: Free Press.

Klein, Naomi. 1999. *No Logo: Taking Aim at the Brand Bullies*. New York: Picador.

Klett, Joseph. 2014. "Sound on Sound: Situating Interaction in Sonic Object-Settings." *Sociological Theory* 32 (2): 147–61.

Knorr Cetina, Karin. 2001. "Objectual Practice." In *The Practice Turn in Contemporary Theory*, edited by Theodore R. Schatzki, Karin Knorr Cetina, and Eike von Savigny. Abingdon, UK: Routledge.

Kopytoff, Igor. 1986. "The Cultural Biography of Things: Commoditization as Process." In *The Social Life of Things: Commodities in Cultural Perspective*, edited by Arjun Appadurai, 64–94. Cambridge: Cambridge University Press.

Krause, Monika. 2014. *The Good Project: Humanitarian Relief NGOs and the Fragmentation of Reason*. Chicago: University of Chicago Press.

Kristeva, Julia. 1980. *Desire in Language: A Semiotic Approach to Literature and Art*. New York: Columbia University Press.

Lakoff, George, and Mark Johnson. 1980. *Metaphors We Live By*. Chicago: University of Chicago Press.

Langer, Ellen J. 2014. *Mindfulness*. Boston: Da Capo Press.

Larkin, Brian. 1997. "Indian Films and Nigerian Lovers: Media and the Creation of Parallel Modernities." *Africa* 67:406–40.

———. 2008. *Signal and Noise: Media, Infrastructure, and Urban Culture in Nigeria*. Durham, NC: Duke University Press.

Lasswell, Harold D. 1938. *Propaganda Technique in the World War*. New York: Garland Publishing.

———. 1995. "Propaganda." In *Propaganda*. edited by Robert Jackall,13–25. New York: New York University Press

Latour, Bruno. 1992. "Where Are the Missing Masses? The Sociology of a Few Mundane Artifacts." In *Shaping Technology/Building Society: Studies in Sociotechnical Change*, edited by Wiebe E. Bijker and John Law,225–58. Cambridge, MA: MIT Press.

———. 2005. Reassembling the Social: An Introduction to Actor-Network Theory. Oxford University Press.

Lazarsfeld, Paul F., and Robert K. Merton. 1948. "Mass Communication, Popular Taste, and Organized Social Action." In *The Communication of Ideas*, edited by Lyman Bryson, 95–118. New York: Harper.

Lee, Jennifer. 2009. "Letters Lost, Meaning Found." *City Room* (blog). November 18. Accessed September 24, 2015. http://cityroom.blogs.nytimes.com/2009/11/18/in-elmhurst-im-hurt-equals-u-r-hurt/.

Liebes, Tamar, and Elihu Katz. 1990. *The Export of Meaning: Cross-Cultural Readings of Dallas*. London: Oxford University Press.

Liebow, Elliot. 2003. *Tally's Corner: A Study of Negro Streetcorner Men*. Lanham, MD: Rowman and Littlefield.

Lizardo, Omar, and Michael Strand. 2010. "Skills, Toolkits, Contexts and Institutions: Clarifying the Relationship between Different Approaches to Cognition in Cultural Sociology." *Poetics* 38:205–28.

Lofland, Lyn H. 1998. *The Public Realm: Exploring the City's Quintessential Social Territory*. Chicago: Aldine Transaction.

Long, Elizabeth. 2003. *Book Clubs: Women and the Uses of Reading in Everyday Life*. Chicago: University of Chicago Press.

Luginaah, Isaac N., Emmanuel K. Yiridoe, and Mary-Margaret Taabazuing. 2005. "From Mandatory to Voluntary Testing: Balancing Human Rights, Religious, and Cultural Values, and HIV/AIDS Prevention in Ghana." *Social Science and Medicine* 61:1689–1700.

Luke, Douglas, Emily Esmundo, and Yael Bloom. 2000. "Smoke Signs: Patterns of Tobacco Billboard Advertising in a Metropolitan Region." *Tobacco Control* 9:16–23.

Lutz, Catherine A., and Jane L. Collins. 1993. *Reading National Geographic*. Chicago: University of Chicago Press.

Maibach, Edward W., and Roxanne Louiselle Parrott. 1995. *Designing Health Messages: Approaches from Communication Theory and Public Health Practice*. Thousand Oaks, CA: Sage.

Makinwa, Bunmi, and Mary O'Grady. 2001. *FHI/UNAIDS Best Practices in Prevention Collection*. Geneva, Switzerland: FHI/UNAIDS.

Malcolm, Anne, and Gary Dowsett. 1998. *Partners in Prevention: International Case Studies of Effective Health Promotion Practice in HIV/AIDS*. March. Geneva, Switzerland: UNAIDS.

Manglos, Nicolette D., and Jenny Trinitapoli. 2011. "The Third Therapeutic System: Faith Healing Strategies in the Context of a Generalized AIDS Epidemic." *Journal of Health and Social Behavior* 52 (1): 107–22.

Mannheim, Karl. 1955. *Ideology and Utopia: An Introduction to the Sociology of Knowledge*. Translated by Louis Worth and Edward Shils. San Diego, CA: Harvest Book of Harcourt.

Mantell, Joanne E., Shari L. Dworkin, Theresa M. Exner, Susie Hoffman, Jenni A. Smit, and Ida Susser. 2006. "The Promises and Limitations of Female-Initiated Methods of HIV/STI Protection." *Social Science and Medicine* 63 (8).

Mantell, Joanne E., Elma Scheepers, and Quarraisha Abdool Karim. 2000. "Introducing the Female Condom through the Public Health Sector: Experiences from South Africa." *AIDS Care* 12 (5), 589–601.

Martin, Gayle H., and David Z. Logan. 2005. *Study of the Social and Economic Impacts of HIV/AIDS in Ghana: Facilitative Studies*. Report funded by the Ghana AIDS Commission, Futures Group International, and Department for International Development (DFID).

Martin, John Levi. 2011. *The Explanation of Social Action*. New York: Oxford University Press.

Mbonu, Ngozi C., Bart van den Borne, and Nanne K. De Vries. 2009. "Stigma of People with

HIV/AIDS in Sub-Saharan Africa: A Literature Review." *Journal of Tropical Medicine* 2009: 1–14.

McClain, Noah, and Ashley Mears. 2012. "Free to Those Who Can Afford It: The Everyday Affordance of Privilege." *Poetics* 40 (2): 133–49.

McDonnell, Terence E. 2010. "Cultural Objects as Objects: Materiality, Urban Space, and the Interpretation of AIDS Media in Accra, Ghana." *American Journal of Sociology* 115:1800–1852.

———. 2014. "Drawing Out Culture: Productive Methods to Measure Cognition and Resonance." *Theory and Society* 43:247–74.

Medrano, Tanya, and Martha Butler De Lister. 2001. "HIV/AIDS Prevention Mass Media Campaign for Young People in the Dominican Republic." In *FHI/UNAIDS Best Practices in Prevention Collection*, edited by Bunmi Makinwa and Mary O'Grady, 28–42. Geneva, Switzerland: FHI/UNAIDS.

Meekers, Dominique, and Anne-Emmanuèle Calvès. 1997. "'Main' Girlfriends, Girlfriends, Marriage, and Money: The Social Context of HIV Risk Behaviour in Sub-Saharan Africa." *Health Transition Review* 7:362–75.

Meekers, Dominique, and Ronan Van Rossem. 2004. "Explaining Inconsistencies between Data on Condom Use and Condom Sales." MEASURE Evaluation Working Paper WP-04-78. Carolina Population Center, University of North Carolina, Chapel Hill.

Merry, Sally Engle. 2011. "Measuring the World: Indicators, Human Rights and Global Governance." *Current Anthropology* 52 (S3): S83–S95.

Merton, Robert K. 1936. "The Unanticipated Consequences of Purposive Social Action." *American Sociological Review* 1 (6): 894–904.

Meyer, Birgit. 1999. *Translating the Devil: Religion and Modernity among the Ewe in Ghana.* Trenton, NJ: Africa World Press.

Meyer, John W., and Brian Rowan. 1977. "Institutionalized Organizations: Formal Structure as Myth and Ceremony." *American Journal of Sociology*, 83 (2): 340.

Mill, Judy E., and John K. Anarfi. 2002. "HIV Risk Environment for Ghanaian Women: Challenges to Prevention." *Social Science and Medicine* 54:325–37.

Miller, David, Jenny Kitzinger, and Peter Beharrell. 1998. *The Circuit of Mass Communication: Media Strategies, Representation, and Audience Reception in the AIDS Crisis.* London: Sages.

Morris, Martina, and Mirjam Kretzschmar. 1997. "Concurrent Partnerships and Transmission Dynamics in Networks." *Social Networks* 17 (3): 299–318.

Mukerji, Chandra. 2010. "The Territorial State as a Figured World of Power: Strategies, Logistics, and Impersonal Rule." *Sociological Theory* 28:402–24.

———. 2014. "The Cultural Power of Tacit Knowledge: Inarticulacy and Bourdieu's Habitus." *American Journal of Cultural Sociology* 2:348–75.

Mulvey, Laura. 1975. "Visual Pleasure and Narrative Cinema." *Screen* 16 (3): 6–18.

Myrick, Roger, Bart Aoki, Steve Truax, Anthony Lemelle, and George Lemp. 2005. "Building Capacity through Partnerships: The Use of Community Collaborative Evaluation and Research to Build Capacity for HIV/AIDS Prevention." *AIDS Education and Prevention* 17 (4): 279–83.

National Technical Committee on AIDS. n.d. *Don't Catch Aids, Know the Facts.* Pamphlet.

Nowack, Glen J., and Michael J. Siska. 1995. "Using Research to Inform Campaign Development and Message Design: Examples from the 'America Responds to AIDS' Campaign." In *Designing Health Messages: Approaches from Communication Theory and Public Health*

Practice, edited by Edward Maibach and Roxanne Louise Parrott,169–85. Thousand Oaks, CA: Sage.

Nyhan, Brendan, Jason Reifler, Sean Richey, and Gary L. Freed. 2014. "Effective Messages in Vaccine Promotion: A Randomized Trial." *Pediatrics* 133:1–8.

Oldenburg, Ray. 1999. *The Great Good Place: Cafes, Coffee Shops, Bookstores, Bars, Hair Salons, and Other Hangouts at the Heart of Community*. New York: Marlowe.

Oster, Emily. 2012a. "HIV and Sexual Behavior Change: Why Not Africa?" *Journal of Health Economics* 31:35–49.

———. 2012b. "Routes of Infection: Exports and HIV Incidence in Sub-Saharan Africa." *Journal of the European Economic Association* 10 (5): 1025–58.

Packard, Vance. 2007. *The Hidden Persuaders*. New York: Ig Publishing.

Palmer, Edward 1981. "Shaping Persuasive Messages with Formative Research." In *Public Communication Campaigns*, edited by Ronald E. Rice and William J. Paisley,227–42. Beverly Hills, CA: Sage.

Patterson, Orlando. 2014. "Making Sense of Culture." *Annual Review of Sociology* 40:1–30.

Patton, Cindy. 1990. *Inventing AIDS*. New York: Routledge.

Peirce, Charles. 1998. *The Essential Peirce, Selected Philosophical Writings, Volume 2 (1893–1913)*, edited by Peirce Edition Project. Bloomington: Indiana University Press.

Pellow, Deborah 1994. "STDs and AIDS in Ghana." *Genitourin Medicine* 70:418–23.

PEPFAR (United States President's Emergency Plan for AIDS Relief). 2007. "Table 3: Approved Funding by Program Area: All Countries." http://www.pepfar.gov/about/82474.htm.

———. 2015. "Partnering to Achieve Epidemic Control in Ghana." http://www.pepfar.gov /documents/organization/199362.pdf.

Perrow, Charles. 1999. *Normal Accidents: Living with High-Risk Technologies*. Princeton, NJ: Princeton University Press.

Peterson, Richard A., and N. Anand. 2004. "The Production of Culture Perspective." *Annual Review of Sociology* 30: 311–34.

Pickering, Andrew. 1995. *The Mangle of Practice: Time, Agency and Science*. Chicago: University of Chicago Press.

Pinch, Trevor J., and Wiebe E. Bijker. 2012. "The Social Construction of Facts and Artifacts: Or How the Sociology of Science and the Sociology of Technology Might Benefit Each Other." In *The Social Construction of Technological Systems: New Directions in the Sociology and History of Technology*, edited by Wiebe E. Bijker, Thomas P. Hughes, and Trevor J. Pinch, 11–44. Cambridge, MA: MIT Press.

Pool, Robert, Graham Hart, Gillian Green, Susan Harrison, Stella Nyanzi, and Jimmy Whitworth. 2000. "Men's Attitudes to Condoms and Female Controlled means of Protection against HIV and STDs in South-Western Uganda." *Culture, Health and Sexuality* 2 (2): 197–211.

Porter, Theodore M. 1995. *Trust in Numbers: The Pursuit of Objectivity in Science and Public Life*. Princeton, NJ: Princeton University Press.

Pratkanis, Anthony, and Elliot Aronson. 2001. *Age of Propaganda: The Everyday Use and Abuse of Persuasion*. 2nd ed. New York: Holt.

Press, Andrea L., and Elizabeth R. Cole. 1999. *Speaking of Abortion: Television and Authority in the Lives of Women*. Chicago: University of Chicago Press.

Pressman, Jeffrey L., and Aaron Wildavsky. 1984. *Implementation: How Great Expectations in Washington are Dashed in Oakland*. Berkeley: University of California Press.

Radway, Janice A. 1991. *Reading the Romance: Women, Patriarchy, and Popular Romance.* Chapel Hill: University of North Carolina Press.

Rivera, Lauren A. 2008. "Managing 'Spoiled' National Identity: War, Tourism, and Memory in Croatia." *American Sociological Review* 73:613–34.

Rogers, Everett M. 2003. *The Diffusion of Innovations.* 5th ed. New York: Free Press.

Rosenstock, Irwin. 1974. "Historical Origins of the Health Belief Model." *Health Education Behavior* 2:328–35.

Rosnow, Ralph L., and Gary Alan Fine. 1976. *Rumor and Gossip: The Social Psychology of Hearsay.* New York: Elsevier.

Rosser, B. R. Simon. 1991. "The Effects of Using Fear in Public AIDS Education on the Behaviour of Homosexually Active Men." *Journal of Psychology and Human Sexuality* 4:123–34.

Rushkoff, Douglas. 1999. *Coercion: Why We Listen to What "They" Say.* New York: Riverhead Books.

Sauder, Michael, and Wendy Nelson Espeland. 2009. "The Discipline of Rankings: Tight Coupling and Organizational Change." *American Sociological Review* 74 (1): 63–82.

Schoepf, Brooke Grundfest. 2004. "AIDS in Africa: Structure, Agency, and Risk." In *HIV and AIDS in Africa: Beyond Epidemiology,* edited by Ezekiel Kalipeni, Susan Craddock, Joseph R. Oppong, and Jayati Ghosh,121–32. Malden, MA: Blackwell.

Schudson, Michael. 1986. *Advertising: The Uneasy Persuasion.* New York: Basic Books.

———. 1989. "How Culture Works: Perspectives from Media Studies on the Efficacy of Symbols." *Theory and Society* 18:153–80.

———. 1995. *The Power of News.* Cambridge, MA: Harvard University Press.

Scott, James C. 1990. *Domination and the Arts of Resistance: Hidden Transcripts.* New Haven, CT: Yale University Press.

———. 1998. *Seeing Like a State: How Certain Schemes to Improve the Human Condition Have Failed.* New Haven, CT: Yale University Press.

Senie, Harriet F. 2002. *The Tilted Arc Controversy: Dangerous Precedent?* Minneapolis, MN: University of Minnesota Press.

Sennett, Richard. 2008. *The Craftsman.* New Haven, CT: Yale University Press.

Setel, Philip W. 1999. *A Plague of Paradoxes: AIDS, Culture, and Demography in Northern Tanzania.* Chicago: University of Chicago Press.

Sethuraman, Raj, Gerard J. Telles, and Richard A. Briesch. 2011. "How Well Does Advertising Work? Generalizations from Meta-Analysis of Brand Advertising Elasticities." *Journal of Market Research* 48:457–71.

Sewell, William H., Jr. 1992. "A Theory of Structure: Duality, Agency, and Transformation." *American Journal of Sociology* 98:1–29.

Sherr, Lorraine. 1990. "Fear Arousal and AIDS: Do Shock Tactics Work?" *AIDS* 4 (4): 361–64.

Shively, JoEllen. 1992. "Cowboys and Indians: Perceptions of Western Films among American Indians and Anglos." *American Sociological Review* 57:725–34.

Singh, Susheela, Jacqueline E. Darroch, and Akinrole Bankole. 2003. *A, B and C in Uganda: The Roles of Abstinence, Monogamy and Condom Use in HIV Decline.* December. Occasional Report no. 9. New York: Alan Guttmacher Institute.

Slavin, Sean, Colin Batrouney, and Dean Murphy. 2007. "Fear Appeals and Treatment Side-Effects: An Effective Combination for HIV Prevention?" *AIDS Care: Psychological and Socio-medical Aspects of AIDS/HIV* 19 (1): 130–37.

Smith, Daniel Jordan. 2004. "Youth, Sin, and Sex in Nigeria: Christianity and HIV/AIDS-Related

Beliefs and Behavior among Rural-Urban Migrants." *Culture, Health, and Sexuality* 6: 425–37.

———. 2007. "Modern Marriage, Men's Extramarital Sex, and HIV Risk in Southeastern Nigeria." *American Journal of Public Health.* 97 (6): 997–1005.

Smithson, Robert. 1996. *Robert Smithson: The Collected Writings.* Edited by Jack Flam. Berkeley: University of California Press.

Snow, David A., E. Burke Rochford Jr., Steven K. Worden, and Robert D. Benford. 1986. "Frame Alignment Processes, Micromobilization, and Movement Participation." *American Sociological Review* 45:787–801.

Snyder, Leslie B., and Ruby A. Rouse. 1995. "The Media Can Have More Than an Impersonal Impact: The Case of Risk Perceptions and Behavior." *Health Communication* 7:125–45.

Sobieraj, Sarah. 2011. *Soundbitten: The Perils of Media-Centered Political Activism.* New York: New York University Press.

Star, Susan Leigh, and James R. Griesemer. 1989. "Institutional Ecology, 'Translations' and Boundary Objects: Amateurs, Professionals in Berkeley's Museum of Vertebrate Zoology, 1907–39." *Social Studies of Science* 19:387–420.

Strathern, Marilyn, ed. 2000. *Audit Cultures: Anthropological Studies in Accountability, Ethics, and the Academy.* Abingdon, UK: Routledge.

Steinberg, Marc W. 1999. "The Talk and Back Talk of Collective Action: A Dialogic Analysis of Repertoires of Discourse among Nineteenth-Century English Cotton Spinners." *American Journal of Sociology* 105:736–80.

Sturken, Marita. 1997. *Tangled Memories: The Vietnam War, the AIDS Epidemic, and the Politics of Remembering.* Berkeley: University of California Press.

Sturken, Marita, and Lisa Cartwright. 2001. *Practices of Looking.* New York: Oxford University Press.

Swidler, Ann. 1986. "Culture in Action: Symbols and Strategies." *American Sociological Review* 51:273–86.

———. 1995. "Cultural Power and Social Movements." In *Social Movements and Culture,* edited by Hank Johnston and Bert Klandermans. New York: Routledge.

———. 2001. *Talk of Love: How Culture Matters.* Chicago: University of Chicago Press.

———. 2009. "Responding to AIDS in Sub-Saharan Africa: Culture, Institutions, and Health." In *Successful Societies: How Institutions and Culture Affect Health,* edited by Peter A. Hall and Michèle Lamont. New York: Cambridge University Press.

Swidler, Ann, and Susan Cotts Watkins. 2009. "'Teach a Man to Fish': The Sustainability Doctrine and its Social Consequences." *World Development* 11:1–15.

Takyi, Baffour K. 2003. "Religion and Women's Health in Ghana: Insights into HIV/AIDS Preventative and Protective Behavior." *Social Science and Medicine* 56:1221–34.

Tanggaard, Lene. 2013. "The Sociomateriality of Creativity in Everyday Life." *Culture and Psychology* 19 (1): 20–32.

Tavory, Iddo, and Ann Swidler. 2009. "Condom Semiotics: Meaning and Condom Use in Rural Malawi." *American Sociological Review* 74 (2): 171–89.

Tepper, Steven J. 2011. *Not Here, Not Now, Not That: Protest over Art and Culture in America.* Chicago: University of Chicago Press.

Thomas, William Isaac. 1927. "The Behavior Pattern and the Situation." *Publications of the American Sociological Society* 22:1–14.

Thompson, Derek. 2013. "JC Penney's 'Hitler Tea Kettle' Sold Out in Hours because This Is the Internet." *Atlantic.* May 29. Accessed September 24, 2015. http://www.theatlantic.com/business/archive/2013/05/jc-penneys-hitler-tea-kettle-sold-out-in-hours-because-this-is-the-internet/276334/.

Timmermans, Stefan, and Steven Epstein. 2010. "A World of Standards but Not a Standard World: Toward a Sociology of Standards and Standardization." *Annual Review of Sociology* 36:69–89.

Timmermans, Stefan, and Emily S. Kolker. 2004. "Evidence Based Medicine and the Reconfiguration of Medical Knowledge." *Journal of Health and Social Behavior* 45:177–93.

Treichler, Paula A. 1999. *How to Have Theory in an Epidemic: Cultural Chronicles of AIDS.* Durham, NC: Duke University Press.

Trinitapoli, Jenny, and Alexander A. Weinreb. 2012. *Religion and AIDS in Africa.* New York: Oxford University Press.

UNAIDS (Joint United Nations Programme on HIV/AIDS). 2012. *Global Report: UNAIDS Report on the Global AIDS Epidemic, 2012.* http://www.unaids.org/en/media/unaids/contentassets/documents/epidemiology/2012/gr2012/20121120_UNAIDS_Global_Report_2012_with_annexes_en.pdf.

Vaisey, Stephen. 2009. "Motivation and Justification: A Dual Process Model of Culture in Action." *American Journal of Sociology* 114:1675–1715.

Vaughan, Diane. 1996. *The Challenger Launch Decision: Risky Technology, Culture, and Deviance at NASA.* Chicago: University of Chicago Press.

Wagner-Pacifici, Robin, and Barry Schwartz. 1991. "The Vietnam Veterans Memorial: Commemorating a Difficult Past." *American Journal of Sociology* 90:72–96.

Weber, Max. 1978. *Economy and Society.* Edited by Guenther Ross and Claus Wittich. Berkeley: University of California Press.

———. 1992. *The Protestant Ethic and the Spirit of Capitalism.* New York: Routledge.

Weeks, John R., Allan Hill, Douglas Stow, Arthur Getis, and Debbie Fugate. 2007. "Can We Spot a Neighborhood from the Air? Defining Neighborhood Structure in Accra, Ghana." *GeoJournal* 69:9–22.

White, Hayden. 1987. *The Content of the Form: Narrative Discourse and Historical Representation.* Baltimore: Johns Hopkins University Press.

Willis, Paul. 1977. *Learning to Labor: How Working Class Kids Get Working Class Jobs.* New York: Columbia University Press.

Wilson, Bianca D. M., and Robin L. Miller. 2003. "Examining Strategies for Culturally Grounded HIV Prevention: A Review." *AIDS Education and Prevention* 15 (2): 184–202.

Woodward, Ian. 2011. "Towards and Object-Relations Theory of Consumerism: The Aesthetics of Desire and the Unfolding Materiality of Social Life." *Journal of Consumer Culture* 11 (3): 366–84.

World Bank. 2005. *Project Appraisal Document . . . Ghana for a Multi-Sectoral HIV/AIDS Project (M-SHAP).* October 18. Report no. 33917. http://www-wds.worldbank.org/external/default/WDSContentServer/WDSP/IB/2005/10/28/000090341_20051028121024/Rendered/PDF/33917.pdf.

———. 2007. *Project Performance Assessment Report: Ghana AIDS Response Project (GAR-FUND).* June 19. Report no. 39557. http://www-wds.worldbank.org/external/default/WDSContentServer/WDSP/IB/2007/10/11/000310607_20071011095403/Rendered/PDF/39557optmzd.pdf.

Wuthnow, Robert. 1987. *Meaning and Moral Order: Explorations in Cultural Analysis*. Berkeley: University of California Press.

Yankah, Kwesi. 2004. "Narrative in Times of Crisis: AIDS Stories in Ghana." *Journal of Folklore Research* 41:181–98.

Zubrzycki, Genevieve. 2011. "History and the National Sensorium: Making Sense of Polish Mythology." *Qualitative Sociology* 34:21–57.

———. 2013. "Aesthetic Revolt and the Remaking of National Identity in Quebec, 1960–1969." *Theory and Society* 42:423–75.

Zukin, Sharon. 1995. *The Cultures of Cities*. Boston: Blackwell.

Index

Page numbers in italics indicate figures